Crowdsourcing
FOR
DUMMIES®
A Wiley Brand

by David Alan Grier

FOR
DUMMIES®
A Wiley Brand

Crowdsourcing For Dummies®

Published by: **John Wiley & Sons, Ltd.,** The Atrium, Southern Gate, Chichester, www.wiley.com

This edition first published 2013

© 2013 John Wiley & Sons, Ltd, Chichester, West Sussex.

Registered office

John Wiley & Sons Ltd, The Atrium, Southern Gate, Chichester, West Sussex, PO19 8SQ, United Kingdom

For details of our global editorial offices, for customer services and for information about how to apply for permission to reuse the copyright material in this book please see our website at www.wiley.com.

The right of the author to be identified as the author of this work has been asserted in accordance with the Copyright, Designs and Patents Act 1988.

Wiley publishes in a variety of print and electronic formats and by print-on-demand. Some material included with standard print versions of this book may not be included in e-books or in print-on-demand. If this book refers to media such as a CD or DVD that is not included in the version you purchased, you may download this material at http://booksupport.wiley.com. For more information about Wiley products, visit www.wiley.com.

For general information on our other products and services, please contact our Customer Care Department within the U.S. at 877-762-2974, outside the U.S. at (001) 317-572-3993, or fax 317-572-4002. For technical support, please visit www.wiley.com/techsupport.

For technical support, please visit www.wiley.com/techsupport.

A catalogue record for this book is available from the British Library.

ISBN 978-1-119-94040-1 (pbk), ISBN 978-1-119-94384-6 (ebk), ISBN 978-1-119-94386-0 (ebk), ISBN 978-1-119-94385-3 (ebk)

Printed in Great Britain by Bell & Bain Ltd, Glasgow

10 9 8 7 6 5 4 3 2 1

Contents at a Glance

Table of Contents

Introduction

*C*rowdsourcing is the latest revolution wrought by the technologies
of computing and communication – a revolution that brings people
together and harnesses their collective intelligence. The power of crowdsourcing is such that it's created political revolutions and toppled governments. At turbulent times, crowdsourcing has deployed *the crowd* – the
group of people who actually do the work required – as a collective witness
to follow the actions of governments, record speeches and monitor elections.
And yet, at a more modest level in everyday life, crowdsourcing can still revo-
lutionise the way you go about things. Crowdsourcing enables you to work
with people who have specialised skills, to engage massive groups of workers, to collect data that you couldn't have gathered previously and to offer
advice that's far beyond experience.

Crowdsourcing can change your life. It connects you to a massive crowd of
people who can bring their skill, experience and knowledge to everything
you do in your business, your non-profit organisation and even in your daily
life. When you work with the crowd, you no longer work alone. You have the
power of the crowd behind you, a crowd that will change the way you work,
the way you plan and even the very way you think.

About This Book

Crowdsourcing For Dummies is here to help you become a *crowdsourcer* – a
person who manages the crowdsourcing process, whether in a business, a
non-profit organisation or just in everyday life. This book gives you the tools
you need for each stage of the crowdsourcing process. I show you:

- How to identify the activities you currently undertake that may benefit
  from crowdsourcing
- How to determine the best form of crowdsourcing to use for your
  project
- How to engage the crowd
- How to get started, see a project through to completion and start again
  with a new project

In this book, I give you a broad perspective on crowdsourcing. I look at the common forms of crowdsourcing, such as crowdfunding and crowdcontests, as well as the lesser-known forms, such as self-organised crowds, so that you can think about different approaches to using the crowd and the ways in which you can best use crowdsourcing to suit your own needs or those of your organisation.

This book is also here to help you understand the information about crowdsourcing that you can find on the Internet. The Internet is constantly producing new information about crowdsourcing and is an important source of reference, but this book puts that information into context.

Conventions Used in This Book

To help you navigate your way through this book, I've set up a few straightforward conventions:

- I use *italics* for emphasis and to highlight new words or define terms.
- I use **bold** to indicate the key concepts in a list.
- I alternate between male and female pronouns in the chapters to be fair to both genders.

What You're Not to Read

You're undoubtedly a wise and experienced individual who can identify the pieces of the book that you should read and the pieces that you can ignore. And although I like to think that you'll be hanging on my every word, I know that you may not want to read the whole book. If you skip bits of it, you won't hurt my feelings.

There are sections of the book that you can skip or put aside for later. Sidebars, for example. I love the sidebars, although they usually contain historical or contextual information that's completely and utterly fascinating but, I admit, not especially useful. Don't you want to know that many basic forms of crowdsourcing were developed in the American Works Progress Administration during the Great Depression? I certainly enjoy knowing that titbit of info, but you may be able to live without it. Certainly you can be a great crowdsourcer without knowing it. That's why such stories are in sidebars. You can skip them if want.

Paragraphs marked with the Technical Stuff icon in the margin are also things you can skip if you want to. This icon marks specialised material that you may not need to know. You can do a lot of crowdsourcing without knowing much about technology. You don't have to make yourself unnecessarily anxious by reading these sections.

One final note: if you're anxious about technical issues, you can completely skip Chapter 16, about workflow, without feeling bad. The ground I cover in this chapter is fascinating but is really useful only to people who are doing cutting-edge microtasking.

Foolish Assumptions

In writing this book, I made the following assumptions about you, the reader:

- You know something about the current state of the Internet and social media. Certainly, you know about email and probably know something about sites such as Facebook, LinkedIn, PayPal and Twitter. You may not use these sites much – I'm okay with that – but you know that they exist and you know what they do.

- You know something about work and how you organise tasks. You may work in an office – large or small – or be part of a non-profit organisation, or you may work for yourself. However, you know how to take a job, think about the resources that you need to do it and then actually do the job.

- You know a little bit about economics. You don't have to know much, but you do have to know the basic ideas of supply and demand. Check yourself on this little example. If you want to hire someone for a job, you'll get more people applying for the position if you offer a high wage for the work than if you offer a low wage. You understand that, right? Good. Then you're fine with this book.

I had wanted to assume that you were deeply interested in the historical and cultural influences on crowdsourcing and how crowdsourcing is part of the great trends of industrial society. My editor, however, convinced me that I was misguided to make that assumption, so I didn't. (However, if you are interested in historical and cultural influences, there's a lovely book on the subject called *When Computers Were Human*, by yours truly. It's a great read, but it won't help you become a great crowdsourcer.)

How This Book Is Organised

Because crowdsourcing is a way of organising people, this book is organised in a way that helps you build your organising skill. It moves from simple ideas to the more complex. The book is split into five parts, and each contains several chapters on the part's theme. Here is an overview of the parts.

Part 1: Understanding Crowdsourcing Basics

Do you know what crowdsourcing is? Do you know how it differs from using social media? Or mob rule? To help, the first two chapters of Part I give you an overview of the material in the rest of *Crowdsourcing For Dummies*. Chapter 1 gives you an introduction to crowdsourcing and helps you understand the potential benefits of crowdsourcing to you, to your work and to any organisation that may want to use crowdsourcing. Chapter 2 guides you into the rest of the book. It offers an introduction to the different forms of crowdsourcing and then points you to the parts of the book that will be of most use to you.

I also include chapters on how to be a crowdworker. Being a working member of the crowd for a while is a great way to learn more about crowdsourcing – and you can earn money while you do it, too.

Part II: Looking at the Different Forms of Crowdsourcing

Part II divides crowdsourcing into its five basic forms – crowdcontests, crowdfunding, macrotasking, microtasking and self-organised crowds – and provides a thorough introduction to each. Each chapter includes a detailed description of one type of crowdsourcing along with examples that illustrate how to apply it. You may only read one or two of these chapters, because you may want to use only one or two forms of crowdsourcing.

Part III: Building Skill

Part III helps you to develop your skills as a crowdsourcer. It offers a chapter on each of the steps you need to take in order to crowdsource. You may not need to read all of these chapters thoroughly, because you may already possess some of these skills, but you can use them to ensure that you have the basic skills to be a good crowdsourcer.

Chapter 14 is an important chapter, because it deals with the basic ideas for managing crowdsourcing. And in Chapter 15, I look at the idea of *continuous improvement*, where you always try to identify the weak parts of your work and take steps to make them better in future.

Part IV: Getting All You Can Get from the Crowd

Part IV presents some advanced topics, such as microtask workflow, large-scale data gathering, prediction markets, election monitoring and innovation crowdsourcing. Many of these topics are becoming more and more common and are increasingly easy to do.

Part V: The Part of Tens

The Part of Tens illustrates the current state of crowdsourcing. It presents innovative crowdsourcing platforms, best practices, success stories and worst practices. The chapters in this part are filled with stories about crowdsourcing. Some will be familiar. Some will be new to you. They're all here to help you understand both the strengths and weaknesses of crowdsourcing, the techniques that work well and those that don't.

Icons Used in This Book

To help you understand crowdsourcing better and to guide you along the way, this book contains icons in the margins that flag different pieces of information:

This icon identifies suggestions and tips that make crowdsourcing easier.

When you see this icon, expect issues that need special attention, or problems that can easily get you into trouble. You ignore them at your own risk.

I use this icon to identify an important point that's worth remembering.

This icon highlights stories that illustrate the ideas in each chapter and demonstrate how you can use them. All examples are based on real stories of real people who use crowdsourcing. Some people have allowed me to use their name and the name of their company. You can identify these by the fact that they have full names and real URLs associated with them. For others, I've camouflaged the source of the example. If an example begins 'Emily started crowdsourcing when she ran a flower shop in Livosk', you can be sure that the source of this story is not named Emily, she doesn't sell flowers and has never been to Livosk.

Paragraphs with this icon are intended for people with experience in IT. You can skip the information and still understand the basic ideas of crowdsourcing.

This icon marks sections that deal with material that's used only for the form of crowdsourcing called microtasking. You can skip the paragraph if you're doing some other form of crowdsourcing, such as crowdcontests.

Where to Go from Here

Chapter 1 is a must-read to get a basic grasp of what crowdsourcing is all about, and Chapter 2 gives you an overview of the different forms of crowdsourcing. From there, you can jump to Part II, where you find detailed descriptions of these different forms. The chapters in that part give you more information about becoming a crowdsourcer.

After you've identified the form of crowdsourcing that you're going to do, head to Part III. There, chapters give you the information that you need to design the job, get it posted and running, and evaluate the results.

Alternatively, you can jump around the book as you like, reading whatever chapter appeals. Use the table of contents to help you navigate your own path. Alongside your reading, I recommend browsing some crowdsourcing websites – you can find examples in Chapter 13.

If you think that you're ready to become a crowdsourcer, take the next step. Turn the page, and start the journey.

Part I
Understanding Crowdsourcing Basics

understanding

crowdsourcing

basics

For Dummies can help you get started with lots of subjects. Visit www.dummies.com to learn more and do more with *For Dummies*.

In this part . . .

- ✔ Bone up on the basics and benefits of crowdsourcing to see what it could do for you and your organisation.

- ✔ Meet the five different types of crowdsourcing and understand the rules that govern how they operate.

- ✔ See the inside view on crowdsourcing and gain valuable experience by becoming a working member of the crowd.

- ✔ Enjoy working in the crowd? Fancy joining a crowdmarket? Want to consider the options open to you? Get the lowdown here on crowdsourcing careers.

Chapter 1

People Power: Getting a Feel for Crowdsourcing

*Y*ou've probably heard about crowdsourcing. If you haven't, you probably won't be leafing through the pages of this book. However, you may not be aware of the many ways in which you can use crowdsourcing to your advantage or of how crowdsourcing is a powerful way of doing work, organising people, gathering information and raising money.

Many people – the unconverted – think that crowdsourcing is nothing more than putting a question on Facebook and waiting for your friends to answer. Yet it's much more than that – and much more powerful.

I can think of no better example of the power of crowdsourcing than what it has done to the encyclopaedia. Putting together an encyclopaedia was once a grand scholarly activity to organise the knowledge of a nation. The French created the first in the 18th century. The British followed with *Encyclopaedia Britannica* in the nineteenth, and the Americans with the *Encyclopaedia Americana* in the twentieth. Now, in the 21st century, they've all been replaced with a crowdsourced encyclopaedia: Wikipedia. Just think about what crowdsourcing could do for you.

In this chapter, I introduce you to crowdsourcing – how it works, the benefits it offers and how you can think about organising the crowd to help you – and the areas that I cover in this book.

What Is This Thing Called Crowdsourcing?

Crowdsourcing is a means of organising and coordinating the labour of individual human beings. You use the Internet and computer software to contact individuals, offer them things to do, and collect the results of their work.

Seeing how crowdsourcing works

Crowdsourcing requires four different elements:

- ✔ A person, usually called the *crowdsourcer*, who manages the process
- ✔ A group of people, called the *crowd*, who do work
- ✔ A market, usually called the *crowdmarket*, that's used to help manage the contributions of the crowd (crowdmarkets are often found on Internet sites that are called *crowdsites* or *platforms*)
- ✔ A means of communicating with the crowd – usually the Internet

Strictly speaking, you can crowdsource without the Internet. You need to have only the crowdsourcer, the crowd and the crowdmarket. However, you can raise a larger crowd most easily if you use the Internet. The Internet reduces the isolation caused by geography and allows you to contact more people, who may have a wider range of skills.

To crowdsource, you put a request on a crowdmarket. You ask for a piece of information, an idea for a new product, a little bit of work, a large task or even a contribution. In return, you offer some kind of compensation. You pay for the worker's services with money, or you offer him gratitude, or give him a gift, or offer him membership in a community.

Just because you may not use conventional money in the transactions doesn't mean that you have no crowdmarket. Even when they're volunteers, workers receive something in the transaction. They get satisfaction from using their skills, pleasure at being part of a group, or a sense of meaning from contributing to something bigger than themselves.

In one of the most well-known examples of crowdsourcing, Wikipedia, almost all the workers are volunteers and work for no payment. Yet they're part of an exchange at a market. They offer their contributions to the Wikipedia encyclopaedia and receive no money in compensation for their efforts, even if their words becomes a fixture in the encyclopaedia. Still, each person feels some kind of satisfaction at contributing to the well-used compendium of human knowledge.

Looking at crowdsourcing forms

Crowdsourcing can take many different forms. You can do it with large groups of people or small teams, or even with individuals. You can crowdsource with people who live near to you or those who live and work on the other side of the planet. With crowdsourcing, you can engage the creativity and intellectual powers of individuals, or you can engage their physical labour, or you can ask for money.

To understand the nature of crowdsourcing and all that it can do, consider the following examples. I indicate the type of crowdsourcing used in each example; for an overview, take a look at Chapter 2.

- ✔ **Creating the best design:** You're preparing an annual report for your organisation. You've written all the text you need but you want it organised with a nice graphic design. You post on a crowdsite or platform a request for proposals for a design for your report. The crowd members submit proposals. You choose the one that best suits your needs and compensate the individual who created it. This form of crowdsourcing is called a *crowdcontest* (see Chapter 5 for more).

- ✔ **Getting a little help with editing:** Every now and then, you write a small article for a professional periodical. You know that your articles would be better if someone edited them. You don't have enough work to hire a professional editor, and so you post a request on a crowdsite for an editor. You find one who meets your needs and hire him to do your editing. This type of crowdsourcing is called *macrotasking* (flick to Chapter 7 for more).

- ✔ **Setting up a new blog:** You need a new blog for your organisation but you don't know how to set up the software. You also need a few special things that aren't usually part of standard blogging software. You describe what you need, post the details on a crowdmarket and ask for bids, and then you choose the ones that best meet your need. This process is called *macrotasking* (the subject of Chapter 7).

- ✔ **Gathering contact details:** You're the marketing manager for a small company and have just been given a list of 10,000 companies that might be potential clients. This list includes no contact information. To get the email address and URL for each firm, you could put the list on a crowdsourcing site and ask members of the crowd for the details. This form of crowdsourcing is called *microtasking*, and is common (head to Chapter 8 for details).

- ✔ **Converting medical records:** You've just finished medical school, passed your exams and are about to take over your Uncle Enda's practice, but here's the problem: your uncle kept all his patient records on paper forms. He kept detailed notes, but they were all in his tiny, slightly messy handwriting. You can either transcribe all his records yourself or hire a consultant to do it for you. Alternatively, you could also divide the records into tiny parts, put each part on a crowdmarket and ask the crowd to transcribe the information. This latter solution is called *micro-tasking* (see Chapter 8) – a technique that has become a common way of transcribing handwritten records.

✔ **Creating a new product:** You've an idea for a new product but you don't know how to make it, how you can market it or even whether you've got the perfect design. You go to a crowdsite that specialises in innovation and post your idea there. First, you get suggestions from the crowd for improving the product. Next, you get ideas that can help you manufacture the product. Finally, the crowd helps you identify an organisation that can help market the final invention. You're doing a form of *self-organised crowdsourcing*, a type of crowdsourcing that's been around for years (refer to Chapter 9).

✔ **Testing new software:** You've created a mobile app but you need to test it to make sure that it works on all kinds of phones, in every different region. To test it, you go to a crowdmarket that specialises in software testing. Members of the crowd download the app, test it in their region, and give you a report. This form of crowdsourcing can be handled by either *microtasking* or *macrotasking*. Either way, it can be very effective and profitable (see Chapters 7 and 8).

✔ **Raising funds for a good cause:** You run a community organisation and want to convert an abandoned car park into a flea market. You need money to buy the land and to erect a shed in one corner. While you may try to raise money through conventional means, you can also do it through crowdsourcing. You post your request on a website and ask for small donations. In doing so, you're *crowdfunding*. (There's more on this kind of crowdsourcing in Chapter 6.)

This form of crowdfunding is *charitable* crowdfunding. The donors expect nothing (or just a gift) in return. A second form of crowdfunding, *equity* crowdfunding, allows people to give money to companies and get a stake in the company in return.

✔ **Solving a big problem:** You're a company or a charity or just a wealthy person who wants to do some good. You're aware of a problem that touches every member of the human race and yet that no one can solve: a dreadful disease, perhaps; an uncontrollable pollution; a desperate poverty. You would like to see the problem solved, so you create a crowdcontest that seeks a solution. You offer a large prize and publicise the activity. As people start working on the problem, you encourage those with good ideas to work together. This form of crowdsourcing is called *innovation crowdsourcing* or *self-organised crowdsourcing* (see Chapters 9 and 18).

✔ **Organising a collection:** After Aunt Emily and Uncle Jared die, you discover that they collected photographs, and had thousands of images stored in boxes that were stuffed into their basement. You recognise a few faces or an occasional vista, but you're unable to identify anything in the remaining photographs or put these pictures into any kind of order. You can identify the images by putting them on a website and asking the crowd to give you information. You can then hire members of the crowd to process the information and put it into order. This is a type of *microtasking*, one that can be done in sophisticated ways. (Find out more about it in Chapters 8 and 16.)

Creating an encyclopaedia. Finding missing people. Folding proteins. Transcribing medical records. Collecting price information. Identifying sales contacts. Running errands. Deciding whether a web page is offensive. Checking the tone of translated text. Answering a question that has stumped you. All these are examples of crowdsourcing.

Considering Why People Crowdsource

You may find a few people out there who are interested in crowdsourcing because it seems to be something new and interesting to do with the Internet, but novelty and technology are never great reasons to do anything. Most people crowdsource simply because of the advantages it offers them. It brings new talent to organisations, enables individuals to do things that they couldn't do before, and allows groups of people to meet and collaborate for their common good. Crowdsourcing is a way of expanding what anyone or any group can do.

Introducing three key strengths

You get different benefits from crowdsourcing, depending on who you are and what you're doing. However, most people who crowdsource are expecting to get at least one of three things. They're looking for:

✔ **Access to talent:** Many people crowdsource to get access to talent that they can't get in any other way. They not be able to find anyone who is an expert app programmer, or knows how to translate French into Urdu, or knows how to optimise a web page in order to get the best ranking on search engines. Crowdsourcing can help you find individuals who have these skills. It can also bring you the talent that comes from the collected intelligence of the crowd, the ability to do things that are difficult for machines to do. For example, crowds are good at recognising handwriting or identifying faces in photographs, or comparing the quality of writing.

✔ **Doing more with less:** Crowdsourcing allows you to do more with your resources. You hire the best person for each job rather than looking for a single person with multiple talents. If you're building a bilingual web page, you don't have to look for a web designer who knows two languages. You can crowdsource one person or team for the task of building the web page. You can crowdsource another team or individual for the task of writing the text in a different language.

✔ **Greater flexibility:** Crowdsourcing allows you to follow trends in the market. It lets you replace rigid organisational structures with simple, flexible processes. Say that you've an office that processes email. Rather than creating a large staff with fixed rules, you can give some of the work to the crowd and let individuals decide the best way to process the material and find the information you need.

Benefitting from crowdsourcing

Anyone can benefit from crowdsourcing. Crowdsourcing expands your capability, giving access to new skills and abilities. It allows you to hire people when you need them and to get exactly the skills that you need at any given time. The following types of crowdsourcer in particular find crowdsourcing beneficial:

✔ **Small businesses:** Crowdsourcing offers skills that small businesses can't easily get any other way. A new business, for example, can use crowdsourcing to stay small and minimise the demands on its capital. You may not have the need for a full-time marketer, but you can get professional marketing skills for each project when you need them. You may not have the need for a full-time finance officer, but you can get financial advice through crowdsourcing.

✔ **Large businesses:** Large businesses often look at crowdsourcing as a way of reducing costs. That's one reason for enterprises to use crowdsourcing, but this reason is often not the best. Large companies often have other ways of minimising the cost of doing business. However, large enterprises should consider using crowdsourcing, because it can make them more creative and more responsive to the market. They can use crowds to do things that they used to think impossible, such as to handle large amounts of data in a personalised way, or get detailed contact information for their sales staff, or adjust their web materials to better engage the market.

✔ **Non-profit organisations:** Non-profit organisations often need specialised skills that they can't find or can't afford. They have to rely on a volunteer for bookkeeping, the friend of a neighbour to design a presentation, the goodwill of the local computer store to create and maintain a web page. Crowdsourcing enables such organisations to hire people with specialised skills on a short-term basis or to use inexpensive services that provide the skills they need.

✔ **Expanding the power of artists:** Artists can use crowdsourcing to expand their role and capacity. Crowdsourcing can offer skills that artists didn't learn in art school and services that they can't provide for themselves. It can give them access to funds through crowdfunding, to collaborators who can expand their art, to business and marketing skills that they couldn't otherwise afford and give them a way of promoting their art to bigger audiences.

✔ **Individuals:** What can one person do? The answer is 'much' if he uses crowdsourcing. Crowdsourcing enables one person with a vision to do things that he can't accomplish by himself. It gives him access to people with different skills, backgrounds and viewpoints.

If you want a good example of how crowdsourcing can expand the power of a single individual, look no further than Linus Torvalds, the person who conceived the Linux computer operating system, or Jimmy Wales, the organiser of Wikipedia. Both these individuals had ideas that they could not accomplish by themselves. However, both were able to rally the crowd to support their work.

✔ **Scientists and researchers:** Research is also a form of production and can make use of new production techniques. Crowdsourcing can allow scientists and researchers to process large amounts of data, gather data from regions that they can't visit, or analyse materials in ways that can't be done by machine.

Considering reliability

Crowdsourcing has its benefits, but you want to be sure that the crowd itself is trustworthy, that it's providing you with good information and not making things up. This is what's called the *reliability problem*. You're putting a task to the crowd – people you don't know and may never meet. You want to be sure that the crowd brings you a reliable result, something that has been done correctly and properly.

Many people resist crowdsourcing because of the reliability problem. They believe that crowd members are lazy, that they traffic in gossip and lies, that they're subject to a mob mentality and want nothing more than to take your money and give nothing in return. Such concerns are valid. The crowd can behave badly. It can take your money and leave nothing in return. But these aren't reasons to avoid crowdsourcing.

A relationship between two people is *reliable* when one of the people can ask something of the other and get a response that's correct and useful. Few relationships are naturally reliable. Unless you live a blessed life, you've probably had a family member lie to you, a worker fail to finish a job, or a colleague give you a wrong piece of information. You have to work to make relationships reliable.

In ordinary relationships, you do a number of things to ensure reliability. You try to pick friends who have the same interests and goals as you. You take advice from several individuals in case one doesn't know he's misinformed. You threaten to withhold a pay cheque from a worker unless he properly completes a task. In crowdsourcing, you also have to work to make the crowd reliable. You get information from multiple points of view, ask multiple members of the crowd to review work and look at the what the crowd has done before you pay for it.

Is crowdsourcing new?

The quick answer is 'no'. People have used crowdsourcing techniques for as long as they've used labour to produce goods and services. You can now do it easily, because you have the Internet and computers, but you can find examples of crowdsourcing throughout history:

✔ In the late 1810s, the English mathematician Charles Babbage hired contractors to help him compute astronomical tables that could be used for stellar navigation. This form of crowdsourcing is called macrotasking (see Chapter 7). Babbage became famous for designing mechanical computers, but he developed several key ideas of crowdsourcing.

✔ In 1891, the state of Washington ran a contest to design an exhibit hall for the upcoming World's Fair in Chicago. It was a form of crowdcontest (see Chapter 5).

✔ In 1914, the National Cash Register Company put a box next to its factory manager's office to collect suggestions from employees. The management announced that it would reward ideas that would reduce the costs of manufacturing. It is an example of how crowdsourcing can be used for innovation (see Chapter 18).

✔ In 1938, the National Foundation for Infantile Paralysis devised a new fundraising technique to support research to find a cure for polio. It asked every citizen of the USA to contribute ten cents to its research fund in what was called the March of Dimes. It was a form of crowdfunding (see Chapter 6).

✔ In 1938, the US Government's Work Projects Administration used crowdsourcing to give jobs to unemployed workers. For example, it created the Mathematical Tables Project, the largest computing office in the world. This project engaged 450 workers at a time to do advanced mathematical calculations. It used crowdsourcing techniques called microtasking (see Chapter 8) and macrotasking (see Chapter 7). It also managed the computations with tools that controlled the workflow (see Chapter 16). This book is dedicated to the leader of the Mathematical Tables Project, the mathematician Gertrude Blanch.

You need to devote time and effort to make crowdsourcing reliable, just as you need to devote time and effort to make any human relationship reliable. In crowdsourcing, you get out what you put in. To get good results from your crowd, you have to think about the process and design it in a way that's efficient and which also catches the crowd's mistakes.

Being a Crowdworker

People become *crowdworkers* – workers who earn their living by taking jobs from a crowdmarket instead of seeking a permanent job in a company – for the same kind of reasons that attract people to social media. Crowdsourcing helps workers overcome the limitations of place, time and creativity. When you're a member of the crowd, you can:

- **Break geographical barriers to using your skills.** Some people have skills that they can't easily use where they live. It's one thing to be a graphic designer in cities that support large advertising industries, such as Chicago or London. It's quite another thing to be a graphic designer and live in a small country town by a lake.

- **Employ skills that you can't fully use in your regular job.** You may have a great job close to home that even uses some of the Spanish language skills that you acquired by attending the University of Santiago for two years. However, you find that reviewing the occasional document in Spanish doesn't really use these skills. By becoming a crowdworker, you might be able to take a job each week that engages all of your languages. For example, you might find a job that asks you to review a Spanish newspaper and summarise the opinion page in English. Something like this may never replace your regular job or add much to your income, but it will challenge you and support a skill that's important to you.

- **Work from home.** Some people, such as new mothers, can't easily leave their home and work in an office.

- **Work to your own schedule.** Some individuals prefer to work at night, for example.

- **Choose jobs you like and avoid work you dislike.** Crowdsourcing does not require workers to do the same job, day after day.

- **Develop new skills.** Many crowdsourcing sites offer training classes for specific skills. You can learn skills that are rarely taught at school, such as how to test software, or expand skills that you already possess, such as those of copy or page editing.

As a crowdworker, you're judged by your skills and accomplishments rather than by your background and training. Even if you didn't go to the right school or come from the right part of the country, you can still do jobs that you want if you can show that you have the skills.

Chapter 4 gives you the lowdown on joining the crowd.

Becoming a Crowdsourcer

If you've read this far, you're seriously considering becoming a *crowdsourcer*, a person who creates and manages the crowdsource processes. A crowdsourcer is a form of a manager. As you find with all forms of management, you can't become a crowdsourcer simply by taking the name of crowdsourcer or by wishing that you can do crowdsourcing. You have to approach the work of crowdsourcing systematically.

When you work as a crowdsourcer, you have to do seven things:

1. **Define the goal.**

   You need to know what you want from the crowd in order to have the crowd help you. It's all too easy to think 'I'll let the crowd solve this' when you're facing a difficult question. But if you don't know what you want, you rarely get anything useful from the crowd.

2. **Design the process of engaging the crowd.**

   To get ideas, look at Part II of this book. It describes the different kinds of crowdsourcing and how you can use each to solve problems.

3. **Post the job.**

   You find a crowdsourcing website – a crowdsourcing site, your own blog or a social networking space – and post your request. You can find information on crowdsourcing sites in Chapters 11 and 12.

4. **Find the crowd.**

   If you're working on a crowdsourcing site, you'll probably find the crowd you need already affiliated with the site. If you need to raise a crowd, you do so using your social network. You contact friends and co-workers to see if they can help you find people who can serve as your crowd. Chapters 10 and 13 offer pointers on recruiting crowds.

5. **Manage the process.**

   Crowdsourcing is an activity that you have to manage. You can't expect it to happen automatically. You can, however, ask one of the crowdsourcing companies to manage the crowd and the work. For more on managing crowds, head to Chapter 14.

6. **Look at the results.**

   You become the best crowdsourcer by learning from what the crowd has done. When the crowd returns your job, it also gives you information about how you should plan your next crowdsourcing endeavour. You can read about learning from results in Chapter 15.

7. **Evaluate the product.**

   You look at what you've done and evaluate the work. You have to ask a few basic questions. Is the final product acceptable? Would I do it again? What changes would I make? After you answer these questions, you can decide to do more crowdsourcing or quit your efforts and go back to conventional ways of doing things.

The good news is that this book takes you through the whole process, so soon crowdsourcing can be a breeze.

Chapter 2

Getting to Know the Forms of Crowdsourcing and Crowdmarkets

In This Chapter

▶ Understanding the benefits of each form of crowdsourcing

▶ Getting to grips with the rules of crowdsourcing

*Y*ou may be as keen as mustard to unleash the awesome power of the crowd. You've heard about all that the crowd can do and you want to use it for your business, for your neighbourhood association or for your own purposes. You might want to use the crowd to design an advertisement for your company, to conduct a poll, to search for a lost child or to have a team of skilled workers behind you.

But whoa there! If you want to be a skilled crowdsourcer and use crowd-sourcing to really transform your work, your business or your non-profit group, you need to understand the basic properties of the different forms of crowdsourcing before you make a headlong rush into starting a project; you need to understand what they can do for you. Each form of crowdsourcing, because it has its own rules, works in a way that's slightly different from how the other forms work. Each is best for certain kinds of jobs and less good for others, and each has certain benefits and drawbacks. Therefore, to get the benefits – to transform your work – you need to know which form will best work for you.

The five forms of crowdsourcing are:

- ✔ Crowdcontests
- ✔ Macrotasking
- ✔ Microtasking
- ✔ Self-organised crowds
- ✔ Crowdfunding

I look at each of these forms more fully in Chapters 5–9, but in this chapter I introduce you to them, to help you get to grips with the basic elements of these forms of crowdsourcing. You'll see here how they differ from one another and how you might apply these forms to certain kinds of jobs. And because each form of crowdsourcing has its own rules, its own purposes and its own form of crowdmarket, you also get acquainted here with the different kinds of *crowdmarkets* – virtual online marketplaces used to help manage the crowd's contributions – and how you can use them to engage the crowd. All this is here, ultimately, to help you match the job that you want to do with the right form of crowdsourcing, and to guide you to the right part of the book that will enable you to become an expert crowdsourcer.

Harnessing the Power of Divided Labour

Crowdsourcing is a powerful means of getting work done by giving that work to a large group of workers – the *crowd*. It gets its power from the idea of *divided labour*, of taking a large job and dividing up the work. Each of the five forms of crowdsourcing involves a different way of dividing the work. Understanding all five ways enables you to work out the best way of dividing your job so as to get the best work back from the crowd.

Keeping the job whole

The simplest way of dividing a job is to keep it as a single task and not divide it at all. If you do this, you give the job to a single person to complete. When you do this kind of division in crowdsourcing, you rely heavily on that single person, so you obviously want the best possible person to do the work. Crowdsourcing enables you to find the best person by letting the crowd compete for your job. You ask the members of the crowd to submit their best work, you choose the best submission and then reward the person who did it. This form of crowdsourcing is known as a *crowdcontest*.

Crowdcontests are commonly used to create a single product quickly and easily and are great for creative activities such as graphic design, package design or video production, and can be useful for other activities such as product development, statistical analyses and financial projections. Crowdcontests are also well suited to activities in which workers believe that they benefit by participating in the contest even if they aren't ultimately awarded the winner's prize, because crowd members can use contests to practise and develop their skills and don't have to invest anything beyond their time and energies.

Caitriona uses crowdsourcing for her cookware store. In addition to standard commercial kitchen utensils, she sells a small line of custom plates, bowls and tableware. She obtains her designs by running crowdcontests. She describes what kind of product she wants and lets the members of the crowd propose designs. She identifies the design that she thinks is best, manufactures it and sells it in her store.

A crowdcontest is for you if you don't want to manage the crowd and you don't have an interest in a long-term relationship with any member of the crowd. Crowdcontests can deliver products quickly and generally don't take much effort to manage.

Crowdcontests do have two drawbacks, though. First, they aren't suited to all kinds of jobs, especially those that take a long time. For any job that requires a lot of work and investment, you have to offer a large prize to get a good crowd. The second drawback is the lack of a long-term relationship with the crowd. You may not, for example, be able to contact the winner of your last contest if you decide that you want to have her help you again.

You can find more about crowdcontests in Chapter 5.

Splitting the job into big pieces

Instead of keeping a job whole, an alternative approach is to divide it into large pieces that each require specific skills. You give each of these large pieces to a member of the crowd who has that specific skill. You manage the process and pay the workers. This form of crowdsourcing is known as *macrotasking.*

Macrotasking is the most flexible form of crowdsourcing because it's an expanded version of freelancing. With it, you can identify a specific skill that you need, find someone with that skill and recruit her to help with your work. The macrotaskers can help you individually; they can join an office team; they can even lead a project for you. Crowdsourcers often use macrotasking to bring specialist skills to an organisation for a short time.

Kwame uses macrotasking in his corporate communications firm, where he helps companies prepare public relations strategies. When Kwame acquires a new client, he assembles a team to help the client deal with its communications problem. That team usually has a manager, a writer and a presentation designer. It may also have several specialised workers, such as a graphic designer, a speech coach or an advertising expert. Kwame tends to hire the specialised workers from a macrotask market.

Macrotasking offers you the broadest set of skills. Not only can you find artistic skills, you can find technical and programming skills, various business and office skills, language skills, communications skills and management skills. Macrotasking also offers you the chance to nurture a long-term relationship with a worker if you find a particularly good macrotasker. It also requires the least amount of preparation, as the work of hiring a macrotasker is just a simpler version of the process of hiring an ordinary employee.

Macrotasking does have its drawbacks, though. Sometimes you may find it difficult to track down exactly the skill you're seeking. Other times, you may find it a challenge to communicate with a macrotasker who lives several time zones away and in a different culture. Finally, managing a macrotask worker can require as much effort as you'd expend to manage a regular employee. If you want a simpler form of crowdsourcing, you may want to consider crowdcontests instead.

You can find out how to hire a macrotask worker in Chapter 7.

Dividing the job as small as you can

Dividing up your job into small or tiny tasks means you can engage more of the crowd and get your job done more quickly. When you do this kind of crowdsourcing, you pay all members of the crowd who work for you. This form of crowdsourcing is known as *microtasking*.

The basic forms of microtasks are simple – usually far simpler than macrotasks. You describe what you want done, post your job on a microtask site and wait for the crowd to respond. You can judge each submission and accept those that are properly done, without having to first review the résumés of potential workers or interview them.

When microtasking, crowdsourcers generally look for a large crowd to do their work, and so they divide it into small tasks that can be done by many, many people. This usually means that the tasks can't require special skills that only one or two people may have. You can microtask if you can find a crowd of ten to help you, but you can't microtask if you can only find one person.

Niall prepares instruction manuals for electronic consumer goods. He has to have the instructions translated into eight major languages and check that the translated instructions are still accurate. He once hired an expert translator to check each version of the instructions, but discovered he can use microtasking to check the translations instead. To do this, he divides each newly translated manual into paragraphs, posts each paragraph on a crowdsourcing platform and invites the crowd to translate each paragraph back into English. He then compares the retranslation with the original English. When the paragraphs match, he knows that the translated instructions are accurate.

Microtasking brings the power of human intelligence to tasks that computers can't do well. It can help you deal with non-textual data such as handwriting or photographs; it can help you collect data from places that you can't reach; it enables you to make judgements about large collections of data, such as the material displayed on web pages or found in big company databases. If you're carrying out elementary tasks with crowdsourcing, microtasking is often the quickest and easiest way to do them.

Microtasking has two drawbacks, however. First, the workers can be unreliable. You have to review each submission to make sure each task has been done properly, and if you're doing a large job, you'll need to create some kind of system to review each submission and verify it. Such a system can be complicated to create and difficult to implement. Second, microtasking can quickly get complicated. You often need to combine multiple macrotasks with the process called workflow to get your results.

Chapter 8 tells you how to prepare and run microtasks (and Chapter 16 can help you see the wood from the trees when thinking about workflow).

Letting the crowd divide the job

In some cases, you don't need to divide the job at all – you can let the crowd decide how to divide it. When you engage in this form of crowdsourcing, you post a job on the crowdsourcing platform, offer a reward for the person or group who does the job best, set a deadline for the job and then let the crowd work. When the deadline arrives, you review the different submissions and reward the best one. This form of crowdsourcing is call *self-organised* crowdsourcing. Self-organised crowdsourcing comes in many forms. *Innovation crowdsourcing*, for example, is commonly used for developing new goods or services. (I look at innovation crowdsourcing in Chapter 18.)

Jamilla has been given the responsibility of reorganising the customer relations department of a large consumer products company. She's concluded that the company's customer relations program is badly broken and that it simply can't handle the unique problems created by the company's products and markets. Rather than hire a consultant to review the system and propose a fix, Jamilla decides to crowdsource a solution. But rather than tell the crowd what to do, she asks the crowd what she should do and lets the crowd form a team to give her advice. She describes the problems with the existing system and gives requirements for a new system, then she posts the information on a crowdsourcing platform and offers a reward for the best system. Since no one person can create such a system, members of the crowd create teams. Usually one member of the crowd is the leader and recruits friends and colleagues to be part of a team. Several teams enter the competition. One, which includes both company employees and a few outsiders, proposes a radically new system that addresses the company's needs.

Self-organised crowds sound great. In theory, you can accomplish anything you want with a self-organised crowd. To date, people have used them to gather information, study markets, monitor elections, create new products and predict the future of the economy. In these applications, you can use a self-organised crowd just as easily as you would use a market survey or focus group. Likewise, software systems such as Ushahidi make it easy to recruit a self-organised crowd and to have it gather data for you. (You can learn more about using self-organised crowds to gather information by turning to Chapter 17.)

Self-organised crowdsourcing has one drawback. It's a new form of crowd-sourcing and isn't as well understood as the other forms. You can spend a lot of time preparing a job for a self-organised crowd and be surprised when the crowd does something completely unexpected. Researchers are working hard to understand how crowds organise themselves, how they cooperate and what they can do. If you're looking to use the crowd beyond the applications that have already been tried and tested, such as innovation crowdsourcing (see Chapter 18), you may become a crowdsourcing pioneer yourself.

Chapter 9 shows you the ropes for working with a self-organised crowd.

Using crowdsourcing to raise money

Crowdfunding is the one form of crowdsourcing where the objective is to raise money rather than do work. In crowdfunding, you use the crowd to raise money for your company, your charity or your artistic endeavour. Crowdfunding has two forms. The first is _charitable crowdfunding_, where you pass a hat to the crowd and ask for donations. The second form, called _equity crowdfunding_, raises money for a company by selling the crowd inexpensive shares of stock. (I cover crowdfunding in detail in Chapter 6.)

While charitable crowdsourcing is common in all parts of the world, equity crowdfunding is not. Equity crowdfunding is regulated by the same government agencies that control stock markets and corporate governance. In some countries, these agencies impose regulations on equity crowdfunding or outlaw it altogether. You need to check with the Security and Exchange Commission in the US, the Financial Services Authority in the UK or the equivalent agency in your country about any regulation of equity crowdfunding.

Tierney is the manager of a rural county animal shelter. The shelter is over-crowded and is no longer able to use part of the building that was damaged in a recent storm. Tierney gets her operating budget from the county council but has to raise money for the building herself. She decided to post a request on a crowdfunding site and used her online social network to notify the county's residents about the campaign. To her requests, she added short videos of children playing with abandoned puppies and kittens in the damaged wing of the building. The campaign got wide publicity in the area and brought in sufficient funds to rebuild the structure. Her crowdfunding campaign engaged more people than any prior fundraising campaign she'd run.

The big drawback to crowdfunding is the work you have to do to get the crowd interested in your project. It requires some effort – you have to recruit a crowd to go to your crowdfunding page and give to your cause – but it does give you a much greater likelihood of success than if you try to raise money through conventional means.

You're most likely to be successful in crowdfunding if you have some fundraising skills. If you review crowdsourcing sites, you'll see that in successful cases the crowdsourcer is able to plan a good campaign, write a good description of the project, draw a large crowd to the site and support the campaign with professional photographs or video.

You can find out more about the ins and outs of crowdfunding in Chapter 6.

Looking at the Rules that Govern How Crowdmarkets Work

Understanding the differences between the five forms of crowdsourcing is important. You can easily distinguish the forms by the way they divide labour, but the other differences are a little more subtle. For example, macrotasking generally handles jobs that have been divided into large pieces, but sometimes you can have the crowd do large tasks with microtasking. Likewise, you can think of self-organised crowds as a form of contest, but you don't have to run them as contests.

The major forms of crowdsourcing are distinguished by the rules they impose on the *crowdmarket* – an online virtual marketplace that is used to help manage the contributions of the crowd.

As a crowdsourcer, in most cases you deal with the crowdmarket through a *crowdsourcing platform* – a website that supports your crowdsourcing. As well as a crowdmarket, platforms offer additional services that support you as a crowdsourcer. Crowdsourcing platforms usually offer a payroll service that pays your workers and files all the appropriate paperwork with Her Majesty's Revenue and Customs (in the UK) or the Internal Revenue Service (in the USA). The platform provider can also help promote your project, give you advice about how to crowdsource, and even help you find specific skills within the crowd.

When a crowdsourcing platform creates a crowdmarket, it usually sets two kinds of rules that determine how that market operates:

- ✔ The first type of rule – often called the contract or contest rule – determines what kind of payments are offered to members of the crowd. When you post a project on a crowdmarket, you can pay the crowd in one of two ways:

    - You can pay every member who contributes to your project. This is a *contract market*, or *pay-all market*.

    - You can pay the one worker who submits the best job. This kind of market is called a *contest market*, or *pay-one market*, because it's similar to a contest.

- ✔ The second type of rule for crowdmarkets determines the way in which the workers collaborate. The market can encourage the members of the crowd to collaborate – this type is imaginatively called a *collaborative market* – or it can require the each member to work in isolation – called an *independent market*.

All forms of crowdsourcing involve markets and exchanges, but not all markets and exchanges involve money. In some cases, crowdworkers donate their earnings to a good cause. In other cases, they work for something other than money, such as satisfaction or status. If a market offers satisfaction rather than money, it's a contract market. Everyone who contributes to the job gets something in return.

I set aside crowdfunding in this section. Crowdfunding is a form of crowdsourcing that's easy to understand and which differs from the four other forms in that you use it to raise money rather than to manage work. You can distinguish these four working forms of crowdsourcing from one another by how they use the crowdmarket. (*Crowdmarkets* are the places where crowdsourcers – the managers of the crowd – meet with the crowd to offer them tasks and accept their work. See Chapter 1 for more about crowdmarkets.)

Distinguishing between contract and contest markets

Two forms of crowdsourcing – macrotasking and microtasking – use contract markets. Contract markets pay the members of the crowd for all work that's done on the contract market site. For macrotasks, the market usually pays by the hour. The macrotask worker works for a certain number of hours on a task and gets paid for those hours of work. In a microtask market, the workers are generally paid by the task. Workers receive the same amount for a task no matter how much time they spend on it.

The other two working forms of crowdsourcing – crowdcontests and self-organised crowds – use contest markets. Crowdcontests use a contest market in a fairly straightforward way. Many members of the crowd submit work to the market; the crowdsourcer picks the best submission and rewards it. This scenario is a contest and nothing more. Self-organised markets, however, use the contest market in a more sophisticated way. The market asks for submissions from the crowd and rewards the team that submits the best work. The team then decides how to divide the reward among its members.

When used for self-organised crowds, the contest market removes an important tool of management from the crowdsourcer and gives it to the crowd. The crowdsourcer no longer evaluates the contribution of each member of the team and rewards it. That work's done by the winning team itself. If the team is strong and well-organised, it will have a good mechanism for dividing the reward and recognising the contributions of each individual. If it's weak and poorly organised, it's likely to have trouble deciding how the money should be divided.

Understanding collaborative and independent crowdworking

When crowd members engage the market, they can either work independently or with other members of the crowd. Crowd members tend to work independently when they complete microtasks or participate in crowdcontests. In both cases, each crowdworker prepares her work without dealing with other members of the crowd and submits that work to the crowd market. In contrast, self-organised crowds are always collaborative affairs. The crowdsourcer poses a question to the crowd and asks the crowd to work together to find a solution.

You can also think of macrotasking as a collaborative effort. You can assemble a team of macrotaskers and ask the individuals to work together on a problem. To be fair, you can also hire a single macrotasker to work by herself on a project. Macrotasking is probably the most flexible form of crowdsourcing and, because it allows for collaboration, you can think of it as a collaborative form of crowdsourcing.

Combining the two rules

Each of the four different forms of crowdsourcing (excluding crowdfunding) represents a different combination of the rules that determine how you pay the crowd and how you encourage the members to collaborate. Table 2-1 demonstrates how the different combinations of these rules determine how the four forms of crowdsourcing operate.

Table 2-1	Different Forms of Crowdsourcing	
	Independent Markets	*Collaborative Markets*
Pay one member of the crowd (contest market)	Crowdcontests	Self-organised crowds
Pay all members of the crowd (contract market)	Microtasking	Macrotasking

Chapter 3

Infiltrating the Crowd

*M*ost of this book clues you in on crowdsourcing from the point of view of the crowdsourcer, the person who designs and manages the crowdsourcing activity. But just as bosses in organisations benefit from getting out on the shop floor, being part of the crowd yourself enables you to gain a good understanding of crowdsourcing.

From within the crowd, you see how the crowd works and how it deals with specific crowdsourced jobs. You notice how individuals interact with the crowdmarket, which tasks are difficult and which are easy, which instructions guide you to do the job well and which are confusing. And you develop a keen sense of which skills are actually needed for a task.

The most experienced crowdsourcers spend a few minutes each day in the crowd. Doing so lets them see whether their crowdsourced job is going well and lets them keep an eye on what their competitors are doing.

In the crowd, no one need know that you're a crowdsourcer. The other members of the crowd need never know that you're someone who's designing and managing crowdsourced activities.

In this chapter, I help you take a walk in the crowdworker's shoes, which can help you gain valuable knowledge to inform your crowdsourcing activities. First, I walk you through the crowdworker's process, and then I pick out key lessons you can take from being in the crowdworker's shoes. Finally, I suggest three major crowdsourcing activities for you to try out: Wikipedia, Amazon's Mechanical Turk and Zooniverse.

Following the Crowdworker's Steps

To undertake crowdwork, you usually take these five steps:

1. **Register at the crowdmarket.**

   The *crowdmarket* is the place where crowdsourcers and crowdworkers meet. *Crowdsourcers* bring tasks that they need to have done. *Crowdworkers* come to do those tasks (for more details, head over to Chapter 2). Sometimes, crowdmarkets don't look much like a market. Wikipedia, for example, doesn't look much like a market, but it is one. Other crowdmarkets, though, such as Amazon's Mechanical Turk or Elance or oDesk, look exactly like markets.

   Because crowdmarkets don't always look like marketplaces, people often refer to them as *crowdsourcing sites* or *crowdsourcing platforms*. Registering at a market is just like registering at any commercial website: you create an identifier and password for yourself and give the site a certain amount of personal information.

   If the market pays its workers, the workers also have to give their tax information. In the USA, a worker has to give his social security number; in the UK, it's the National Insurance number; and in Australia, it's the tax file number. The worker may also have to give details of a bank account or PayPal account so that the market can transfer his earnings.

2. **Verify your skills.**

   Crowdmarkets usually ask workers to demonstrate their skills. They verify your skills in different ways, depending on the kind of crowdsourcing that you're doing. (For more on different types of crowdsourcing, check out Chapter 2.)

   • **Crowdcontest** markets sometimes ask for your credentials, but they often ask only for your submission. Crowdcontests are more concerned with your submission than with the background of the workers.

   • **Macrotask** markets usually ask for information about the background of workers, requesting academic credentials and examples of prior work.

   • **Microtask** markets ask potential workers to do sample tasks to show that they can complete the work correctly. Often, these sample tasks are associated with specific collections of tasks. If you move from one group of tasks to another – from transcribing business cards to reviewing web pages, for example – you complete a new sample task to demonstrate your skills.

- **Self-organised crowds** generally avoid tests to check the skills of the individual workers. Instead, they rely on reputations. Self-organised crowds recruit members who are connected to existing members of the crowd, who have a portfolio of work, and who post their accomplishments on the crowdmarket. The crowd quickly finds out if a new worker has exaggerated his reputation or can't do the work.

- **Crowdfunding** generally asks only for your credit card. If your money is good then the crowdsourcer is happy with you.

3. **Choose a task.**

If the market deals with crowdcontests, microtasks or macrotasks, it displays the tasks in lists or lets you search a database of tasks for specific kinds of jobs. In these types of tasks, you can generally read the full description of the job before you accept it.

Most markets let you return a job after you've started it. If you conclude that you've made a mistake, you can click a Return button and send the task back to the market. Returning a job you don't want to do is always better than completing it badly. If you make errors in a task, those errors reflect on your reputation score.

Crowdfunding sites give you a list of projects that are seeking funds. They work much like microtasking or macrotasking sites.

Sites promoting self-organised crowds provide lists of groups that you may want to join.

4. **Do the work.**

As a crowdworker, you often complete the task at your computer. Some of the tasks take a lot of time, others very little. The better markets give you an estimate of the effort that you need to expend on a task.

Some tasks require you to do research on the web. Others ask that you use resources of your own. Many ask you to use a piece of software that they developed. Often this software is connected seamlessly into the market. When you use Zooniverse, for example, you use this kind of software to count craters on the moon or look for planets of distant stars.

5. **Submit your work.**

After you complete the task, you send your work to the market. When your work is at the market, it's reviewed by the crowdsourcer to make sure you've done it properly. He checks to make sure that you've followed the instructions and that every part of the task is complete. In some circumstances, such as for microtasks, this review happens very quickly. At other times, notably in crowdcontests and macrotasks, the review takes several hours or even a couple of days.

While the completed task is under review, you can select another task and start work on it.

Taking Lessons from Your Time as a Crowdworker

As you live the life of a crowdworker, you begin to gain an understanding of the nature of these workers. You discover that crowdworkers aren't invisible individuals, that they need training, that they need clear instructions. If you work long enough, you also discover that crowdworkers have the power of movement. If they don't like a job, they can leave it and move on to another.

Lesson 1: Crowdworkers have names and reputations

When you work in crowdsourcing, you're quickly reminded that it's a human activity and that crowdworkers are real people with goals and reputations that shape the way they work. You can easily forget these facts when you're planning or managing a large crowdsourcing job. It's also easy to forget the value of a good reputation to a crowdworker.

The first thing you learn from working in a crowdmarket is that crowdworkers have names and reputations. Often, names are masked by identifiers applied by the market, but the reputations are not. Good reputations enable workers to get the best jobs or to demand the highest pay. Mediocre reputations force workers to take uninteresting work or low-paying tasks.

Crowdworkers often try to protect or improve their reputations. They try to gain qualifications for new skills or get crowdsourcers to give them a top review on a task. If a reputation is summarised in a numerical scale, as it is at many crowdmarkets or crowdsourcing sites, workers may protest a low score or a claim that they didn't complete a job correctly.

At most crowdmarkets or crowdsourcing sites, crowdworkers can't easily abandon their reputations and build a new one from scratch. When crowdworkers register at crowdmarkets, they're required to give their real names and their real tax identifications. Only if you're working for free can you can hide behind an invented handle.

Lesson 2: Crowds need training

When you spend some time as a crowdworker, you quickly learn that training's important. Workers can't just log on to a crowdmarket and become an expert crowdworker, just as you can't expect to be a great writer simply by turning on a word processor, or a great game player by merely logging in to a game. You always need to find out what to do.

Even the simplest tasks require training. When you prepare a task for the crowdmarket, think about how you'll prepare the workers for that task. You need to teach them how to get the information that they require, how to go through the steps of the task, how to check to see that the work's properly done, and how to return the work to the market.

When training crowdworkers, you may have to spend a little time helping them to deal with ambiguity. Sometimes, the workers will start a task and conclude that the work they have to do doesn't quite match the instructions they're supposed to follow.

For example, suppose the crowdworkers are transcribing a short audio file, which is a common task on crowdmarkets. The instructions tell them to listen to the file, type the words that they hear into a field on the site, and then push a button marked Submit.

Those instructions sound complete enough, but think about what the workers should do if they don't understand all the words, if they hear two people talking at the same time, if the words are in a language that they don't understand, or if they hear something that the crowdsourcer never anticipated.

In this example, you'll want to train your workers to take a specific action when they can't complete the task. You might ask them to write 'cannot transcribe words' if they can't transcribe even a part of the tape.

If you don't tell your workers what to do, each worker will make a different judgement when they can't understand the words. Some will make a valiant effort and guess the words. Some will do only part of the task. Some will return the task untouched. As a result, you, as the crowdsourcer, will have to review the work for each task and determine what each worker meant.

Albert Einstein said, 'Everything should be kept as simple as possible, but no simpler.' This principle certainly applies to training crowdworkers.

Lesson 3: Crowds want clear instructions

Nothing frustrates crowdworkers more than an instruction they don't understand. And if they don't understand what you want, they won't take your job.

On all crowdmarkets, you find jobs that the crowd rejects. When you see a job that's sitting untaken in the crowdmarket, you may be tempted to think that the job's underpriced. A better price, you may conclude, would attract more workers to the job. Technically, you may be right. A higher price would attract more workers to the task. However, the real problem may be a badly written set of instructions.

Good, clear instructions tell crowdworkers the:

✔ Actions to take

✔ Data to find

✔ Judgements to make

✔ Format for the work

The guidelines for writing clear crowd instructions are no different from the guidelines for writing any form of instructions:

✔ Keep sentences short.

✔ Use a direct voice.

✔ Use plain English.

✔ Whenever possible, test the instructions on a friend.

As you read more and more crowd instructions, you'll find that pictures can be more powerful than words. You can't always describe complex instructions in simple sentences. A diagram or picture can guide the crowd through your work more easily.

Lesson 4: Crowds are free to move

'Plenty more fish in the sea' is the advice you may give a young person whose relationship has failed. For crowdworkers, the sea is filling up with more and more fish every day.

Crowdworkers aren't bound to a single job. They're free to move about. If they don't like a task or become bored with it or get angry because their payments are delayed, they can go in search of other work. Just because you have a crowd today doesn't mean that you'll have a crowd tomorrow.

Yet crowdworkers do develop loyalties. They find certain kinds of work satisfying. They enjoy building skills on specific kinds of tasks. They like to identify with a specific institution, even if they occasionally disagree with the goals or ideals of that institution.

As a crowdsourcer, you want to keep the crowd interested in your work and your tasks. You develop a reputation just like a crowdworker, although most markets don't yet keep a reputation score for those who provide jobs.

One of the ways to encourage workers to stay at your crowdmarket or crowdsite is to offer recognition for workers who have completed a certain number of tasks. You might call these recognitions bronze, silver and gold stars. When they've completed 50 tasks, for example, you give them a bronze star, you give a silver star for 100, and a gold star for 200. You can keep a leaderboard to show the names of everyone who's received stars and, perhaps, each week you might also a small financial reward to the workers who've completed the most tasks that week. These techniques are often part of a process known as *gamification*.

Joining the Staff of Wikipedia

If you want a simple starting point to find out about crowdwork, head to Wikipedia (www.wikipedia.org). Wikipedia is one of the most visible and accessible crowdsourced activities, and it illustrates the basic structure of crowdsourced work (see the earlier section, 'Following the Crowdworker's Steps'). You register as a worker, choose a task, complete the task, and submit the task for evaluation. The only step you don't do is demonstrate your ability to do the work before you take a task. Wikipedia judges all work by the quality of the submission, not by the qualifications of the contributor.

Registering as a worker

To register as a contributor to Wikipedia, simply go to http://en.wikipedia.org/wiki/Main_Page, click the 'Create account' link in the top-right corner of the screen, and type in a username, password and (optional) your email address.

That's it! Because Wikipedia doesn't pay its contributors, it doesn't require you to give any information for tax identification. You also don't have to give your real name. However, your user name is identified with your contributions. If you're a reliable contributor, the editors recognise your ability. If you're unreliable or regularly violate the Wikipedia guidelines, you acquire a poor reputation. Eventually, one of the senior volunteers will notice your reputation, especially if you make a lot of changes to a small group of entries. If that volunteer decides that you're causing more trouble than you're worth, he can ban you from participating in Wikipedia again.

Choosing a task

Most commonly, you will be editing an existing entry. Wikipedia is now a large and comprehensive encyclopaedia that already has articles on most common subjects and many uncommon ones. Still, you may find a topic that lacks an entry and be the first to create one.

Completing a task

In the article you want to modify, click the 'Edit' tab at the top of the page, which gives you access to the editor.

You can use the editor as you would any word processor to select words, delete text and write new sentences. However, you have to follow the guidelines for Wikipedia contributions as well as the mechanics of editing.

As one of its five pillars or principles, Wikipedia claims that it has no firm rules. However, it does have general guidelines for contributors, which you can find at `http://en.wikipedia.org/wiki/Wikipedia:Wikipedia_ in_brief`. These guidelines ask you to:

✔ Write from a neutral point of view.

✔ Target an encyclopaedia audience.

✔ Avoid original research.

✔ Avoid plagiarised or copyrighted materials.

✔ Keep to the facts.

Submitting a task

As with many crowdsourcing markets, Wikipedia asks you to submit your complete work in a formal manner. After you complete your writing, you review your work for errors and then you scroll down to the bottom of the page to the 'Edit Summary'. There, you fill in details of the nature of the changes you've made to an article and then click the Save Page button to send the material to an editor. Wikipedia publishes the changes immediately, but editors can remove them if they believe that the modifications aren't appropriate.

In the formal submission, Wikipedia also notifies you of all the legal require-ments for contributors. As a contributor, you have certain rights and obliga-tions that you acknowledge when you submit your work.

Leaping into the Market with Amazon's Mechanical Turk

At the time of writing, Amazon's Mechanical Turk (www.mturk.com) is the largest and most heavily used crowdsourcing platform. The site is really a nothing more than a simple job market. On Mechanical Turk, you can find large jobs that offer large payments or small, quick tasks that pay pennies. Individuals, academic researchers and large crowdsourcing firms use the platform.

Mechanical Turk workers (they sometimes go by the name 'Turkers') go through the five steps for crowdworkers outlined in the first section in this chapter.

To learn how Mechanical Turk operates, go ahead and do a couple of the tasks that are common to the site. For example, a common task is to find the number of people who 'like' a certain product or artist on their Facebook page.

Registering as a worker

Go to www.mturk.com and click the link in the upper right-hand corner. Doing this enables you to log on to the crowdmarket as a worker. (Amazon's Mechanical Turk uses its own terms to describe crowdsourcing. They often call crowdsourcers by the name of *requesters*.)

Registration is much like that for any commercial site. You have to give your correct name and, when you reach the last page, you have to give your tax information. In the USA, you have to enter your social security number. If you live outside the USA, you can get a US social security number by filing a foreign worker form with the Internal Revenue Service. The Mechanical Turk software helps you do this. If you don't have a US social security number, you have to take your earnings in the form of Amazon products.

What's a Mechanical Turk?

Amazon's Mechanical Turk takes its name from an 18th-century machine. The machine's designer, the Austrian Baron Wolfgang von Kempelen (1734–1804), claimed that the machine could play chess, but it was really a fraud.

The Mechanical Turk consisted of a dummy dressed in clothes associated with the Ottoman Empire, seated at a desk in front of a large chess set. The dummy was able to move its arms and manipulate chess pieces on the board. Von Kempelen claimed that these arms were controlled by machinery, but they were actually directed by a colleague of his who was both an expert chess player and a very small man who could hide among the gears and levers of the machine.

Von Kempelen toured the Hapsburg empire with this machine and challenged people to games of chess. As his expert was a good player, the machine generally won. The Turk had a long history that ended after it was sold to a museum in Philadelphia and was then destroyed in an 1854 fire. A reproduction can be seen in the Deutsches Museum in Munich.

The story of the original Mechanical Turk is completely unconnected with crowdsourcing. However, Amazon often uses the image of von Kempelen's machine to advertise its job marketplace.

Selecting the task

Mechanical Turk calls the basic task the *Human Intelligence Task*, or *HIT*. It lists these tasks on a screen such as the one shown in Figure 3-1. Each of the rounded rectangles describes one set of similar tasks or HITS. The group with the largest number of available tasks is listed first.

The title of each task is given in the upper left-hand corner of the record. For example, the title of the top set of tasks is 'Find the Facebook page URL and number of "Likes" for certain music labels and music artists'.

From the record, you can also see the payment or reward offered for each task and the number of tasks of this type that are available. In this case, the requestor's offering $0.03 and has 953 individual tasks or HITs in its pool.

You find the two key pieces of information about the tasks in the middle of the record. The *HIT Expiration Date* tells you that these tasks can be found on Mechanical Turk until 30 December or until they're done, whichever is first. *Time Allotted* tells you that Mechanical Turk will give you five minutes to complete the HIT after you start it. If you haven't completed it in five minutes, the program withdraws the task.

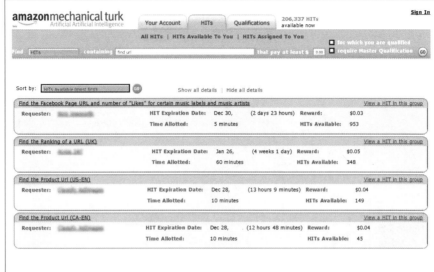

Figure 3-1:
Tasks
(HITS) on
Amazon's
Mechanical
Turk.

To see an actual task in this first group of HITS, click on the text that reads 'View a HIT in this Group' in the upper right-hand corner of the rectangle. Next, the screen shown in Figure 3-2 will appear. This screen describes the task in detail and shows the work that you'd have to do to complete it. This task is pretty easy. It asks you to find the Facebook page of a band called The Future Sound of London, and gives you instructions to find the number of people who like this band. It also has two fields. In the first, you put the address (or *URL*) of the band's Facebook page; in the second, you put the number of people who 'Like' the band.

If you like the task, you can click the Accept HIT button at the bottom and go ahead and do the work. If you decide that it doesn't interest you, you can click on the Skip HIT button and go on to another task.

Qualifying and completing the task

Now that you've accepted the task, you need to become qualified. Each requestor has its own way of qualifying crowd workers. Usually, the crowd-sourcer asks you to do a special task. These tasks look like any other tasks but have an answer that the requestor knows. If you get the right answer, you can do more tasks; if you don't, you have to correct your answer before you can proceed to the next step.

Often, the step that asks you to demonstrate your skill is also the step that trains the workers. The requestor creates examples that guide the workers through the different steps and help them understand what they're to do. For more on training, see the earlier section 'Lesson 2: Crowds need training'.

After you've completed the example task, click the Submit HIT button. If you don't like what you've done, click Return HIT and your answers won't be recorded.

Some requestors require you to do only a single example task before you can start to work. Others require several test tasks. In all cases, the requestor can check your responses to these examples and reject you if you aren't doing the work properly.

After you qualify to work on this specific pool of tasks, you can return to the starting screen (Figure 3-1) and request a new task. You complete this task and click the Submit HIT button, which sends the task for the requestor to review.

You're not automatically paid when you submit the task. The requestor has the right to review the work and reject if it you haven't done it well.

Donning the White Lab Coat: Zooniverse

Crowdsourcing isn't always done for profit as it is with Mechanical Turk. For generations, scientists have used crowds to gather process data. After all, scientific research is a form of production. (One well-known scientist joked that research merely took the raw materials found in caffeinated beverages and turned them into important scientific results.)

One of the more prominent scientific crowdsourcing markets is Zooniverse (`www.zooniverse.org`). Scientists place projects on Zooniverse and ask the crowd to analyse photographs, gather data, look for patterns in data, and transcribe old documents. Zooniverse doesn't pay its crowd in money. Instead, the workers at Zooniverse gain satisfaction from doing this work, because they feel they're contributing to a cause that's bigger than themselves.

The Zooniverse marketplace is simple, because Zooniverse is a volunteer site. Potential workers have to register with the site, but they don't have to provide much information. You have to create a logon name, which can be your real name or a name that you've invented. You also have to create a password, so that someone doesn't try to use your identity, and give an email address so that Zooniverse can keep in touch with you. Zooniverse also asks for your full name, because sometimes scientists want to thank everyone who worked on the research. However, you don't have to give your name if you don't want to.

The homepage of Zooniverse gives a list of projects currently on offer. One of the projects you can get involved in is called Old Weather (see Figure 3-3).

As a rule, meteorologists are people who stick close to their desks and never go to sea. They get a better understanding of weather by processing data then by standing in the rain. Meteorologists have found great value in the log books of the British Royal Navy, which contain one of the most complete records of global weather data. Once the sun never set on the British empire, and it certainly never set on the British naval officer who had to record weather data six times a day.

The logs of the British Navy are handwritten, and no computer can scan them successfully. Examples include: 'Pistols explode,' 'Seamen abscond with dinghy,' and 'Prayer services held.' Even the best programs may not realise that these events had anything to do with the weather.

For each task, the crowd is shown a single page of a ship's log. When they see something of interest on the page, they're supposed to move the cursor to that point and click. The Zooniverse interface then opens a little window, which allows the worker to transcribe the information. The boxes for weather data have specific fields for wind, temperature and barometric data (see Figure 3-3).

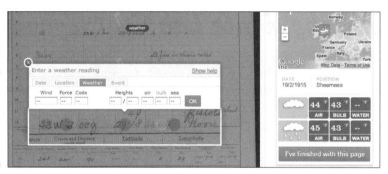

Reproduced with permission from Zooniverse.

Figure 3-3:
Old Weather
project
screen on
Zooniverse.

Old Weather is a good example of a project that engages the hearts and imaginations of the crowd. The world is apparently filled with people who dream of standing at the head of the mast and ruling the Queen's Navy. Over 27,000 people have volunteered for the project, even though they never receive personal recognition for their service or even have the privilege of seeing their words in print, as they would in Wikipedia.

Chapter 4

Joining the Crowdforce

. . . .

. . . .

*A*ll the crowdsourcing websites out there encourage visitors to join the crowd. 'Click here to become a worker!' they say. 'Find a job here!' 'Learn about our opportunities!' 'Become part of the workplace of the future!' These invitations are so enticing, but they don't always tell you what you need to know about being a crowdworker.

You may become a crowdworker for many different reasons, and you can find many different kinds of careers as a crowdworker. Some are full-time careers that will support you and your family; others are part-time jobs that will supplement your income or allow you to develop your skills. Some are little activities that might not have been called a career ten years ago but could be an important part of your life.

Perhaps the most common form of career in the crowd is that of a mac-rotasker. If you choose this kind of career, you'll find that you're working with a crowdmarket to find jobs that match your skills. Some people pursue careers in crowdcontests, looking for new contests that they might enter and win. Microtasking offers another kind of career to crowdworkers, although microtasking is often a supplemental career where workers do a couple of microtasks instead of playing a game on their computer or chatting online. Following a career in self-organised crowds is often an opportunity to be part of a bigger world. You might be working as part of an innovation team trying to bring a new idea to the market, or working on a disaster relief project and trying to help other people.

And if you look for a career in crowdfunding, you'll probably be looking to help people identify good projects and convince the crowd to provide contributions for these projects. The happiest crowdworkers are those who manage their careers, who think about the things that they want from crowdwork, who know how to find the best opportunities for their skills and who know what to realistically expect out of crowdwork.

This chapter is here to help you understand what kind of career opportunities you might find in the crowd and how you can follow one of those careers.

Deciding to Join the Crowdforce

Many people start thinking about their careers by discussing the amount of money they want to earn. That approach is usually not the best way to make good career decisions, although, of course, anyone who makes a career plan without thinking about money at some point will get what they deserve.

A better approach is to start your discussion by asking 'What things do I want to do with my life?' and 'What skills do I want to use in my career?' When you've answered those questions, ask 'Is crowdwork the best way to achieve my goals?' To help you answer that question, consider whether any of these four circumstances sound like your own, in which case crowdwork may be a good career for you:

✔ **You can't work a conventional schedule outside your home.** Many successful crowdworkers are people who have to stay at home. You might be a young mother, for example, who has to stay with your children, or be caring for relatives. In such cases, crowdsourcing can provide a good career.

Testing software as a stay-at-home mum

Lakshmi was a stay-at-home mother from Slough with two babies and a technology degree. She knew nothing about software testing until she learned that a neighbour had starting working as a crowdsourced software tester. Lakshmi was interested, so she went to a software testing website, took the qualifying test, passed it and started work as a basic tester. She worked with some of the training materials and became qualified for more advanced testing work. 'If I wanted to work full time,' she said, 'I could probably support the whole family.'

Instructor to representative

Fiona was a composition teacher at Mega Local University before she became a crowdworker. She had 60 papers to grade a week, three terms every year, and the same class lessons to run, time after time. She stumbled onto TaskRabbit (www.taskrabbit.com) when she was looking for a way to supplement her income. TaskRabbit is a crowdsourcing site that specialises in personal jobs such as running errands, cleaning the garage and assembling furniture.

Fiona says, 'I thought it was just a way for me to earn a little bit more money by doing errands for people. If I needed to go to the grocery shop, I could look at the site and see whether anyone had posted a task for grocery shopping. If so, I would take the task and deliver the groceries.'

Eventually, Fiona found that she liked running errands more than correcting the syntax of students. 'I'm my own boss,' she said. 'If I want to stay in bed some mornings, I can.' She added 'Of course, I don't do it often, because when I stay in bed, I'm wasting my own time.'

✔ **You have skills that you can't use in your neighbourhood.** You might be a graphic designer living in the highlands of Scotland, or a Java programmer with a home in Wyoming's Wind River Mountains. In both cases, you may be able to find some local jobs to employ your skills, but you'll find many more opportunities as a crowdworker.

✔ **You have skills that won't find you a full-time career anywhere.** Programmers often find themselves in this situation. They know the deep inner workings of some esoteric piece of software. Some companies need their skill once in a while, but no company needs anyone to work on that software full time.

✔ **You love the excitement and variety of working for yourself and learning new tasks.** Crowdwork has many, many opportunities for people who like to work in this kind of environment.

Crowdsourcing can also work for you if you like to move to your own rhythm. Unlike many other forms of work, crowdwork allows you to start you career at your own pace. You can try crowdwork while you hold down another job or are acquiring skills, and you can take on as many tasks as you can handle. When you feel ready, you can do it full time. However, if you need to start a crowdwork career at a moment's notice, you can. Just go to a crowdsourcing site, register as a worker, and – hey presto! – you're ready to go.

Getting your due

Crowdsourcing companies generally pay their workers through electronic transfers of money. Some use their own system; others use PayPal (www.paypal.com) or some other commercial system. Usually, you have to have an account at PayPal or a bank that accepts your payments.

Some crowdsourcing sites are able to pay workers who live in certain countries. Others have special forms for workers who live in certain regions. For example, Mechanical Turk pays all workers who live outside the USA as if they're non-resident workers. It requires these workers to file a special form with the US Internal Revenue Service.

Most importantly, crowdwork gives you a tremendous ability to plan your own career. You can learn about the career as you work, and adjust it day by day. If you have any concerns about your ability to do certain tasks or to earn a living from crowdwork, you don't have to commit to that kind of career until you get answers.

Money remains an important consideration, though. Whether you can earn your living as a crowdworker depends on your abilities and on the field in which you work. Many people earn their living as crowdworkers, and some do very well. However, not all crowd careers provide all workers with an income that fully supports their lives. If you're a PHP programmer, for example, you can find enough work in the crowd to give you an income good enough to support you in most parts of the world. If, however, you want to spend your days doing nothing but transcribing business cards, you probably can't.

Considering Your Options

If you're considering a career as a crowdworker, you can easily start it by taking a look at microtasking, macrotasking or crowdcontests. For these three forms of crowdsourcing, you can go to a website that specialises in these kinds of work, register and be ready to go.

If you're interested in crowdfunding or self-organised crowds, you should be able to build a career in either field, but you may not be able to just go to a website and register for a new career. You have to be a little clever.

Looking at microtasks

For the crowdworker, microtasks offer the simplest introduction to crowd-sourcing. The crowdsourcer has taken a large job and broken it into smaller tasks, and you take on one or several of these small tasks.

Microtasking is a good way to find out about crowdsourcing, even if you don't intend to do microtasking for long. You can find out about the mar-kets, about getting paid, about dealing with problems. Microtasks generally don't require you to have special skills or take any special tests, and because they're small, they rarely lead you into trouble.

You can easily register to be a microtask worker. Just go to the crowdmarket, choose a job and demonstrate your ability to do the work.

A commonly used crowdmarket for microtasks is Amazon's Mechanical Turk. To become a microtask worker at Mechanical Turk, you simply go to the website (www.mturk.com), register and follow the instructions. When you've registered, go to Mechanical Turk's task market and start selecting tasks. Many tasks require you to take a test to qualify yourself. When you've quali-fied for a task that you want, you're ready to work.

You can become a worker at other microtasking sites through a similar series of steps. Other sites include:

- ✔ CrowdFlower (www.crowdflower.com)
- ✔ Trada (www.trada.com)
- ✔ tagasauris (www.tagasauris.com)

You can find more microtask sites at www.crowdsourcing.org.

Of all the forms of crowdsourcing, microtasking is probably the most flexible. You can choose jobs at a moment's notice and do as many as you like. If you get bored with one set of tasks, you can move to another. You can work in the night. You can work in the day. You can manage your time as you see fit.

At the same time, microtasking is probably the most isolated form of crowd-sourcing. You have no contact with other crowdworkers and little, if any, with the organisations that are offering jobs. However, although you work by yourself as a microtasker, you're part of a community. All the major micro-task markets have community forums that allow workers to talk, share ideas and discuss crowdsourcing. Workers at Amazon's Mechanical Turk use the forum TurkerNation (http://turkernation.com) to express ideas, dis-cuss different kinds of tasks, and even offer tips and tools that make micro-tasking easier. TurkerNation also provides subforums for organisations that place jobs on Mechanical Turk.

For more information on microtasking, head to Chapter 8.

Competing for the contest

Crowdcontests, in which you compete to have the winning entry, require more specific skills than microtasks. You need to demonstrate that you've mastered graphic design, statistical analysis or whatever skill is required by the contest. Usually, your accomplishments are more important than your academic credentials. If you can create something that's capable of winning the contest, you have sufficient qualifications for the work.

In crowdcontests, you're likely to have more contact with the contest organiser than microtask workers have with the crowdsourcers of their jobs. The contest organisers can offer feedback on your entries, suggest changes and encourage you to develop your design in certain ways. When the contest is over, however, you're unlikely to have further contact with that organiser. You move to a new round of contests.

In crowdcontests, you have little contact with other members of the crowd, because you often compete against them. However, most crowdcontest markets have forums that allow crowdworkers to talk with each other and share ideas. For example, you can find the forum for the graphic design crowd marketplace 99designs at `http://99designforum.com`.

 Workers often consider crowdcontests to be an easy way of finding out about crowdsourcing, for those with the right skills. You can enter them easily and build a portfolio of work. Many workers, however, don't consider them to be a permanent form of work, and they quickly move on to macrotasking.

For details on crowdcontests from the organiser's point of view, take a look at Chapter 5.

Lining up for macrotasks

All macrotasks require you to have specific skills and to be able to demonstrate those skills. The nature of macrotasking is that the crowdsourcer puts a large job on the crowd market and seeks one individual or one team to do the work.

Macrotasking also offers you the opportunity have more contact with the organisers of the tasks and even with other crowdworkers. You're likely to have regular meetings with the person who hired you for the job. You may also have contact with other crowdworkers.

To get started in macrotasking, you first need to identify a skill that you intend to use. That skill may be something you've developed through formal education, such as programming or accounting, or something you've learned on your own, such as office organisation or copy editing. When you've identified this skill, you need to find a market that offers tasks that require this skill, and register. Some popular macrotask markets are:

✔ oDesk (`www.oDesk.com`) – a general purpose macrotask market

✔ Elance (`www.elance.com`) – a general purpose macrotask market

✔ TopCoder (`www.topcoder.com`) – a specialist macrotask site for computer programmers

You can find more macrotask sites at crowdsourcing.org.

Registering at a macrotasking website is easy. Just go to the site, find the registration button and provide the information required, including tax identification numbers, which allows you to work. As soon as you're registered, you're ready to work. However, at most macrotasking sites, you'll be best able to win jobs if you have a portfolio that shows what you can do. You can learn more about portfolios in the 'Building your portfolio' section later in this chapter.

Many individuals use macrotasking to expand their skills. They register at a macrotask market with one skill and then start working to develop a new skill so that they can take tasks that are more interesting to them or offer higher pay. For example, you might start as a web developer who knows only HTML, but start to build skills with PHP programming or animation and look for tasks that require those skills.

You can learn more about macrotask work by joining one of the various online macrotask discussion forums. There, you can get tips from other workers and learn what you need to do to be a success. Most of the big macrotask markets have forums for their workers. The forums for the markets Elance and oDesk are at `https://www.elance.com/q/forum` and `http://oDesk.com/community`.

Wading into self-organised crowds

Self-organised crowds offer a couple of opportunities for potential crowd-workers. You can find tasks to do in innovation crowdsourcing (see Chapter 18) and crowdsourcing that gathers news or responds to natural disasters (see Chapter 17).

In *innovation crowdsourcing*, the most common opportunity is similar to a crowdcontest. In these situations, an individual or organisation is looking for a new idea and is offering a prize for the individual or team that can create that new idea. The crowdsourcer posts the description of what's required and the prize at a crowdmarket. As an individual worker, you go to the market, review the contests and look for teams that may need your skills.

You can learn more about opportunities in innovation crowdsourcing on websites such as:

✔ Innocentive (www.innocentive.com)

✔ Chaordix (www.chaordix.com)

The jobs for crowds that respond to natural disasters are useful opportunities, although they're rarely careers that would support an individual. Still, these jobs are opportunities to contribute to the welfare of other people. You can often find news about organisations that are trying to develop such crowds at the Daily Crowdsource (www.dailycrowdsource.com). The Ushahidi Foundation (www.ushahidi.com) has lists of such projects that use its software.

Searching for careers in crowdfunding

Can you find a career in crowdfunding? Almost certainly. People and organisations often need help planning and executing crowdfunding campaigns. But can you find a job in crowdfunding by registering at a crowdfunding site? No; at least, not at the moment.

The way to start a career in crowdfunding is by being good at crowdfunding and by using the tools of social media. To be a little more specific, I'm talking here about careers in charitable crowdfunding (or other forms of crowdfunding that don't involve selling stocks or raising equity). If you want to carve out a career in this field, your first step is to run a successful campaign – a crowdfunding campaign that meets it target. If you haven't done this before, then start simple. Join someone else's campaigns by going to one of the crowdfunding sites and volunteering for a campaign. Rally all your friends in your social network and help bring the campaign to the attention of other donors.

When you've helped with someone else's campaign, your next step is to run one of your own, helping a friend, a neighbourhood project, a small business or a local charity. Crowdfunding platforms love to keep news of successful campaigns on their sites for a long time, so if your campaign is a success you can take advantage of this and use that campaign to promote your skills. Post links to the news from your social media sites such as Facebook and LinkedIn. Identify yourself as a successful crowdfunder and let people see that you know how to raise funds and that you can be of benefit to them. Sign up as a worker on the big macrotasking sites and identify yourself as a crowdfunder.

If you're looking for a career in crowdfunding, you have to be a pioneer and cut a new path through the forest. You'll get that career by showing the world what you've done – not what degree you have or what training you've had. You'll spread the news of your accomplishments through your social media and get it to people who need help with crowdfunding.

Getting Up and Running on a Macrotask Crowdmarket

When you're ready to become a crowdworker, you generally have to complete four steps before you can work. You choose a market, register at the market, identify and demonstrate your skills, and finally build a portfolio.

Choosing a market

You're not restricted to a single crowdmarket. You can register at as many as you like. However, you may not want to be registered at a market that has no use for your skills. For example, you don't want to be a graphic designer on a site that specialises in computer programming, or a bookkeeper trying to sell your services on a website that offers creative skills.

When you look at crowdmarkets, consider:

- ✔ **The kind of work they offer.** Make sure that other people who have skills similar to yours are registered. While you may feel that these individuals are competing with you, they're really the sign that you're joining an active market and that organisations are placing tasks that you can do. No self-respecting crowdsourcer would place a task on a website that offers only a single person who is able to do the job.

- ✔ **The typical payments that specific jobs offer.** Some macrotask websites get you higher payments than others. Generally, the sites that have a reputation for offering the best workers get you the best-paid jobs.

- ✔ **Policies for crowdworkers.** Some macrotasking sites have policies that guarantee that you're paid for every hour you work. Some sites let the crowdsourcer decide which hours will be compensated and which won't. Be sure to read the workers' policies before you agree to take any task.

When you join most crowdmarkets, you agree to let the site arbitrate in any disputes between you and any individual who offers a job. If a crowdmarket has a reputation of settling disputes in favour of the individuals who offered the job, you may want to look elsewhere.

Setting yourself up on the market

Registering at a crowdmarket is much like registering on any commercial website. You give your name, address and email. Unlike most commercial sites, you have to give your tax ID in case you need to pay taxes on your earnings.

After you register, you have to identify your skills. Most sites give you three ways of showing your skills. You can:

- ✔ Identify your skills on a profile.
- ✔ Upload a portfolio of work.
- ✔ Take a test to demonstrate your skills.

Figure 4-1 shows the profile page for Elance, one of the major macrotasking markets. It requires workers to identify their skills with standard keywords that the market has defined. When Elance presents you on its web page, it wants to do so in a way that's well understood by both workers and potential employers.

Like most macrotask markets, Elance allows you to post your own résumé, give details of your education, and add a portfolio of your work. It also allows you to take tests on some of your skills. Figure 4-2 shows the test results for one set of skills.

When you register on a macrotask market, you generally give a range for the hourly wage that you'll accept. Scan the records of workers with similar skills and backgrounds to see what values they post.

Tell us your skills and expertise.

Enter your skills. This helps clients find you.

Content Writing X   Business Writing X   Creative Writing - Non-fiction (U.S. Version) X

English Editing - AP (US) X   Online Article Writing and Blogging (U.S. Version) X

Report Writing X   WordPress 3.1 X   *Enter new skill*

Browse All Skills

I'm Finished   Skip for Now

Top Skills in Demand: Eng. & Mfg. ▾

3ds Max 9   AutoCad 2007

Networking Concepts   Mechanical Engineering

Manufacturing Design   Civil Engineering

Skills Related to WordPress 3.1

Wordpress 3.0   HTML5   CSS 3.0

Joomla! 1.5   jQuery

Figure 4-1: Identifying skills in a macrotask market.

Skills			▪ Tested ▪ Self-rated	Edit

Skill	Score	
Content Writing	▪▪▪▪▪▪▪▪▫▫	Test Now
Business Writing	▪▪▪▪▪▪▪▪▪▫	Test Now
Creative Writing - Non-fiction (U.S. Version)	▪▪▪▪▪▪▪▪▪▫	Test Now
English Editing - AP (US)	▪▪▪▪▪▪▪▪▪▫	Test Now
Online Article Writing and Blogging (U.S. Version)	▪▪▪▪▪▪▪▪▪▫	Test Now
Report Writing	▪▪▪▪▪▪▪▪▪▫	Test Now
WordPress 3.1	▪▪▪▪▪▪▪▪▫▫	Test Now

Figure 4-2:
Test results.

Reproduced with permission from Elance.

Building your portfolio

In macrotasking, you benefit if you have a strong portfolio and profile. As you work, you want to collect your best work and add it to the portfolio. You also want to collect recommendations and comments from employers who have been satisfied with your work.

The portfolio allows you to expand your abilities beyond your formal training. When you start macrotasking, you start with your best skills and adjust your payment requirements so that you start to get jobs. As you complete more and more work, you start adding the best pieces to your portfolio and start to increase your payment requests.

You can also use your portfolio to expand your work into new fields. If you see a job that appeals to you but requires new skills, you can bid for it by pointing to work that's similar. When you start to get such new jobs, you can add the results to your portfolio and use them to help demonstrate your new skill.

Protecting Yourself as a Macrotasker

As a macrotasker, you want to be protected from the consequences of bad jobs as much as possible. You also want to control the material that you produce:

✔ **Protecting your assets:** Risk is the big issue. When you're a crowd-worker, you're considered to be an independent contractor. You don't work for the market, be that market oDesk, Elance, 99designs or Amazon's Mechanical Turk. The market merely connects you to someone who wants to purchase your services. Because you're a contractor, you're responsible for your mistakes. If you make a mistake in a micro-task or macrotask, you risk not getting paid for the work. If you knowingly make a mistake, you may be liable for any damage that the mistake causes. If you regularly work on large, complicated jobs, you may want to consider professional liability insurance to limit your financial risk. You could get such insurance from an insurance company.

✔ **Holding intellectual property:** Many crowdmarkets have policies that transfer all intellectual property rights from the worker to the employer when the job is finished and the payment is made. (These policies differ from market to market.) For many kinds of job, such policies present no trouble to you.

However, if you've a certain kind of intellectual property that's associated with you, you may need to check the policies. You may have a certain graphic style, a way of dealing with accounting problems, or even a unique way of editing reports. You don't want to find that your signature approach has been transferred to a single employer.

Even though you don't work for the crowdmarket, you agree to certain things when you register for the market and ask to take work. You usually agree that any disagreement between yourself and an employer will be handled by a process that the crowdmarket oversees. Generally, these processes try to balance the rights of workers with those of employers. The crowdmarket, not the employer, holds the payment until it has reviewed the case and decided whether the worker should get the money or the employer can withhold payment.

The policies of crowdmarkets are written in a way to protects the interest of the market itself, not the employer or the worker. Furthermore, no two crowdmarkets have the same policies. Read the polices carefully before you take work.

If you have questions about policies, contact the site. If have any concerns about legal issues, contact a lawyer.

Making the Bid in Macrotasking

In general, only macrotasking requires you to place a formal bid. In crowd-contests and in microtasking, you just take the assignments and do the work. In macrotasking, you have to tell potential employers that you want their job and how you intend to do that job. You use the proposal, the covering letter and your résumé to convey the crucial messages.

The proposal

The *proposal* is a short document that responds to the job description. In it you:

- ✔ State that you can do the job.
- ✔ Show who you'll do the job for.
- ✔ Estimate the time and effort.
- ✔ State the cost of the job.

Occasionally, the proposal responds to the original job description and modifies it. If you can see a faster or more efficient way of doing the task, you should suggest a modification in your proposal. However, if you prepare a proposal with a modified job, you should probably prepare a proposal for the original job as well.

In the proposal, you can state your qualifications to do the work and try to convince the employer to hire you. However, most people keep the proposal simple and don't try to sell themselves in it. They make their pitch for the job in the covering letter (see the next section). Figure 4-3 gives a sample proposal and shows how simple a proposal can be.

The covering letter

Your covering letter should send one simple message: if you choose me, I'll do a great job. You use the covering letter to sell your services and make the case that you're the best person to do the job.

The covering letter should be simple and straightforward. Start with a formal greeting. You're never wrong to start a letter 'Dear Mr' or 'Dear Ms'. But if you start it 'Hey, Employer' you may offend someone who may be able to offer you a job.

Summarise your proposal in one or two sentences. Then write a paragraph explaining why you're a good choice for the job. You'll make a good case for yourself if you can point to jobs that you've already done and to employers who are satisfied with your work.

Figure 4-4 shows a simple covering letter. Like the proposal, it need not be long and complicated. Get to the point, but explain that you're the best.

End the letter with a second quick summary of your proposal and then state that you'll do a good professional job on the task that will satisfy the potential employer.

Proposal: Copy edit manuscript

Statement of Work:
I will copy edit the 100-page manuscript.
I will put the text into the standard Chicago style.
As I edit I will correct typographical errors, punctuation and spelling.
I will also do light re-writing. I will fix sentences that are awkward or overly complex. However, I will leave the basic paragraph structure intact.

Final Product:
The final product will be a Mircrosoft Word Document with tracked changes. You will be able to see all the changes to the manuscript before you accept all the changes and get a clean manuscript.

Effort Required:
The work will take roughly 20 minutes per page. I estimate that it will be completed after slightly less than 40 hours, at $18 per hour for a total cost of no more than $720 plus the fees for the crowdmarket. The job will be billed on an hourly basis.

Start and End of Work:
I can start work on the project next Monday and can finish it in 10 calendar days.

Figure 4-3:
A sample proposal.

Dear Ms Author,

Attached you will find a proposal for copy editing your manuscript. The work as described will take about 10 days and will cost no more than $720 plus fees.

The editing will be of the highest professional quality. From my résumés, you can see not only that I was trained as a professional editor but that I have worked on several high-profile projects, including Carrie Hannah's novel, *Retail Shoes*, which won a New York Book Critics Award and the screenplay for the movie, *Oval Office*.

I have read your manuscript and think that I can turn it into a professional, polished document. I have worked with authors with many different backgrounds and have good working relationships with all of them. My résumé contains a list of writers who have worked with me and are willing to recommend me. They will explain that I worked well with them and was able to help them produce a better manuscript.

The price of $720 is highly competitive for the quality of work that I deliver. I look forward to hearing from you.

Figure 4-4:
A sample covering letter.

The résumé

You have a profile on the crowdmarket, but consider including a résumé in your bid to help show why you're the right person for the job. Don't include a full résumé unless the employer asks for it. Just prepare a short résumé that describes the experiences that are relevant to the job you're seeking.

The résumé should demonstrate two things: skills and maturity. Show that you've developed the skills to do the work and that you have the experience to complete the job on time, on budget, and without needless conflict. List the jobs that are most relevant to the project that you're hoping to undertake. Then summarise other jobs. After giving the details of three or four recent jobs that you've completed, you can add, for example: 'In addition, I've done 44 other debugging jobs on platforms ranging in size from handhelds to servers.'

You can put awards on your résumé, because they show recognition of your work. You can also describe your educational background. In crowdsourcing, however, educational history is less important than in traditional résumés. In traditional résumés, your education communicates the kind of community to which you belong and hence the kind of values or skills you may have. In crowdsourcing, people are more interested in what you can do than in what school you attended. Hence you can often reduce the amount of space you give to your education. Eventually, you have just a few lines:

> Principia High School, 1993; college prep program, pre-science
>
> University College Dublin, 1998; BSc Cum Laude Mathematics, Computer Science
>
> Harvard University, 2006; Certificate, Higher Education Administration

An inconsistent résumé that does not seem to make sense is a big problem. Lying is bad too. Nothing ends the opportunity of getting a job faster than a résumé that's inconsistent or false. Potential employers ask 'What isn't right in this résumé?' but don't spend time finding the answer. They just move on to the next one.

Setting the price

At first, one of the hardest things to do is to set the price. You often don't know what you're worth as a crowdworker and don't understand the competition. You need to set your price based on the market. You can't get top fees if everyone in the market's offering their services at half price. At the same time, don't feel that you always need to underbid. If you're offering high-quality work, you can expect a higher price.

Crowdsourcing involves markets. You always have to monitor the markets to make sure that you're offering the right prices. As you explore the market, check to see what others are asking for similar jobs. At the start, you may need to underbid other workers to get your first jobs. After you've done a few jobs, you may want to start raising your prices.

Crowdmarkets don't always reward the lowest bidder. Some employers conclude that a worker who's offering a low price isn't a good worker. As soon as you can point to successful projects in your portfolio, you want to raise your prices.

Learning from the process

You won't win every job you bid on. It's not personal. It's a market. Whenever you lose a job, try to see whether you can read the winning proposal. Sometimes you find that the winner offered a lower price. However, you may also find that the winner was offering more work for the money or had a more impressive portfolio. Look at what the winner has done and see whether you can adjust your future bids.

Completing the Macrotask

You always put yourself in a strong position if you complete the work well, however much you may feel tired or inclined to rush towards the end of it. At the very least, doing a good job earns you a stronger recommendation from the employer. The following sections are here to help you impress the crowdsourcer.

Remembering the goal

When you start crowdsourcing, you see how easy it is to forget the original goal. You spend two or five or ten weeks on a project, and you discover that you're doing something quite different from the original statement of work. Such a drift can cause problems between crowdworkers and employers. To avoid it, you need to keep the goal in front of you. Regularly ask 'Am I still making progress?' or 'Am I getting closer to my goal?'

As you work with your employer, regularly review the goals of the project and check that you're making progress. Because you aren't part of a permanent team, you miss some of the discussions that keep projects focused: the conversations in the office, lunches with other workers, and those short little discussions at the end of the day.

You may be asked to do some additional work, and you have to make a choice. If the work is just more of the work that you've already been doing, you may take the assignment and not worry about it. If the work takes you into a new project, you may want to ask the employer for a new statement of work. (For more on statements of work, head to Chapter 11.)

You're a crowdworker and are reviewed by your accomplishments. If you're distracted from the original goal, you can find you've worked a large number of hours and are still far from completing the original project.

Communicate, communicate, communicate

If your employers don't communicate with you, you should communicate with them. You don't need to communicate a lot. An email in the morning. An email at the end of the day. An email in the middle if that seems good. Because you're working at a distance, you need to be sure that you're doing the work that the employer wants. If the employer isn't telling you, you need to ask.

If your employer isn't giving you much information, you may need to resort to the technique of asking repeated questions. Ask three nearly identical questions:

- ✔ Is this the right thing to do today?
- ✔ Am I making progress towards the goal?
- ✔ Is this going to be satisfactory to you?

If the answer to all three questions is similar, then you can be reasonably sure that you're getting a consistent message from the employer.

Most macrotask crowdmarkets use some kind of technology to track the number of hours you work. However, your employer usually needs more information than just the number of hours you worked. Keep the employer aware of the tasks that are hard, the tasks that are easy, and the progress you're making.

Working across cultures

Crowdsourcing is a global activity. You can easily find yourself working with an employer from another culture. The barrier between the two cultures may make it difficult for you to understand what you need to do. The employer may not be able to explain the task completely. You may not be able to understand what needs to be done.

If you're working with an employer from a different culture, you need to be sure that you're getting the right information. Sometimes, the best way to ensure that you're fully communicating with your employer is to ask multiple questions. Use the strategy I lay out in the preceding section of asking the same question in multiple ways. If the answers are consistent, then you can be pretty certain that you have the right information.

Never take a simple 'yes' or 'no' as the final direction you receive. Ask for clarification. 'Do you mean "Yes, you're doing the right job" or "Yes, you need to change your approach to the work."?'

Keeping good records

Keep good records. The crowdmarket also keeps records of the job and your employer. You may need to contact the employer if you need a recommendation. You may need to defend yourself from the claim that you've not been working on the right project. You'll always find it useful to have your own set of records.

In general, you should keep records of the job, the proposal, the hours that you work, and your contact in the organisation. This material not only helps you understand what you've done, but also helps you prepare more proposals for other clients.

Getting an extra recommendation

As the job comes to an end, ask for an extra recommendation. Most crowd-markets solicit one from the employer, but I recommend asking for an independent letter. Your value as a crowdworker comes from your reputation. You can build that reputation with outside letters that the employer did not *have* to write.

You can also use outside letters at other crowdmarkets. Your reputation can't be easily moved from market to market. If you move into a new market, you're starting with no reputation. If you have a letter, you have at least some part of your reputation that can move with you.

Part II
Looking at the Different Forms of Crowdsourcing

Five Distinct Ways to Go Crowdsourcing

- ✔ **Crowdcontests:** Keep a job as an undivided, single task and give the job to a single person to complete. Because you rely heavily on that single person, you want the best possible person to do the work. Let the crowd compete for your job by asking crowd members to submit their best work. Choose the best submission and reward the person who did it.

- ✔ **Macrotasks:** Divide a job into large pieces that each require specific, specialist skills. Give each of these large pieces to a crowd member who has that specific skill. Manage the process as you go, and pay the workers.

- ✔ **Microtasks:** Divide up your job into small, straightforward tasks to engage more of the crowd and get your job done more quickly. Judge each submission and accept those that are properly done, without having to first review the abilities of potential workers or interview them, then pay the crowd members who work for you.

- ✔ **Self-organised crowdsourcing:** Let the crowd decide how to divide a job. Offer a reward for the person or group who does the job best, set a deadline for the job and let the crowd work. When the deadline arrives, review the different submissions and reward the best one.

- ✔ **Crowdfunding:** Use the crowd to raise money for your company, charity or artistic endeavour. Pass a hat to the crowd and ask for donations, or raise money for a company by selling shares of stock.

To access the handy *Crowdsourcing For Dummies* cheat sheet, go online and head to www.dummies.com/cheatsheet/crowdsourcinguk.

In this part . . .

- ✔ Rouse and engage with the competitive crowd to generate new ideas with crowdcontests.

- ✔ Raise money for your company, charity or artistic endeavour in small donations from a large crowd with crowdfunding.

- ✔ Use the market to engage the crowd and find the specialist skills you lack, but which you need to complete a job, with macrotasking.

- ✔ Break down a large job into small, straightforward tasks for the crowd, and tap into the crowd's energy, with microtasking.

- ✔ Accomplish goals, learn from the crowd and let the crowd organise itself by harnessing the power of self-organised crowds.

Chapter 5

Creating Crowdcontests

Crowdcontests are perhaps the simplest form of crowdsourcing. Announce that you're looking for some kind of product or idea. Establish the rules. Set a deadline. Advertise your contest. Wait for the results.

You don't run a crowdcontest, however, simply because you like a good contest. You run a crowdcontest in order to generate new ideas. Those ideas can be creative products, new innovations, a snapshot of a big market, a strategic plan, or even just a solution to a problem that you've not been able to solve.

In this chapter, I take a look at why – and how – crowdcontests can work for you.

Reaping the Benefits of Crowdcontests

So what's so great about crowdcontests? Well, three things:

✔ **Crowdcontests generate new ideas.**

Crowdcontests are often associated with creative work such as logo design, T-shirt design, video production, photography and music production. However, you can use them to generate any kind of new idea, from innovative concepts for new services and processes to unique ways of using old objects. You can even find some organisations, such as Kaggle (www.kaggle.com), that use crowdcontests to create statistical analyses and financial projections.

✔ **Crowdcontests give you access to talent that you may not have in your organisation.**

Not every organisation employs a full-time graphics designer, an ad copywriter or a financial analyst. With crowdcontests, though, you can access hundreds of talented people and choose the one who best meets your needs for your current project.

✔ **Crowdcontests are simple.**

You describe what you want, offer an award and choose the submission that best meets your needs. You don't worry about the background or education or credentials of the individuals who submit to your contest. The proof, as they say, is in the submission. You merely choose the submission that best meets your need.

Take these three considerations together and you have a process that you can use to solve thousands, if not thousands upon thousands, of problems.

Deepening understanding

Many organisations run contests in order to better understand their customers or their community. They run a contest for a specific idea, make a judgement, and reward the winner. However, before doing so they analyse the *entire* collection of submissions to get a complete picture of all the people who entered the contest. (See the later section 'Understanding Types of Crowdcontest' for more on general research contests.)

For example, lots of companies run contests to determine how they should support charitable organisations. They ask for proposals for charitable projects from the crowd and also turn to crowd members to be the judges, giving money to the projects that get the most votes.

Crowdcontests not only give the company good ideas for charitable work, but they also tell the company about the values of its customers.

Hoover Park Hardware runs an annual room-makeover contest. According to the rules, the store is seeking to produce a low-cost makeover kit – a selection of products it can offer to customers at a discount. Contestants must submit a picture of a room they'd like to redecorate and a list of the materials they'd need. The staff of the hardware store choose the entry that they like best and award a prize: a large amount of in-store credit. In the process, the store learns how its customers would like to redecorate rooms and the products they'd need to do this.

Taking a lesson from design contests

You can discover a lot about crowdcontests by looking at contests in the artistic fields. The fields of both graphic design and architecture have long histories of relying on contests to identify good ideas. The design of the Vietnam Veterans Memorial in Washington DC, USA, was chosen in a contest. So was the design of Brasilia, the capital city of Brazil. So are many advertisements, logos, stamps and other artistic creations.

In design contests, established professionals compete with new students, and those who live near the organisation site face those who live on different continents. The organisers are usually trying to identify new and talented designers and artists who may not know how to contact a traditional organisation. They try to reach to the broadest pool of talent, and often make special efforts to reach young artists just starting their careers. The designer of the Vietnam Veterans Memorial, Maya Lin, was 21 when her design won the competition.

The American Institute of Architects has developed a set of guidelines for architectural contests (*The Handbook of Architectural Design Competitions*, American Institute of Architects, Washington DC, USA, 2010). These guidelines are useful for a crowdcontest if you're developing an expensive or complex idea. They're also of interest to businesses and organisations that want to know more about professional competitions.

Good ideas don't always come from special expertise. They often come from long-term experience. The crowd often understands the strengths and weaknesses of a product better than the engineers who designed it do. The engineers may have special expertise. The crowd is likely to have far more experience of the product, so by engaging the crowd, you deepen your understanding.

Faster, better, cheaper

Compared with conventional methods, crowdcontests can get ideas:

- ✔ **At a lower cost:** As with all forms of crowdsourcing, you pay for just the talent you need for your project.

- ✔ **More quickly:** You can get results without having to search long and hard for talent. You can tap in to a crowd that's waiting to demonstrate its skills.

- ✔ **Of better quality and variety:** You reach out to a bigger pool of expertise than you can get in your organisation or your own neighbourhood. Crowdsourcing is a means of combining expertise, especially expertise that may be overlooked. You may discover that the guy who volunteers at your organisation is a good graphic designer, or that a woman who walks dogs up the street knows everything about your city. These skills may be overlooked in an ordinary organisation. In crowdsourcing, they can contribute to the good of all.

Sometimes, running a crowdcontest within a crowd that's limited to a specific group of people is useful. This *private crowd* may comprise the employees of a company or the residents of a neighbourhood. Members of a private crowd often have useful experience that they can bring to an organisation, even if they don't have all the skills of a larger group. See the later section 'Using a private crowd'.

Understanding Types of Crowdcontest

Crowdcontests can take many different forms, but generally fall into four different categories:

- **Single-request crowdcontest:** The most common form. As the name suggests, you put a request to the crowd and ask for a response. The request can be for a new T-shirt design or for a new process to manage a multinational transportation fleet; the crowdcontest for each request works in the same way.

The East Bellows Falls girl scouts troop needs a web page to advertise its activities. The page can be simple; nothing fancy. It just needs basic information: meeting times, a contact list, news of recent activities, and so on. The trouble is that none of the volunteer leaders know how to make a web page. Furthermore, the girl scouts know they want the site to look different from that of the West Bellows Falls girl scouts troop. A crowdcontest could easily handle this problem.

- **General research crowdcontest:** To the crowd, a general research contest looks just a like a single request crowdcontest. The crowd receives a request and tries to find the best possible submission to answer that request. However, the crowdsourcer isn't as interested in the winning entry as in the information that's found in the entire collection of submissions. The crowdsourcer is trying to understand a consumer market or a social group or a collection of institutions.

Tiber Groceries, a regional food chain, asks the crowd to identify the most creative school in the world, and offers a grant to the top ten schools that are identified as the most creative. From the submissions, the store's managers find out where crowd members are located, the things they identify as creative and the extent to which they're prepared to support a local school. All this information can be useful in the store's effort to reach customers.

- **Student crowdcontests:** Student contests, as the name implies, are contests for a restricted crowd. Such contests are generally single-request crowdcontests, but they also have an educational purpose. The crowdsourcer establishes a formal procedure for the contest that's intended to teach certain ideas to the crowd or develop specific professional skills.

The Briand Business Foundation, a group interested in promoting international trade, runs an annual business plan contest. The contestants must be students at one of 20 schools that work with the foundation. The contest helps one student start a business and identifies other potential leaders among these school students. The students submit a plan for an international business that can be started with less than $100,000 ($63,000) and that meets certain goals of the foundation. The foundation will create a business from the winning plan, provide the necessary capital and business expertise, and take a small ownership of the firm. Finally, the foundation will recognise and promote ten more plans that it judges to be of high quality.

✔ **Professional crowdcontests:** Professional crowdcontests are for a restricted crowd. To enter, an individual must have specific professional credentials, belong to a specific group such as a professional organisation, or be employed by a specific company. These crowdcontests are similar to contests traditionally held to identify the architect of a new building.

Professional crowdcontests are intended to minimise risk for an expensive or sensitive project. Some projects, like the design of a building, require specific skills in order to do the job properly and prevent trouble later. Other contests require the crowd to work with sensitive information that the members shouldn't disseminate to competitors or to any other group. Such issues are best handled by professional crowdcontests, which allow only qualified entrants.

The leaders of Addison County decide to hold a contest to determine how to use an abandoned piece of land near the centre of the county. They recognise that they probably can't open the contest to all county residents, because the site is polluted in a way that may rule out some uses. Instead, they decide to hold a contest that's open to landscape professionals – individuals who know how to handle former industrial sites. The contest is judged by exerts appointed by the county but, to keep county residents engaged, they allowed residents to review the submissions and vote for their favourites. The final decision combines both the expert opinions and the votes of the residents.

Running a Crowdcontest

Essentially, crowdcontests are easy to run. You need a statement describing the goal of the contest, a set of rules, a place on the web where you can post your contest, and a mechanism for collecting the submissions. The first two items – the description of the contest goal and the set of rules – are both examples of instructions that you give to the crowd. You can find an in-depth description of how to write instructions for the crowd in Chapter 11, so you may want to refer to that chapter.

In this section, I look at ideas that you can use specifically for crowdcontests. For example, in a crowdcontest you need to write rules about the intellectual property that is submitted to the contest but doesn't win. You may also need to write rules that describe how you'll publicise the results of the contest. Many people participate in crowdcontests for the publicity when they win rather than for the prize.

As you read this section, you may find it useful to keep two example crowdcontests in mind: designing a bottle for a brand of iced coffee, and developing a new business process for a company. You can see that both forms of crowdcontest follow the same pattern.

Stating the goal

When you describe the goal of the crowdcontest – the thing that you hope to get from the contest – you're writing something like a statement of work (see Chapter 11). However, the description of the goal of a crowdcontest is slightly different from a statement of work for microtasking or macrotasking. When you describe the goal of a contest, you're trying to make sure that you get what you want, while simultaneously encouraging the creative skills of the crowd. In contrast, when you write a statement of work, you're generally trying to make sure that the crowd members work as you'd like them to work.

To write a good goal for the contest, you have to navigate between two contradictory forces. You want to write the description with as much specific detail as possible, so that you get the kind of result you want. At the same time, you want to keep the description as broad and open as you can, so that you attract the most talent and allow the crowd to think freely.

A well-written goal has five parts:

- ✔ **General description of the submission and its purpose:** Describe what idea you want out of the crowdcontest and what you intend to do with that idea. Make the description easy to read for any potential contestant. For example, you may say that you're asking for a logo design, and that this design is to appear on products and websites.

- ✔ **Description of the context for the submission:** Give background information about the idea you're trying to crowdsource. Explain the constraints on the idea and outline other ideas that you're currently using or have tried in the past. Start with broad and general statements and then move to technical details. Following the example of the logo design, you can give a list of previously used logos and say that a new logo has to capture some of the same spirit as its predecessors.

✓ **Properties for a successful submission:** Include a section on elements that the idea must have in order to be considered. In the logo example, you may say that the logo must contain at least three interlocking circles, and that the company name must be written in Helvetica font.

✓ **Properties that the submission can't have:** Identify any elements that you don't want in the final idea. Sometimes you exclude things because you've tried them and they don't work. Sometimes you exclude things because another organisation has the rights to them.

✓ **The form of the submission:** In many crowdcontests, the form of the submission is merely a message describing the idea. However, for other forms, especially those that involve artistic endeavours, you want to describe the submission format in detail. Do you want a certain kind of graphics? How big can the file be? Where should the crowd place that file?

Writing the rules

After you have a description in mind of the goal you're seeking from the crowd, you can write the rules for your crowdcontest. Rules should be straightforward and simple. Keep in mind that they convey a lot of information to the crowd.

Be clear about what you want. Crowds don't like ambiguity. If crowd members don't understand the rules, they may ignore them or even invent their own rules. You may get submissions that you don't want, can't evaluate or can't use. Ambiguous rules can easily make the entire contest useless.

Crowds don't like rules that change. If you change the rules, you may communicate that the crowd isn't able to provide you with what you want, that your description doesn't adequately express what you want, or even that you're not sure what you want.

Setting the deadlines

You usually want to keep your deadlines short, because deadlines that stretch into the future encourage people to delay their submissions. Still, you may need a certain amount of time to notify the crowd and get people with the right experience and talent to respond.

For many crowdcontests, a rolling deadline is useful. You can tell the crowd that you'll begin accepting submissions immediately, that you'll start judging them at a certain date, and that you'll keep receiving submissions until you've found a submission that's satisfactory.

Finding the skill to name a company

When the computer companies Burroughs Corporation and Sperry Rand merged, the corporate leaders decided to create a new name for the combined corporations. Rather than hire a marketing firm to create the name, they held a crowdcontest among the new firm's employees. The employees were told what the name needed to convey and were told to submit an idea. Most of the employees gave no thought to the impact that the company name would have on the market. One and all, this majority submitted the obvious pun on the name of a common bird: 'Sperroughs'.

However, a few members of the crowd thought more carefully about the new name. None of this group had formal marketing skills but all could appreciate the kind of image that a company name should project. One of them, a mid-level software manager, submitted the name 'Unisys', which was judged the winner and became the name of the company.

Finding your crowd

When you run a crowdcontest, you're usually looking for crowdworkers who have certain kinds of skills. You're looking for graphic designers, video producers or financial analysts. When you open your contest, you need to publicise it to a community of individuals who are likely to have those skills or know people who have those skills. If you're using a commercial crowdcontest firm, you can usually assume that the firm has built a crowd of people with the appropriate skills.

Often, crowdcontests turn the process of recruiting a crowd upside down. You have a crowd that's interested in the goal of your contest, but you don't know which individual members of the crowd may have the right skills to win the contest. A common example of such contests is one that creates a logo or name for a company. The employees of the company have an interest in the new logo, but only a few may possess the skills necessary to produce such a logo. A crowdcontest can pull the talented people out of the general crowd.

Qualifying the crowd

If you're dealing with a student crowdcontest or a professional crowdcontest, then you want to make sure that each member of the crowd has the appropriate credentials. You can do this task in one of two ways:

- ✔ **One-stage process:** You ask for the credentials of each worker when he submits to the crowdcontest. If the worker doesn't have the right credentials, you can reject the submission. This form is simple to administer but you don't control the flow of information. You can, however, identify good submissions from people who aren't technically qualified.

✔ **Two-stage process:** You ask potential members of the crowd to submit their qualifications to you first. After you've determined that people are qualified, you let them join the crowd. This technique is most commonly used in professional crowdcontests, contests in which you want submissions only from people who have specific training or credentials. In most crowdcontests, you'll only be concerned with the results, not with credentials, so in such cases you'll not need a two-stage process.

Judging the submissions

You want to tell the crowd how you intend to judge the submissions. In many cases, you may be the only judge. For complicated ideas, you may want to have a panel of experts.

You'll often find it useful to have more than one person judging the crowdcontest. By having more than one person involved, you talk about the brief, and try to better understand what it means and how the different entries capture that meaning. At the same time, too many judges can make it harder to select a single winner.

Setting the criteria for winning

As you plan your crowdcontest, you want to develop a clear set of criteria to determine the best entry. You may be tempted to say, 'I can't describe it, but I'll know the winning entry when I see it.' However, this strategy leads to vague descriptions and open-ended contests that generate nothing of value.

Although the criteria must be clear, they can be broad and open to the inspiration of the crowd. You can ask for a logo that's forceful, for example, without saying what forceful means. You can ask for an idea that simplifies your operations, without specifying exactly how the idea should achieve that simplification. Remember, though, that you get the best results when you know exactly what you're seeking.

Compensating the best entry

Crowdcontests generally compensate only a single individual, a team of workers or perhaps a small group. The simplest form of compensation is the ordinary prize: compensation given to the person who submitted the entry judged to be the best. However, you can consider two other forms of compensation:

✔ **Contingency compensation** awards the prize in two stages. You give the first compensation, usually the smaller, to the winning entry immediately at the end of the contest. Then you give a second, usually larger, payment after the idea has been tested and proven to be effective.

Contingency compensation is a way of encouraging new and innovative ideas while minimising the risk to the crowdsourcer. You get time to test the idea to ensure that it actually works.

✔ **Value-added compensation** is similar to contingency compensation.
You award the prize in two stages. However, the second stage is directly
connected to the amount of revenue the idea generates or the reduction
in costs that it creates. You use this form of compensation to get people
to submit bolder ideas while keeping the risk to the crowdsourcer low.

Deciding about intellectual property

You need to have a policy on the intellectual property of all submissions,
both those winning and losing. You usually want all the rights to the entry
that you select as the best. To get those rights is why you run the contest.

But you also have to decide what to do with the intellectual property of the
entries that don't win the contest. The standard way of handling these rights
is to claim that you, as the crowdsourcer, own the intellectual property of all
submissions. To understand why you might want to claim ownership of all
submissions, consider a case where you're running a crowdcontest for something that'll be closely identified with your organisation, such as a brand, a
logo or a product container. You don't want to see a losing entry in the hands
of a competitor, who might use that entry to confuse the public into thinking
that its product is the same as your product.

It is, of course, unethical to use entries that you didn't select without compen-
sating the individuals who submitted them. In some cases, it's actually fraudulent and doing so can get you in legal trouble.

Publicising the results

You have to do some publicity at the start of the contest in order to attract
the appropriate crowd. Often, the hardest thing about crowdsourcing is
bringing the first members of the crowd to your activity. After the first
members of the crowd have started to come, they bring other members to
the site.

Nothing requires you to publicise the result of a crowdcontest. However,
doing so has benefits for you and the crowd, in terms of:

✔ **Boosting your reputation:** Your reputation as a crowdsourcer helps you
get the best submissions to future contests. You get better submissions
from the crowd if you run fair contests, compensate the winners well
and are able to identify top-quality work.

✔ **Helping out the crowd:** In crowdcontests, as in many forms of contests,
an individual gains compensation from winning. That compensation
takes the form of an improved reputation, which, for example, may make
it easier for the winner to get a job later. By publicising the results and
identifying the winner, you're allowing that individual to capitalise on
his accomplishment.

You can also improve your own reputation among the crowd by publicising the list of top considerations. Doing so also allows more members of the crowd to claim improved reputations, because they were able to separate themselves from the general crowd.

✔ **Checking for submission violations:** By publicising the results of your contest, you have an added check on the integrity of the winning submission. Because you want the rights to that submission, you want to know that the individual who submitted can claim the intellectual property rights to the idea. Verifying intellectual property rights is difficult unless you publicise the winner of the contest.

Of course, if someone claims that the winning idea was actually his, you can't be certain that the winner stole the idea without further investigation. Still, if you don't publicise the winning submission, you may find yourself in a position one or two or three years after you've invested in the winning idea of discovering that the entry was stolen.

You can do a great deal to protect yourself from this situation by simply searching the web. If you're crowdsourcing graphical images, you can try the search-by-image Google function (`www.google.com/images`), and if you're crowdsourcing videos, check out YouTube (`www.youtube.com`).

Improving the Crowdcontest

The simple crowdcontest sounds like a straightforward and fair way of getting information from the crowd, but is not always the most efficient method. If you follow the basic model in which you describe what you're seeking, set the rules, and wait for the entries to arrive, you're missing an opportunity to really get the best out of the crowd members and engage them fully. The following sections help you communicate with the crowd, split the contest into multiple stages, build a professional crowd or even run a whole series of crowdcontests.

The simplest way of giving information to the crowd is to talk with members. You can do so in three ways:

✔ **Give general updates on the contest.** As the contest progresses, you may want to give the crowd information about the contest, without directly commenting on any of the submissions. You can say how many submissions you've received, how many days are left in the contest, and what issues you see developing.

Use a general discussion to repeat the basic requirements of the contest. Don't just send the crowd additional copies of the original description. Put the idea in a new context, describe it in a new way or offer new insights.

✔ **Make general comments on the submissions received.** Listen first and then present your ideas. In this way, you're giving useful information to the crowd that shapes the members' approach to the contest. Tell the crowd your impressions of the work. You can identify the strengths and weaknesses of the current submissions and let the intelligence of the crowd respond to your comments. You can also take questions from individuals about the contest and offer the answers to the entire crowd.

Don't refer publicly to any specific entry. If you embarrass someone in front of the crowd, that person can easily react to your comments and may stir up the crowd. If you comment on an individual entry, do so only to the person who submitted it.

✔ **Sit down for a chat with the best.** Often the most effective form of feed-back is to provide comments directly to the individual members of the crowd. You can look at a submission and tell the crowd member what you like about it or what aspects don't meet your requirements. You can respond when a participant asks for your opinion, or you can identify promising submissions and contact their creators.

If you run repeated crowdcontests, think about renewing your crowd – about inviting new members to join the crowd. If you don't find new participants for new contests, your crowd tends to shrink. People who don't win a crowdcontest aren't always interested in trying a second or third contest by the same crowdsourcer. If people aren't compensated in a market, they tend to leave the market.

Splitting the contest

You may find it useful to run the contest in stages:

1. **Ask the crowd to submit an intermediate product.**
2. **Identify a small number of participants and offer them a small compensation.**
3. **Ask that small group to prepare a complete final submission.**

Some fields lend themselves to multi-stage crowdcontests. In video produc-tion, crowdsourcers often run their contests in two stages. In the first, they ask for a storyboard – a drawn representation of the final video. Such storyboards are relatively easy and inexpensive to produce. After they've collected storyboards from the crowd, the crowdsourcers select five or six and compensate the authors of these storyboards. The crowdsourcers then ask that group of authors to complete finished videos based on their storyboards.

Building a stronger crowd

You can improve the quality of the result of a crowdcontest by increasing the quality of the crowd through two methods: creating a private crowd or increasing the size of the crowd.

Using a private crowd

A private crowd is only open to a select number of people. You can create a private crowd by recruiting people from a specific organisation, such as your company, or by trying to get people with recognised skills.

Recruiting people from your company is the easier of the two approaches, but it doesn't always work. You get a crowd that may share your goals and that's easier to track. Such a crowd always makes it easier to control any sensitive information that you may need to give to the crowd. However, the talent pool is limited, and members of the crowd may not have the skills you need.

Recruiting a crowd with specific skills is harder. One strategy for building private crowds is to recruit skilled individuals from open crowds. At the end of every open crowdcontest, you review the top submissions and invite those individuals to join the private crowd.

Attracting more participants

You can often build a stronger crowd by increasing the payment for the winning submission. This process doesn't work in all forms of crowdsourcing. However, it can be effective in pay-one markets where you pay only one winner. (For more on market types, see Chapter 2.)

By increasing the payment for the winning submission, you attract all sorts of new people to your crowd. You're likely to attract a few new highly qualified individuals who'll do a good job for you. The higher prize makes it worth their while.

The higher prize is also likely to attract many people who aren't especially qualified for the work. In a crowdcontest, you don't have to worry about getting more entries from less-qualified participants, other than the fact that you have to review their submissions.

Increasing the payment for work usually increases the quality of work in crowdcontests. However, doing so doesn't always improve quality in other forms of crowdsourcing.

Running a series of contests

If you're trying to crowdsource a complicated solution or develop an answer to a difficult problem, you may find it worthwhile to run a series of crowdcontests. You start with simpler contests and use them to build a crowd that understands your needs and desires.

If you're trying to crowdsource an advertising campaign, for example, you may start with some elements of that campaign. So you crowdsource a brand or logo, and then you follow this crowdcontest with one that develops a catchphrase or theme. From there, you build to more complicated elements of the campaign.

As you deal with a complicated series of crowdcontests, you may discover that you have to backtrack and ask the crowd to review an earlier judgement. Such backtracking is part of the process of learning. As you find out more about the crowd and what it can do, the crowd is finding out more about what you want.

Considering an Example: The Business Logo

As mentioned earlier in this chapter, a simple example to use for a crowdcontest is the business logo, a bit of graphic art that you use to identify your organisation or activity. Logos are easy to crowdsource, and the process of running a logo crowdcontest shows you much about crowdsourcing.

Running a logo contest yourself

Here are the steps you take:

1. **Decide the goal.** You need to have a clear idea of the kind of logo you want and how you want to use it.

2. **Write the brief.** Describe the elements of the logo. You may want the organisation name or specific imagery in the logo. You may want a certain font or colours. You can also include a list of adjectives to describe your logo, such as strong, rugged, feminine or minimalist.

3. **Set the rules.** Describe:

- Who can participate in the contest and how you want to receive the designs, such as by email to you in a standard file format or put onto a website of your design.

- The deadline. A logo is a fairly simple piece of graphic design, so you can probably have a fairly short deadline. You may select two weeks if you've a ready crowd, or four weeks if you haven't.

- The criteria for winning. Clearly state what the logo is trying to accomplish and the qualities it needs to possess.

- Who's to judge the work. Generally, you want professional judges – individuals who have the skill to understand the criteria for winning and know how to apply it. If your crowd contains students or skilled professionals, these judges give the crowd the best feedback. If you're trying to find good work among a crowd of amateurs, professional judges are best able to recognise the gold among the dross.

- The compensation for winning. In crowdcontests, bigger prizes tend to attract a larger crowd that contains higher-quality entries.

- Intellectual property terms. For the winning entry, you want all intellectual property rights in all media. Because these logos are being designed for your organisation, they contain elements that identify your organisation. Therefore, you probably want to state that all entries to the contest become your property.

4. **Publicise.** If you don't publicise the contest, you won't raise a crowd. You can advertise the contest to members of your organisation or to local art schools. You can also send a Tweet to national design organisations, such as AIGA (former American Institute for Graphic Arts) for example, to let its members know about the contest.

5. **Talk with the crowd.** Talk with designers and tell them what you like about the design and what you don't. You're far more likely to get a satisfactory design that way.

Using a contest service to run the contest for you

You can run a crowdcontest without any special computer software. You can use a simple web page or even your Facebook page to describe your business-logo contest. Tell the world about what you're doing with a few Twitter feeds and you're running a crowdcontest.

However, if you feel that you need help running a crowdcontest, you can find plenty of companies interested in assisting you. They offer specialised software, expertise with rules and, most importantly, access to large crowds of workers. Working with such a company can be considerably easier than running a contest by yourself. It can also provide you with access to large and highly talented crowds.

A good way to find a list of crowdcontest companies that specialise in graphic design is to go to crowdsourcing.org (www.crowdsourcing.org) and look at the list of crowdsourcing firms under the Crowd Creativity tab. Among the firms there, you'll find 48hourslogo, 99designs, DesignCrowd and Logo Design.

All of these firms provide a standard template for running a contest. These sites provide you with fixed outline for the brief and a fixed set of contest rules. You can create simple, one-stage contests or more complicated two-stage contests where you identify a set of designers to work on a final design. You can communicate with the designers or you can let them work on their own. These sites handle all the financial transactions, recruits the designers and have a standard set of policies for intellectual property.

You may want to turn to one of these crowdcontest companies to handle your contest for four reasons:

- ✔ You're interested only in getting the result of the crowdcontest, and never plan on running a crowdcontest again. In this case, you really have little reason to try to run it yourself.

- ✔ You've never run a crowdcontest before and aren't sure where to start. Crowdcontest sites can show you examples of successful contests that have produced high-quality work.

- ✔ You don't have access to a good crowd, and you want to have the best crowdworkers participate in your contest.

- ✔ You're simply too busy to do the work that's needed for a contest and are willing to pay others to do that work.

Chapter 6

Raising Money with Crowdfunding

*U*nlike other forms of crowdsourcing, crowdfunding is not about work. Crowdfunding is about raising money in small donations from a large crowd of people. You can quickly identify two fundamentally different kinds of crowdfunding: crowdfunding for charity and crowdfunding for commercial companies.

The easiest type of crowdfunding to understand is *charitable crowdfunding*, where you go to a crowd and ask each member for a donation to a cause. That cause can be an organised charity, a personal need (such as a medical expense or home repairs after a natural disaster), a community activity or an artistic endeavour.

Some crowdfunding sites identify another kind of charitable crowdfunding, usually called *fund-your-dreams crowdfunding*, where you try to raise money to do something that you've always wanted to do, such as travel to Rwanda to see the mountain gorillas, learn to drive a high-speed sports car or collect flags from every country on earth.

When commercial firms engage in crowdfunding, they usually do so to raise funds to help build their operation. To do this, they either sell shares of stock in the company or ask the crowd for a cash advance. The first kind of commercial crowdfunding, usually called *equity crowdfunding*, is a new form of crowdfunding, although it has roots in earlier forms of finance known as penny stocks. Because equity crowdfunding is new, many countries (including the USA) don't have a complete set of rules to govern it.

The second form of commercial crowdfunding is sometimes called *cash advance crowdfunding* because the company is asking for a cash advance from the crowd. The firm often repays the cash advance by offering the crowd goods and services, when they become available, at discount rates.

Crowdfunding, while similar to the other types of crowdsourcing, has a few features that distinguish it from those other forms. In particular, crowdfunding requires you to take an active role in assembling your crowd, whereas for macrotasking and microtasking you usually rely on others to find your crowd. Building your crowd is where this chapter comes in handy.

Knowing the Basics of Crowdfunding

In crowdfunding, you take an active role in assembling your crowd. In many other forms of crowdsourcing, you can go to a crowdsourcing platform and find the crowd that you need. You can go to Guru (www.guru.com) to find general macrotaskers, or tagasauris (www.tagasauris.com) to get micro-taskers able to create labels, or TopCoder (www.topcoder.com) for macro-tasking programmers. At the major crowdfunding platforms, you find a crowd with some people who may be interested in your ideas. However, you have to expand that crowd. More importantly, you have to bind that crowd into a community.

General crowdfunding is a form of charitable fundraising and hence is governed by local laws and regulations. Your area may require you to keep a list of all donors, or notify the tax authorities of large donations, or do certain other things in order to follow the law. The major crowdfunding platforms can help you satisfy the law, but make sure that you understand the local requirements when you begin crowdfunding.

Seeing crowdfunding as a community activity

Like all forms of crowdsourcing, crowdfunding is nothing new. Until the industrial age created large, wealthy foundations, fundraising was almost always done on a small scale. A shilling in the collection plate. A penny for a Buddy Poppy. A dime to cure polio. Small contributions accumulated and allowed a community to address an issue it had identified.

The tools of modern crowdsourcing allow fundraising to move beyond a local neighbourhood or small town and engage people around the globe. However, the small neighbourhood remains the central image of crowdfunding. Don't think that you'll collect money from complete strangers, although you may not know all the people who donate to your campaign. You collect money from a community that's identified your project as something of value. You may not know the members of this community personally. You may live nowhere near them. Yet you all have a common purpose and a common interest. You're bound into a community through that purpose and interest.

More than almost any other form of crowdsourcing, crowdfunding is about building a sense of community. That community may exist only for a short time, but it decides to support your activities.

Using the crowdmarket

At the centre of crowdfunding is the crowdmarket. As with all other forms of crowdsourcing, a transaction is at the heart of crowdfunding. Instead of offering work, the crowd offers money as its part of the transaction. In return, the members may possibly receive many things. They may receive a gift from you in appreciation: a T-shirt, a coffee mug, a little thing to put on the desk. They certainly receive a note of gratitude and a receipt. Many, if not most, benefit from knowing they've been *altruistic* – the feeling that they've done something good for someone else. However, all receive membership of your community.

In making a donation, the crowd is stating that it believes in what you're doing and wants to identify with you and your work. Members may not want to make that identification in a public way. They may not want to wear a T-shirt with your name on it, or put a sign on their door that promotes your cause. Still, they've offered you money. By doing so, they've said that they stand with you. Your task, then, is to pull this crowd into your community, to make the members feel that they want to belong to you.

Of course, the techniques of building a community around a market are the techniques of mass marketing. To rally a crowd for your crowdfunding campaign, you build a market for your idea and try to engage that market. This steps in this process are much like those of an advertising campaign:

1. **Try to make people aware of your activities, and get enough knowledge to understand what you're doing.**

2. **Get people to like what you're doing and develop a desire to identify with you and your project.**

3. **Get people to act – in this case, to pledge a donation.**

In crowdfunding, you can rely on all the techniques of modern marketing and advertising. However, you're primarily relying on two things:

- ✔ **Personal connections within the crowd:** People are more likely to join your community if they already know someone who's in it.

- ✔ **Low cost of contributing:** People are more likely to contribute if the cost is low.

Consider using a professional crowdfunding platform that can help you satisfy the local fundraising regulations. Although you can do crowdfunding with nothing more than a Facebook page (see Chapter 12) or website that directs people to make a contribution at a PayPal account, this approach works well only if you're raising money for an established charitable organisation that knows how to handle donations. Head over to Chapter 13 for details of picking a platform and examples of crowdfunding ones.

Deciding between all-or-nothing funding or partial funding

As you prepare for your crowdfunding, you'll find that most crowdfunding platforms use one of two kinds of market rules: the all-or-nothing funding rule or the partial funding rule. Both have advantages and disadvantages and work best in specific settings. The following sections explain each rule.

Most of the major crowdfunding platforms put a deadline on each fundraising call. You can keep your request on the platform until that date. After the deadline comes, you have to take the request off the site. You can avoid the problems of deadlines only if you're crowdfunding from your own site.

Understanding the power of all-or-nothing funding

If you're using the *all-or-nothing* market rule, you've set specific fundraising targets for your campaign and are collecting pledges from the crowd towards that goal. You also have a specific deadline by which you need to meet that goal. If your pledges exceed that goal before the deadline, you receive all the money that's been pledged. If your pledges don't exceed the target, you receive nothing.

The all-or-nothing rule is generally used to fund specific projects. In project funding, you're doing a specific task in a fixed period of time with a budget. Perhaps you're making a film, or building a playground or remodelling a building to house a charitable organisation.

If you don't get the entire budget, you can't do the project. Half a film or two-thirds of a playground isn't a worthwhile result. In all-or-nothing funding, your donors don't give money to create half a project. They make their pledges anticipating that you can do the entire project. So if you don't raise all the funds, you have to return the pledges.

Many crowdfunding platforms state that they're funding projects only and require you to use the all-or-nothing market rule.

Choosing to ask for partial funding

In *partial* funding, you have a fundraising goal and you have a deadline. However, you don't need to raise the entire budget in order to be able to start work. In this case, you still get some money if you fail to get enough pledges to cover the budget. When the deadline arrives, you get the amount that's been pledged to your work.

Partial funding is most useful when you're doing work that you can easily expand or shrink. You may be trying to raise money to feed 100 people for a month or offer concert tickets to 200 people. If you raise money to feed 50 people or give tickets to 120, you can still do good.

 If you're trying to use crowdfunding to support the ongoing activities of an organisation, you may want to establish your own crowdfunding site. Use a website or a social networking site to keep the crowd aware of your activities, and use a financial service such as PayPal to collect money.

Understanding the fee

As you draw up your budget for crowdfunding, include the fees that you pay the crowdfunding platform. Usually, you pay two kinds of fees:

✔ **To the crowdfunding platform that promotes your fundraising efforts.** Most crowdfunding platforms charge you a fee if you run a successful campaign on their platform. If you post a campaign and that campaign isn't successful, they charge you nothing. All partial-payment campaigns are considered to be successful, even if you don't collect the full amount that you request.

Generally, these fees are roughly 10 per cent of the money that you collect. Each platform should give you a clear statement of the fees that you can expect to pay. If you don't see such a statement, use another crowdfunding platform.

> ✔ **To the financial firm that handles the transfer of funds for the platform.** For example, Amazon or PayPal may take a fee. Typically, a financial organisation charges between 3 and 5 per cent of the amount that you collect.

Raising money over the Internet offers many possibilities for misunderstanding and fraud, so use only crowdfunding platforms that publish all their fees and policies. Also consider using only platforms that are accredited by one of the industry groups that promotes integrity and ethics in fundraising. One such programme is the Crowdfunding Accreditation for Platform Standards, one that's run by crowdsourcing.org.

Running a Crowdfunding Project

You're ready to start crowdfunding. You have a project. You understand the basic idea. The following sections provide guidance for getting your project off the ground.

Preparing to crowdfund has much in common with the work of describing your tasks for other forms of crowdfunding. So, you may want to take a look at Chapter 11, which explains how to write instructions for the crowd.

In crowdfunding, the instructions are very simple. You simply want the members of the crowd to give money or encourage their friends to give money. However, you need to explain to the crowd members why they should give money, and to do that, you need to start with the reasons why you need the funds. You need to start with the budget.

Writing the budget

After you've decided on a platform (Chapter 13 helps you here) and have decided between all-or-nothing funding or partial funding (see the earlier section 'Deciding between all-or-nothing funding or partial funding'), you need a budget. The budget should lay down the amount of money that you need and the way in which you intend to spend the money. Be sure to include any fees that you need to pay (see 'Understanding the fee', earlier in this chapter).

Use the budget to make the case for your crowdfunding activity. The budget isn't merely a statement of how you plan to spend money, but is actually a statement of your values. It may show that you'll be spending the money on people rather than on things. It may demonstrate that an eager group of volunteers needs only one piece of equipment to be more effective. It may reveal that you'll be donating substantial labour and equipment that you already own to the project.

Keep the budget as simple as possible. Many crowdfunding platforms publish only the total amount that a crowdfunder is seeking. Furthermore, the crowd has a decidedly low tolerance for figures. If it sees a detailed budget with lots of figures, it'll skip your request and go to the next project.

Describing your project

Benefits, benefits, benefits.

When you write the description of your project, remember the first rule of crowdfunding: emphasise the benefits to the crowd. The crowd will fund your project if it identifies with your work and believes that the work will do good. The crowd members often won't care about how brilliant the idea may be or how beautiful it may look. They want to see a benefit to the crowd.

Of course, many members of the crowd may not directly benefit from your project. However, if they can see a connection between those who do benefit and themselves, they may see enough good to offer their contributions.

Here are some helpful hints for writing descriptions:

- ✔ Start the description with a strong sentence that emphasises the value of the project.

- ✔ Tell people what they're contributing to the project, not how the project will be done. See the nearby sidebar 'Explaining benefits' for an example.

- ✔ Use the words *we* and *ours* rather than *I* or *mine* to emphasise the community nature of the fundraising.

- ✔ If the platform allows, include photos and videos that emphasise the benefits of your project. A good video can be a powerful fundraising tool. With it you can explain your project, demonstrate the benefits of your work, and explain the things that may not be easy to understand in your pitch.

The Vancouver restaurant Besties produced a three-minute video that showed the two partners talking about their planned restaurant. They explained some of the food they'd serve, including a German street food called currywurst, and showed how they were developing the restaurant by themselves. The video helped the firm raise $10,000 (or £6,300). Check it out online at www.indiegogo.com/bestie.

Don't exaggerate the value of your project. In the long run, exaggeration damages your reputation as a crowdfunder. For a time, you may be able to convince some people that your project's better and more important than it really is, but you won't be able to do it over an extended period. Communities on the Internet are usually able to uncover exaggerations and hyperbole.

Explaining benefits

In writing a description of your project, you can simply describe what you're doing, but describing isn't always the best way to attract a crowd. A simple description may read as follows:

> I'm going to use the funds for this project to purchase a 5-metre net climber that I am going to put in a vacant lot owned by the city. Some of the money I will use to rent a backhoe to dig a hole for the foundations of the climber. I will also will purchase some concrete for the foundations. This climber will be part of the playground.

You can make a more persuasive case by stressing the benefits of your project to the crowd:

> The funds will be used to help build a safe and clean playground for an urban neighbourhood that's not had a good playground for 20 years. It will allow a growing group of young families to have their kids play near their homes rather than go across town to find a good play area. A group of parents have banded together to create the playground. One has convinced the city to donate a strip of land. We are all working to clear the lot. One of us is skilled in construction and will set up the equipment. The funds will be used to purchase a 5-metre net climber for the playground.

Setting a deadline for a decision

Most crowdfunding platforms allow you to set the deadline for your crowdfunding campaign, usually a date between one and ten weeks after your posting. You're responsible for driving most of the crowd to your platform, so choose a date that reflects how much time you need to contact your crowd. Most members of the crowd will make a decision shortly after they hear about your campaign. If you set a date that's too close, you may not get enough of the crowd to know about your campaign. If the date is too far in the future, people may forget about the campaign.

Campaigns often see a surge of activity at the start and at the end. When the campaign is new, you get people visiting your presentation to see what you're doing. At the end, you can rally people to the cause and encourage them to donate once more. If too much time elapses between the start and the end, the crowd may forget about your campaign and react with surprise when you start telling them that the deadline is near. You get the best reaction if you set a long enough deadline so you can build a big response at the start, keep regular contributions coming in to the campaign, and have a big push at the end while the idea is still fresh in the minds of the crowd members.

Crowds are often smaller than you may expect. On small crowdfunding projects, you can quickly find that your crowd has a small number of members who are communicating among themselves only. If this happens, you may find that the crowd tires of your project and doesn't respond when you try to raise funds at the final deadline.

Contacting the crowd

Before you start the campaign, you should take a moment to think about the crowd that you hope to find. Ask yourself:

- Who may be the members of the crowd?
- How do I contact them?
- Who do they know?
- What ideas can I use to get a response from this crowd?

To contact the crowd, you use the standard tools of digital communication, like email and phone, and social networking (for more on social media, see Chapter 12). You send messages to your friends and colleagues to tell them of the campaign. You ask these people to fund the campaign and to notify their friends. You look for institutions and organisations that may help you by sending messages to their employees, customers, friends or members. You keep your crowdfunding fresh and active by adding news of your progress and ideas that you've gained during the campaign.

As you run the campaign, try to use images and ideas that identify your crowd and encourage people to join it. If you're funding a neighbourhood project, use pictures of the neighbourhood. If you're doing something that doesn't have geographical boundaries, such as an art project or an effort to support certain kinds of animals, use images that identify your project and encourage people with such interests to join. If you know a prominent individual who's willing to lend her name to the project, you may find that her doing so expands your crowd.

Here are a few other ways to reach out to the crowd, many borrowed from traditional fundraising:

- **Find an inner core of supporters to start the campaign.** It takes money to raise money. People are more likely to pledge money to campaigns that have already attracted some money. Early contributions are evidence that people like your project and have confidence in your leadership. Therefore, before you start advertising your crowdfunding campaign to the world, raise some money from friends and family so that you can open your campaign with some real pledges towards your goal. In crowdfunding circles, these early donors are known as your *inner core of contributors.*

   The inner core can be very helpful to your campaign. As well as giving early donations, they can contact their friends and family and ask them to donate to your campaign and provide a second round of contributions midway through the campaign to encourage other people.

✔ **Use matching challenges to bring donations.** If you know someone who's willing to make a large donation, ask her to give it as a challenge. Instead of her donating $100 ($63), have her say that she'll double the contributions of ten individuals up to $10 ($6.30), and then challenge your crowd to find $10 donations. In crowdfunding, you can also use a challenge to match the gifts of individuals who bring new people into the crowd.

✔ **Give gifts.** You can offer gifts to people who make donations of a certain size or to individuals who bring a certain number of contributors to the crowd.

✔ **Use multiple social platforms.** Not everyone uses Facebook. Not everyone uses Twitter. Not everyone uses Net2. Not everyone uses the neighbourhood listserv. Not even everyone uses email. Promote your project on as many platforms as you can. If doing so seems appropriate, you might even use traditional forms of media – notes on the supermarket bulletin board, talks to organisations, calls to friends.

✔ **Look for volunteering opportunities.** Some people find it easier to give labour than to give money. Find a way to engage people in working for your project. Have them gather to support the neighbourhood activity, create the artwork, support the cause. Post information about that contribution on your project page to show that you're making progress towards your goal.

✔ **Have a gathering.** Invite the people who support your project to gather in a physical location such as a park or a coffee shop. At the event, encourage the participants to contact their friends over social media to donate to your project.

✔ **Offer a webinar.** Organise a *webinar* – an online conference – on one of the social media sites such as Google+. In the webinar, you can explain your project and the need that you have for funds. You should be able to capture the webinar and replay it for other people.

Considering an Example: Creating a Playground

A group of neighbours want to build an urban playground for their children. They've identified a piece of land that's owned by the city and have obtained the permission of the city council. They've been able to find several old playground structures that they can use, but they want to purchase and install a climbing structure. The city has no funds for the project, so group is raising money through crowdfunding.

Building a budget

The group identifies a make and model of climbing net that costs $14,999. (£9,400). The group has to install it themselves, so it needs concrete, construction equipment and a city permit. The members estimate that they need $18,642 (£11,600). When they remember that the crowdfunding platform is likely take about 10 per cent, they decide to ask for $19,000 (£12,000). Figure 6-1 shows their budget.

1	14' Netclimber BE-3144	$14,999
2	Shipping	$780
	Tax - none	
3	Backhoe rental	$750
4	Concrete	$124
5	City Permit	$125
6	Total	$16,778
7	Fees (10%)	$1,864
8	Total Need	$18,642
9	Contingency	$358
10	Total Request	$19,000

Figure 6-1: Budget for a crowdfunding project.

Writing a letter

After they create the budget, the members of the crowdfunding group draft a letter describing the project. The basic idea is short and straightforward. The letter describes the project as providing a safe and clean playground for young children. After they complete the description, the group open an account on a crowdfunding platform and create a project. Figure 6-2 shows that project and the description on the crowdfunding site WhenYouWish.com.

Setting a timeline

The group decides that it should be able to raise the money in a month. Because the neighbourhood has a diverse group of families, the group members decide on a deadline of 35 days to make sure that the timeline cover the paydays of all the families. The members believe that some people are most likely to give when they've just received a pay cheque.

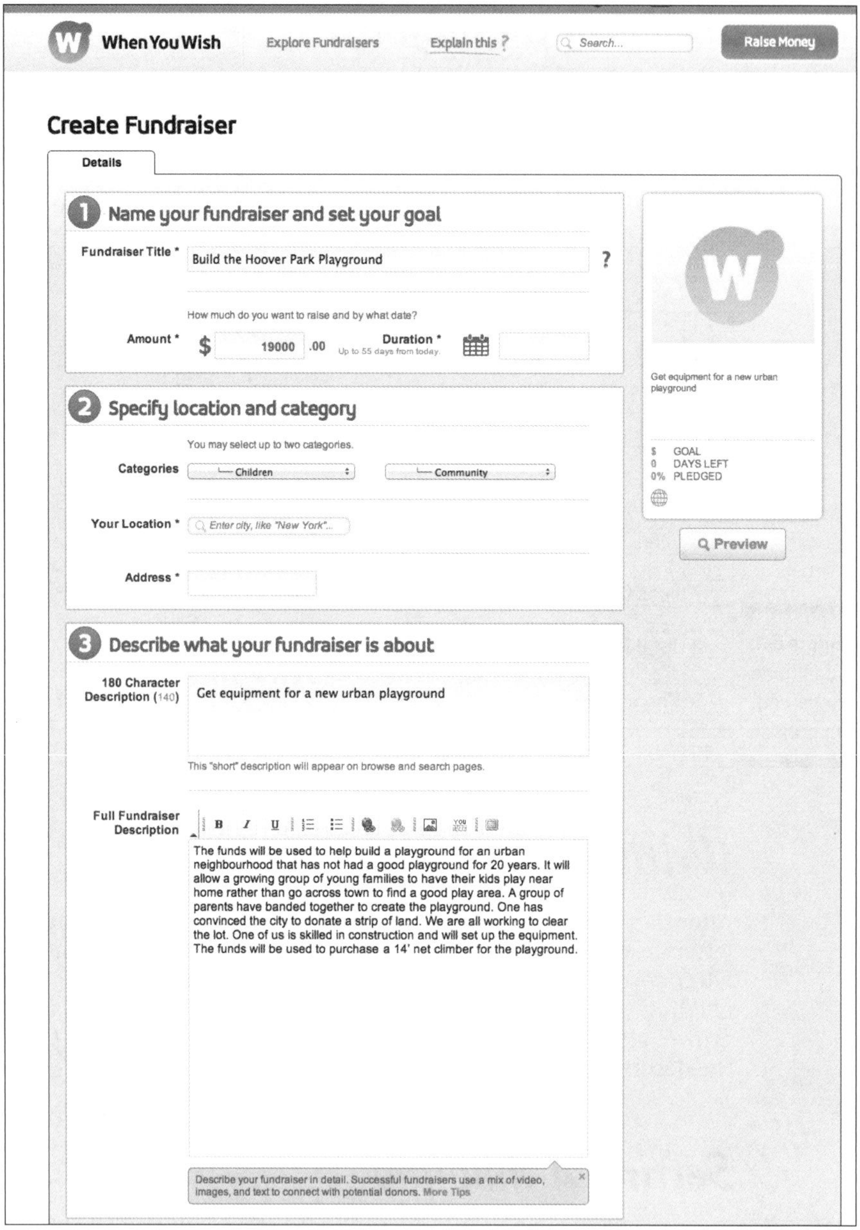

Figure 6-2: Project on a crowdfunding platform.

Reproduced with permission from When You Wish.

Getting the crowd

After they place the project on the crowdfunding platform, the group members start calling the crowd to the platform. Ten families donate $100 ($63) each, so the group can start the project with $1,000 ($630) already pledged. The members then start inviting the crowd. They contact their own families and friends, the people who subscribed to the neighbourhood newsletter, and the local shops and schools. The fund begins to build and soon meets the goal. The group doesn't even have to use matching funds, prizes or a big push at the end to get the final money.

Accumulating Equity for a Company

In *equity crowdfunding*, you're raising money for your company. Instead of just asking for donations, as you would in ordinary crowdfunding, you sell a little bit of the ownership in your company to members of the crowd. As with charitable crowdfunding, you expect the crowd to buy the ownership of your company in small units. Instead of selling large shares of stock worth $40 ($25) or $100 ($63), or even $1,000 ($630), you sell shares for $1 ($0.63), or $5 ($3.15) or $10 ($6.30).

Crowdfunding is tightly regulated in most countries. You have to meet the regulations of the country where you're attempting to raise money. Before you do any equity crowdfunding, make sure you know the crowdfunding regulations for the country where your company is incorporated and for the country where you're trying to raise funds. Check the crowdsourcing industry website (www.crowdsourcing.org) to see whether it has any information about regulations in your country, and also look at the website of the government agency that regulates banking and investment – usually the best place to start looking for such regulations. If you have any questions, get professional help.

At the moment, equity crowdfunding is in a state of flux. It became legal in the USA only recently, and at the time of writing, the American Government is still in the process of creating regulations to govern this form of crowdfunding. When it's created these regulations, the number of firms that offer equity crowdfunding services will expand quickly. Many of the firms that provide charitable crowdfunding, such as Indiegogo, WhenYouWish and Kickstarter, will likely offer equity crowdfunding services.

In the following sections, I use the UK firm Crowdcube as an example of an equity crowdsourcing firm. Crowdcube follows the model that most experts believe will become the standard for the equity crowdfunding industry.

Before you start equity crowdfunding, find out more about the state of the field at information sites such as crowdsourcing.org (`www.crowdsourcing.org`) or Daily Crowdsource (`www.dailycrowdsource.com`), and check the services offered by other firms involved in crowdfunding.

Making a pitch

Equity crowdfunding works much like charitable crowdfunding. You decide how much money you need for your company – the target goal for this funding campaign. You also decide the percentage of your company that you're willing to exchange for that amount of money. You post this request on a crowdfunding platform.

You can set your request low or high. Most platforms have a minimum value that you must request. Some have a maximum amount. All crowdfunding platforms encourage small investments, but most establish a minimum investment. At Crowdcube (`www.crowdcube.com`), a crowdfunding platform in the UK, you have to ask for at least £10,000 ($16,000). Crowdcube has no maximum request, but it does require all investments to be at least £10 ($16).

When you're deciding how much you should request and how much equity you'll sell, you're determining the value of your company. The amount you request is equal to the value of the fraction of the company you sell. If you believe that your company is worth $5 million (£3.15 million) and you want to raise $500,000 (£315,000), then you sell 10 per cent of the equity in your company.

If you don't know how to put a value on your company, seek the advice of a commercial banker or investment advisor who knows how to do it. If you don't, you run the risk of selling too much of your company for too low a price. Essentially, the value of your company is the price that someone would pay for it on the open market. However, most investment organisations employ an economic model that includes the assets of the company, the amount of income that the company can generate, and the business risk that the company faces.

In addition to setting a target goal, you also set a deadline, usually two to three months in the future. If the crowd meets your goal by the deadline – if it provides all the funds that you're seeking – then you sell the piece of equity in your company, issue stock certificates and get the money you need. If the crowd doesn't meet your goal, the platform returns the money that's been pledged and you get nothing.

Using a platform

You carry out equity crowdfunding on special platforms regulated by the local government. You can't do equity crowdfunding on platforms for charitable crowdfunding.

When you do equity crowdfunding, you have to provide substantial information about your company: the business plan, recent financial statements, financial projections for the coming years. You also need to show how the company would provide a return on the investments it'd like to receive.

Figure 6-3 gives the first part of the application for a posting on Crowdcube. The application is much like the form for a charitable crowdsourcing campaign. It asks for a few pieces of technical information such as your company number, an acknowledgement that your company is indeed a UK limited liability company, and the investment that you've already secured.

 You'll be most successful with your first attempt at crowdfunding if you pitch your offering as a good investment rather than trying to describe your organisation as a good company. Most investors want to know that your company will make their money grow, that it will return their investment, and that it has a promising future. Many first-time crowdfunders spend too much time trying to describe their product or service. They want to explain why the product is good rather than why the investment is good.

Figure 6-4 shows the second part of the Crowdcube application for equity crowdfunding. In this part, you have to provide the information that describes your business. You provide a business plan, financial forecasts, and details of the number of employees, funding, revenue and profit. The form also asks you to state the funds you require and the percentage of the ownership in your company that you're willing to sell in exchange for the money.

Paying the fees and getting the funds

When you do equity crowdfunding, you tend to pay four kinds of fees, as follows:

- **Posting fee:** The fee that you pay to the crowdfunding platform to register and post a pitch for funds. This fee is usually a small amount. At Crowdcube, the fee is ₤250 ($400).

- **Success fee:** A percentage of the amount of money raised through the crowd. Typically, this fee ranges from 3 to 8 per cent. At Crowdcube, the fee is 5 per cent of the total money you raise.

✔ **Transfer fee:** The money paid to a financial institution to transfer the money to your account. Crowdcube transfers the money to the bank of your choice and doesn't charge a fee.

✔ **Processing fee:** Covers all the costs of paperwork and legal filings. Crowdcube charges a flat fee of £1,750 ($2,800).

Figure 6-3:
Initial information for an equity crowd-funding campaign.

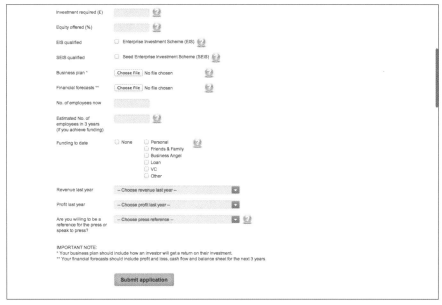

Reproduced with permission from Crowdcube.

Figure 6-4: Business information for crowd-funding.

Attracting the crowd

When a crowdfunding platform has accepted your application for equity crowdfunding, you can start directing the crowd's attention to your campaign.

You have to help build the crowd. Most crowdfunding platforms have at least a small group of investors, but they rarely have enough to fund your request completely. You have to recruit more members of the crowd through your network and the networks of other members of your company.

In equity crowdfunding, you may have to limit what you say when you promote your company's crowdfunding request. You can certainly draw the crowd's attention to the platform and tell it that the campaign represents an investment opportunity and that the platform has information that explains the quality of the investment. But you may be restricted by government regulations from making additional claims about the quality of the investment.

As with charitable crowdfunding, assemble an inner core of investors so that you can show that a substantial fraction of your request has been filled on the first day. You can then use the network of this inner core to call new members to the crowdfunding platform.

You can recruit new members to the crowd by using the same techniques that you may employ in charitable crowdfunding. After you start with an inner core of investors, you can turn to neighbours and local institutions. You can have events that gather investors together. You can have volunteer activities for investors. You can even offer investors a modest gift for their investment, such as a shirt, an item for their desk, or an early version of your product. (You may also want to use an early version of the product to raise funds without selling equity; see the later section 'Using non-equity funding'.)

Waiting for results

Generally, you can't change your pitch after you've posted it. Some platforms let you increase the amount of equity that you're offering, but you can't change the amount of money that you hope to get out of the campaign. However, you can add information to show the progress that your company's making.

As with charitable crowdfunding, you may have to make a push at the end to achieve your goal. In this final stage, you may find that the most likely investors are those who've already pledged. Because they've already made an investment, they're often interested in seeing you succeed.

 Be careful during any final push to avoid frightening investors. Most crowdfunding platforms allow investors to withdraw their investment at any time before the deadline. If you send messages that suggest that you're in desperate shape, you may find that some of your investors decide that your company isn't a good place for their money.

Examining the results

No matter what happens at the end of your campaign, look at the results and try to understand what happened.

When all goes well, you get the money, pay your fees, and get back to work. However, consider how much effort you put into the campaign. If you got the money quickly and with little effort, you may have undervalued your company. If you had to work hard and barely made your goal, you may have overvalued the company. In either case, you want to think carefully about how you approach the crowd for a second round of funding.

Investing in crowdfunded companies

What if you want to invest? Well, as in all forms of investing, be cautious when you invest in a crowdfunded company. If you enter with low expectations and invest no more than you're willing to lose, you'll never be disappointed.

Crowdfunding is designed to be a process for small investors. If you're going to invest a substantial sum, you probably have to register with the platform as a large investor. Crowdcube, for example, requires anyone who's going to invest more than £5,000 ($8,000) to register as a high net worth or sophisticated investor.

Crowdfunding uses social networks to raise funds, which changes your risk in two ways:

✔ You may know the leaders of the company or perhaps know someone who knows them. From this connection, you may have a better appreciation of their business. You may better know their skills, the quality of their work, the value of their products, and the likelihood of their success.

✔ You're part of the business's community, and you may care about the leaders and their business more. You may be more willing to take a risk with this business than with a stranger.

When crowdfunding doesn't work, you've overvalued your company or failed to convince the crowd that the company was indeed a good investment. You can return to the crowd for a second attempt of crowdfunding, but before you do, take time and prepare yourself. Ask yourself what you can do to make your company better value and how you can better communicate that value to the crowd.

Spark Devices attempted to use crowdfunding to raise $250,000 ($155,000) to start manufacturing a device that would enable people to connect electric lights to the Internet and control those lights with a computer. The campaign began with great enthusiasm and ended six weeks later with pledges for $125,000 ($77,500). However, by the rules of Kickstarter, the firm got nothing, because it failed to meet its goal.

The record of Spark Devices' campaign (available on the Kickstarter website at www.kickstarter.com) suggests that the firm made two mistakes. Firstly, it set its fundraising target too high. The campaign could have raised a substantial amount if the firm had set their target lower. Secondly, a close look at the contributions suggests that the firm overestimated people's willingness to give large sums of money to the campaign. Few people were willing to give more than $100 ($63), even though the company offered gifts, products and other opportunities for large contributions. According to the campaign budget, the firm anticipated getting at least $40,000 ($25,200) more in contributions from large donors.

In general, the crowd responds to actions rather than to figures. Can you get the product out the door? Can you get a new contract? Can you improve the quality of your service? These sorts of things impress the crowd and may make your next attempt at crowdfunding more successful.

Using non-equity funding

You may want to avoid equity crowdfunding for as long as you can. When you're selling equity, you're selling some control in your company and some of the claims on future income. When you sell equity as a small company, you're selling it dear. Generally, the longer you can wait before you sell equity in your company, the more money that equity brings.

Crowdsourcing offers small start-up companies an alternative to equity crowdfunding. Instead of selling part of your company, you can raise capital through donations. Although people rarely give gifts to profit-making companies, you can reward the gifts with early versions of products or specialised versions of products.

The Pebble Watch provides a dramatic example of how funds can be raised for a company without selling equity in the company. The firm posted a request for funds on the crowdfunding platform Kickstarter. The request offered rewards for the donations. If you gave $99 (£62), you got one watch. If you gave $220 (£138), you got two. If you gave $235 (£147), you got early access to the developers' kit that allowed you to create software for the watch. A gift of $1,000 (£625) got you ten watches. Given that the firm planned to sell the watch for $150 (£94), these rewards were really preliminary orders for the watch. However, the firm was able to raise more than $10 million (£6.25 million) through Kickstarter and use that money to expand its organisation without having to sell equity.

Chapter 7

Making Use of Macrotasks

*W*elcome to the world of *macrotasking* – a new form of freelancing where you (as the crowdsourcer) go to the crowdmarket with a job that requires a specific skillset. You use the market to engage the crowd and find one person with the skills needed to do that job. Macrotasking is so similar to freelancing that a new term – *elancing* – has been coined to describe it.

As with all forms of crowdsourcing, macrotasking has led people to think about jobs in new ways. In the traditional model, organisations are supposed to be self-contained, possessing all the skills and talents they need among their employees and managers. If an organisation needs a specific skill to complete a task, it either needs to find that skill among its employees, hire a new employee or decide that it doesn't need that skill. Macrotasking gives managers another option: to look for specific skills outside the organisation.

In this chapter, I help you come to grips with macrotasking so that you too can use it to your benefit.

Getting to Grips with Macrotasking

Macrotasking is the professional form of crowdsourcing. It uses the crowd-market to match workers who operate as freelancers or independent contractors – and who have special skills or experience – with complex jobs that require advanced skills or training. These jobs usually require several hours or days of work. The term *macrotasking* is used to distinguish this type of work from *microtasking* – the form of crowdsourcing that focuses on short tasks that may not require advanced skills. Workers involved in macrotasking can be writers, editors, web designers, programmers, graphic artists, proofreaders, accountants, statisticians or people from many other professions.

In some cases, macrotasking is similar to freelancing, although it's freelancing on a global scale. If you're a worker, you can find jobs anywhere in the world. If you're an employer, you can search that same world to find talented workers. Perhaps the most important aspect of macrotasking is that it occurs in an open, public market. Anyone can post a job or offer their services. You don't need to send your résumé to hundreds of individuals to find a job, or to struggle to find the right kind of worker. You have a public market that can help you find both.

Macrotasking also differs from freelancing in that an organisation helps manage the relationship between you and the contractor, handles payments to the contractor, files any necessary governmental paperwork, monitors the macrotasker and verifies the number of hours worked.

I regularly receive emails from small local businesses who're looking for a worker who has specific computer skills. 'Help,' these emails say, 'I need a student who can create a spreadsheet' (or design a SQL database, program an app, configure a network or do some other technical task).

What the people who write these emails don't admit (or realise) is that they don't really want a student. What they want is a trained, mature worker who has the skill to do their task and do it professionally. However, they don't have enough work to warrant hiring a full-time employee with these skills. Instead, they may need a speedsheet programmer for just 20 hours a year, or a database designer for a day every other month.

One strategy that such a business might employ is to hire someone who has the necessary technical skills and also the ability to do some other kind of job, such as accounting or sales. However, such a strategy's rarely effective, because finding people with an unusual combination of skills can be tricky, and secondly, these people are always better at one job than another. For example, you may get a first-rate programmer but have to accept a second-rate accountant in the deal.

Of programmers and plumbers . . .

Orion Plumbing Contracting is an organisation well known for fitting high-quality plumbing systems within existing structures. A couple of senior employees who were able to design complicated systems, calculate how to bend pipes to create the system, and then assemble the pipes into the final system achieved the company's good reputation. To keep the company competitive, the owner, Liam, needed to capture the knowledge of those senior employees and make it available to all the plumbers who worked for Orion Plumbing. To do this, he came up with the idea of producing a program that works on a tablet computer, whereby the plumber takes a picture of the structure and sketches the pipes, and the program then tells him how to construct the system.

Programming, however, is not plumbing. Orion had many plumbers but no one who could program. Liam had three obvious choices: hire a programmer, look for a company to create the program, or produce the program through macrotasking. The first option, of hiring a programmer, didn't appeal to him. Liam believed that a programmer wouldn't be kept busy. The second option, of finding a company to create the program, was too expensive for Liam's budget. The third option, macrotasking, was the most appealing. Liam would be able to hire a skilled programmer for his job, but wouldn't then have an employee with time on his hands. He'd pay only for the hours needed to create the program.

In the end, the macrotasking solution cost more than Liam anticipated, although the cost was still far less than that of a new employee or a contract with a software firm. Liam discovered that he not only needed the programmer to write, debug and install the program, but also to monitor the software and add new features. He found that he could re-contract with his macrotask worker later to review the software and add new features.

Macrotasking enables you to separate the skills and hire workers on a task-by-task basis. You can hire the right kind of programmer for your programming jobs and the best accountant for your accounting problems.

Seeing the Benefits of Macrotasks

Many people are cautious about macrotasking. Some are concerned that, by sending work out, they'll lose control of a project. Others worry that they'll be unable to manage a worker who's not physically near their office, or that they may compromise sensitive information or intellectual property. All these issues represent real concerns that you must handle in any macrotask. However, many people resist this form of crowdsourcing because they simply can't see the opportunities for macrotasking in their organisation. And that's a shame, because macrotasking has some great benefits:

Macrotasking for the home

Every household has jobs that need to be done. A new piece of furniture has arrived and needs to be assembled. The pest inspector is coming next week, and someone needs to be there to meet him. The garden needs tidying. In an earlier time, you might have hired a local worker or handyman to do these tasks. However, handymen have become hard to find. In many neighbourhoods, handymen have been replaced by macrotaskers. For example, you can request a helper through a macrotask service such as TaskRabbit (www.taskrabbit.com) or PinDone (www.pindone.com). At these sites, you can post a job that needs doing in your home or personal life, state how much you want to pay, and find a member of the crowd to do it. This way, you get the job done on your terms but match it more closely with someone who has the necessary skills (a handyman was often a jack of all trades but master of none) – simple!

✔ **You get the skills you need.** In conventional organisations, you often get skills that are only similar to the ones you want. A member of your sales staff can do a little programming. A member of your delivery organisation is a bit of a writer. In macrotasking, you hire a person with exactly the skills you need.

✔ **You get what you pay for.** If you're running a small business or working as an individual, you may not have enough work for a full-time PHP programmer or English–Russian translator. Through macrotasking, you hire a person for only the work that you have.

✔ **You get access to a global talent pool.** No matter where you live or work, macrotasking gives you access to talented people around the globe. You may know no one in your area who can write advertising copy, create 3D models or work with Japanese government documents, but macrotasking gives you access to people who can do those things and more.

✔ **You can benefit from it, no matter who you are.** Macrotasking is commonly associated with small companies or entrepreneurial start-up firms. These organisations can gain much from macrotasking, because they often lack people with specific skills and are unable to hire a full-time employee for certain tasks. However, macrotasking is also useful to individuals (see the sidebar 'Macrotasking for the home') and large organisations. It can be used in any situation that needs a specific skill to get a job done.

Identifying Macrotasks

Pinning down the macrotasks in a small start-up organisation is fairly easy. Small organisations always have some kind of project that current employees can't handle. For example, a small organisation's team may have basic business skills but lack any individual who can design a web page, or plan a marketing campaign, or draft an annual report. In a small organisation, then, you identify potential macrotasks when you find a project that needs skills that aren't currently available in your organisation.

Identifying potential macrotasks within large organisations is trickier. Potential macrotasks can be hidden, because large organisations can almost always find someone to do a job. Some of these potential macrotask jobs may be handled by people who don't truly have the appropriate skills, experience or training. Nonetheless, they do the tasks. So how do you know which jobs to macrotask? The following sections help you root out macrotasks.

To determine whether a task can be macrotasked, you need to examine it carefully and decide whether the work can be done independently, takes a fixed amount of time and requires special skills.

Thinking process, not organisation

When you think of organisations, you often think in terms of positions and titles. You think that your organisation has an assistant financial officer, or a manager of customer support, or a youth outreach director. In fact, you don't build an organisation by identifying the positions that you need and deciding what to do with them. You determine what the organisation *does*, the work processes that it handles. Then you decide what kind of positions you need to carry out those processes.

So when you go looking for macrotasks, start by looking at the main processes of the organisation. Ask yourself, how does the organisation:

- ✔ Create a product and deliver it to its customers?
- ✔ Deal with its suppliers or the other companies?
- ✔ Handle its basic business activities?
- ✔ Organise a service and perform that service week after week?

After you identify the processes, you can break them down into individual steps, look at the way each step is performed, and ask whether that step should be handled by a permanent member of the organisation or by a macrotasker.

The National Association for the Promotion of Goodness and Virtue (NAPGV) is a lobbying group that promotes, as the name implies, things that are good and virtuous, and holds an annual conference for its supporters. The leadership, having watched the annual convention become more and more complex, has decided that it'll try to improve the management of the conference by crowdsourcing some of the work.

To identify possible macrotasks in the conference, the NAPGV management looks at the process that's used to create and manage the conference programme and the speakers and organisations who address the meeting. The leader of the organisation, Kamal, decides that the process to create a programme for the conference has five steps:

1. Identify and contact speakers.

2. Collect speech titles and biographies from speakers.

3. Edit a conference programme.

4. Contact speakers a week before the conference and get their presentations.

5. Edit the presentations into a standard form and put them on the conference computer.

Of these five steps, steps 2, 3 and 5 are good candidates for macrotasking. They are well defined, easy to describe, and require specific skills. Step 2 requires the skills of an administrative assistant, someone who's organised and persistent. The work is easy to describe, and checking that it's been done is easy. Step 3 requires the skills of an editor and document designer, and may be best divided into two macrotasks: an editor to review the material, correct problems and put it in the proper order, and a designer to format the material so that it looks good in a programme or on a web page. Step 5 requires the skills of presentation editor. Like steps 2 and 3, this task is easy to define, easy to describe and easy to check when it's been done.

Steps 1 and 4 are difficult to macrotask. Step 1 requires a clear understanding of the goals of the conference and a knowledge of the potential speakers. Neither of these is easy to find at a macrotask market, and both are best done by a senior member of the organisation. Step 4 is difficult to macrotask because the task isn't as well defined as it appears. When you contact speakers a week before a conference, you encounter problems that you didn't anticipate. Perhaps one speaker forgets that she was going to talk. Another may ask whether he can give the same talk that he gave last year. A third may respond with cryptic messages that seem to indicate that he's going to make up the speech on the platform of the conference. You can't easily instruct a macrotask worker how to handle all these different circumstances, so step 4 is best done by someone within the organisation.

Identifying independent tasks

The tasks that are easiest to macrotask are those that can be done independently. In effect, you identify an activity, give it to a macrotask worker, and let him go work by himself. After the macrotasker finishes, you incorporate his contributions into your organisation.

In fact, you can be a little more specific about the nature of an independent task. Independent tasks are those that are:

- **Easy to describe:** In some cases, the tasks are easy to describe because they're simple tasks. If you're asking someone to proofread a document and find any grammatical errors, you're describing a relatively simple task.

  However, many complicated tasks are also easy to describe. The description is easy because the task relies on complex ideas that professional communities have spent years developing. For example, if need a purchase and sales agreement that's valid in certain countries, you're asking for a highly complex item. However, anyone who's qualified to draft such a document quickly knows what you need.

- **Based on obvious goals:** You should be able to identify exactly the kind of work product that you expect and criteria that you'll use to judge whether the work's been properly done.

- **Simple to coordinate:** The jobs should require only limited contact with the others who're working on the bigger process. If the task requires the worker to talk with other members of the team several times a day or requires him to meet the rest of the team often, then it probably isn't a good macrotask.

Choosing what's important

In macrotasking, you need to focus on your goals. You may be looking to:

- Create a more flexible structure that can quickly respond to changing conditions
- Get a higher-quality operation
- Improve your organisation
- Reduce costs

After you identify potential macrotasks, examine each and ask:

- Is it an independent task?
- Is it simple to describe?

✔ Does it have a fixed deadline?

✔ Does it require special skills?

If you answer 'no' to all these questions, the task may not be suitable for macrotasking. If you answer 'yes' to at least one of the questions, you may have found an activity that you can macrotask.

Every organisation has different managerial skills and different abilities to macrotask. Some organisations can manage only the simplest macrotasks. Some had can handle highly complicated tasks. Some are able to macrotask only the jobs that require highly specialised skills. Others feel comfortable macrotasking with any kind of macrotask, including jobs that can be done by full-time employees if they have the time. You have to determine the tasks that can be best handled by your organisation.

Finding a fixed deadline

Good candidates for macrotasks are short-term jobs. The work of preparing sales material for a new market is a good candidate for a macrotask. A macrotask worker should be able to do that job in a fixed time. The bigger task of opening a new market for your products is probably not a good macrotask. Such a task could easily require more time than anyone anticipates.

However, macrotasks aren't limited to short-term work. You may have a job that's done regularly that doesn't require a deep or permanent knowledge of your organisation. You may find several jobs that are done once a year and require limited knowledge of what was done the previous year, such as designing a conference logo.

If you're looking at jobs that recur regularly, ask, 'Would I be satisfied if a new person did this job each time it's needed?' If the answer is 'yes', the task is a good candidate for macrotasking.

Requiring special skills

If a task involves special skills that you normally don't require in your organisation, consider macrotasking. The skills of a videographer, for example, may not be common in your organisation. You may not regularly need the skills or a copywriter, or a graphic designer, or a web designer.

A job needn't require special skills to be a good macrotask job. Many organisations need to expand their workforce for a short period each year. They may choose to macrotask an aspect of work that their staff normally handle during the rest of the year.

Preparing the Macrotask

After you identify a macrotask, you need to prepare it. You can quickly see that macrotasking can be powerful, but it's not magic. Like all forms of management, macrotasking requires careful preparation. By preparing carefully, you're more likely to get the job done well, on time and on budget. You're also in the best position to get the full benefits of macrotasking.

After you've identified a macrotask, you need to decide how it'll fit into your organisation. If you work by yourself, you have few decisions to make; you've identified the macrotask, you'll hire the macrotask worker and you'll determine when the job is done properly. However, if you're working in a larger organisation, you may have to decide how the macrotasker will interact with the other employees. You may have identified the macrotask, but you may not be the right person to manage the macrotask worker or determine when the task is done. The macrotask worker may be managed by an employee who reports to you, or may be part of a team of people who work together as equals, or may be able to work without having any contact with anyone in your organisation.

When you macrotask a job, you're responsible for making sure that the macrotask worker fits into your organisation. That's where this section comes in.

Naming the manager

Macrotaskers need to have a manager or point of contact. In general, macrotasking should follow the most fundamental rule of management: workers need a single manager. That manager should be the person who hires the macrotasker, gives directions to the macrotasker, and determines when the macrotask has been properly completed.

Macrotaskers usually have only limited contact with your organisation. They aren't part of the informal dynamics of your office. They may not be able to determine who has real influence and who doesn't, whose opinions are more important and who's merely repeating gossip. To make effective use of macrotasking, carefully define how the macrotasker is to engage with your organisation, and then follow that definition.

Putting together a statement of work for macrotask workers

As with all forms of crowdsourcing, the statement of work is at the centre of your relationship with the macrotasker. In the statement of work, you describe what the macrotasker needs to do.

Chapter 11 contains heaps of helpful guidance on preparing a statement of work. Here, I offer some specific tips for elements of a macrotasking statement of work:

- **Cost:** You need to decide what to pay the macrotasker. The wage of the worker relates to the skill and reputation of the worker, which is generally connected to quality of work, speed of work and the ability to communicate easily and well with the employer. For macrotasking, you have a choice:

  - **Fixed fee:** You encourage the worker to get the project done quickly and with the least amount of effort. However, you need to be able to create a good estimate, one that's close to the actual effort required. If you don't, you overpay for the work or the task may be unfinished.

    A fixed fee offers one substantial benefit to the crowdsourcer: under most fixed fee arrangements, the crowdsourcer need not pay the macrotasker for the work unless the entire project is done properly. You, as the crowdsourcer, decide whether the project has been properly done.

    Because the fixed-fee scheme puts some risk on the workers, macrotaskers don't like it as much as hourly payment. Hence, they tend to ask for a fixed fee that's higher than the rate that they'd get if they were paid for the same job by the hour.

    Crowdsourcing platforms handle fixed fee payments in different ways. Some don't offer them. Others don't allow the crowdsourcer to refuse all payments to a worker if the job's done badly. You should check the policies of the website that you plan to use before you offer a job to a worker.

  - **Hourly rate:** Most sites post the wages of sample workers and let you cap the number of hours worked on a project. The hourly model is easier to adjust when you don't have a good estimate. However, it gives little incentive to the worker to minimise the effort.

    When you use the hourly rate for paying macrotaskers, you pay for the work done. Few macrotask websites guarantee the quality of the work. If you think that the work's not being done well, stop the work and cease payment for any more work. However, you're obligated to pay for all the work that the macrotasker's already done.

The amount that you offer directly affects the quality and number of people who make a proposal for your task. A low price attracts only low-skilled workers. A higher price attracts both low-skilled workers and higher-skilled workers. The project cost will also come up in negotiations with potential macrotaskers. See the later section 'Reviewing the proposal'.

✔ **Delivery date:** Here's an old joke: 'If you don't set a deadline, the project will never be late.' You need to determine when you want the macrotask completed and set a deadline.

In macrotasking, workers are often tempted to juggle several tasks at the same time. At any given moment, they may work on the project that interests them most or that promises the greatest payment or has the most pressing deadline. You can't control the interests of the macro-tasker and you've only limited influence over the relative value of your task. However, you can set a firm deadline – but the macrotasker may try to negotiate.

✔ **Intermediate milestones:** Tracking the progress of a macrotask isn't easy. You won't be working in an office with the macrotasker, so you can't drop by the macrotasker's desk and ask, informally, how things are going. To track your macrotask, you need to have concrete milestones or intermediate products. These products show the progress that the macrotasker is making. Intermediate products may be things such as an organisation chart for a web page, a storyboard for a video project or a rough draft of an annual report.

Many of the commercial macrotasking sites have software that allows you to follow the number of hours that the macrotasker's working and to collect intermediate products.

✔ **Final requirements:** The statement of work should include a description of the final item product to be delivered to you and the criteria that you'll use to determine whether the work's been well done. For certain macrotasks, you need to describe how the work product is to fit into a bigger product or system. For example, you may be macrotasking animated graphics for your website. You want to see both the original graphic and the graphic after installation on the web page.

✔ **Additional requirements:** You may want to describe other aspects of the macrotask, such as the kind of tools that the macrotasker should use or the places where he should find data, or any other aspect of the job that you think important.

Describe as few additional requirements as possible. In crowdsourcing, you rely on the wisdom of the crowds, and hence you want to give your macrotaskers ample opportunity to express their wisdom.

✔ **Specific skills:** In some cases, you want the worker to have specific skills for your macrotask. You want programs written in certain languages, analyses conducted in certain ways, documents drafted following a certain style. Be sure to include these skills in your statement of work. But because you're relying on the wisdom of the crowd, not their individuals' credentials, put in this section only the skills that the macrotasker *must* have.

When you're starting to crowdsource, spend time browsing macrotasking websites. Look at the successful jobs. Because the site is advertising these jobs, you've reason to believe that they were done well and that the crowd understood the kind of work needed. You can examine statements of work and borrow ideas and ways of describing a task.

Beginning the Macrotask

In theory, you can macrotask using any website, because macrotasking is a global form of freelancing. You can macrotask from your home page, from a classified advertising service such as craigslist or even from Facebook. For some specialised tasks, you may find that such a form of macrotasking meets your needs.

However, you can accrue many benefits from macrotasking with a website that specialises in macrotasking, such as oDesk (www.odesk.com), Elance (www.elance.com), Guru (www.guru.com), uTest (www.utest.com) or one of many other sites. Posting a job on a macrotask website brings you many advantages over a request posted on craigslist or Facebook, such as:

✔ **A crowd of workers ready to take your macrotasks.** Platforms that offer macrotasking have crowds of workers ready to take jobs. If you're working on your own site or on Facebook, you may not have such a crowd waiting for your call, and you'll have to recruit a crowd. (Skip to Chapter 10 for more about recruiting your own crowd.)

✔ **A portfolio for each worker that lets you see what workers have done on previous jobs.**

✔ **Software for keeping track of the hours worked.** You don't have to rely on the macrotasker to do this or keep track yourself.

✔ **A system for keeping track of all the payment and tax issues.** You pay the website, and the site pays the worker, any taxes and other payments.

✔ **A mediator who can help resolve any problems.** If you and the macrotask worker get into a disagreement, the website mediates to help resolve the issue. In cases where a macrotask worker hasn't completed a job properly, some websites offer a refund.

Choosing a site

When looking for a good macrotasking site, you're looking for two things:

- ✔ **A crowd that's capable of doing your macrotask:** Different macrotasking sites specialise in different kinds of crowds. Some specialise in web development. Some specialise in smartphone app programming. Some specialise in graphic design. All advertise what they do and give examples of typical jobs. You can find out a great deal about the website simply by reading job descriptions and trying to match them to your task.

- ✔ **Tools that help you manage the macrotask:** All the reputable crowd-sourcing sites help you manage the macrotasker. Most require the macrotaskers to keep a log or have a software system that keeps track of the time they spend on the project. The sites have standard forms for statements of work and standard ways of presenting the skills and reputation of the macrotasker. Most also have a mediation service that helps you resolve a disagreement with a macrotasker, and a refund policy that helps you if things go badly wrong.

Read the site information carefully. When you start to macrotask, you're taking more responsibility than you normally do when you order a book or an electronic gadget online. When you're macrotasking, you're contracting with a worker. Contracts always involve rights and responsibilities.

You can find good lists of current sites at www.crowdsourcing.org.

Posting the project

When you've selected a site, the next step is to post the statement of work for your project. This involves putting your description of the job on the website, together with details of the amount that you'd like to pay the worker and the deadline for the task. When you do this, you ask for members of the crowd to respond with a proposal.

The members of the crowd read the description of your job and decide whether they want to apply for it. If they want to apply, they'll send you a proposal – a letter stating their interest – explaining how they'll do the job and giving their opinion of how long it'll take and how much it'll cost.

Set yourself a deadline for reviewing the proposals. This deadline can be as short as a day after the posting or as long as a week. Determining how much time you need to get a good response to your posting is your job.

Inviting workers to your job

As well as waiting for the crowd to respond to your job description (see the preceding section), you can also take the initiative and select members of the crowd who you invite to respond. Most macrotasking websites allow you to review the portfolios of workers at the site and to ask them to respond to your job posting. For these macrotask workers, you can search for specific skills, look at their qualifications, review the work they've done and read recommendations.

To find the best macrotaskers for your job, examine reputations. Each macrotasker has a reputation score. For macrotasking, this score is usually based on subjective evaluations by people who've hired the worker. A few sites incorporate other information into the reputation, such as the cost of the jobs or the reliability of the worker in meeting deadlines. For more on reputation, skip to the later section 'Checking the reputation'.

As you look through the lists of workers, you may see a few that you'd like to invite to apply for your job. You can click on their names and send them invitations. An invitation doesn't guarantee that macrotaskers apply, however. Most good macrotaskers manage their project load carefully and only apply for jobs that fit into their plans.

Choosing a Macrotasker

When the deadline for responding to your posting has passed, you should have received a number of proposals from macrotaskers who're interested in your job. To select the right macrotasker for your job, you have to review these proposals on the macrotask platform. These sites show you the proposals you've received and enable you to contact the workers. Most provide you with several ways to contact workers, including by email, text, Twitter and a phone service such as Skype.

Your next task is to review the proposals and select a macrotask worker to do the job. On most macrotask websites, you generally receive five things from each macrotasker who applies for your job:

- ✔ **A covering letter expressing interest in the work**
- ✔ **A proposal that describes how the macrotasker would approach the work and the wage that he would like**
- ✔ **A portfolio that shows what the macrotasker has done in the past**
- ✔ **References and reputation scores**
- ✔ **A résumé that shows the macrotasker's qualifications**

In some ways, selecting a macrotask worker is similar to hiring a new employee in a traditional organisation. You look at the materials that you receive and try to identify one macrotasker who's best qualified for the job and best able to work with you. However, in the world of macrotasking, as in other forms of crowdsourcing, accomplishment is more important than formal training. The best macrotaskers are those who can demonstrate that they complete jobs on time and under budget, and who also have a reputation for working well with those who employ them.

Reading the covering letter

From the cover letter, you should be able to get an overall impression of the macrotasker, his interest in the project and his ability to do the work. The macrotasker will generally say that he's very interested in your project, has done such work before and has a portfolio of successful projects.

Macrotaskers often apply for many jobs, so they frequently reuse covering letters and proposals. Nothing's wrong with this practice, provided the modify the contents to show that they understand your task and are bidding on it, not on a generic task that falls within their set of skills. Look at the covering letter carefully and make sure that the applicant understands your project. If he doesn't, move on to the next macrotasker.

Reviewing the proposal

Of all the parts of the application, the proposal should be the part most tailored to your job. In the proposal, the macrotasker must demonstrate that he understands what you're trying to do and present a strategy for completing the task. If you're not happy with the proposal, don't go with that macrotasker.

In the proposal, the macrotasker may suggest a higher price for the job and a longer deadline. Such suggestions are a natural part of the negotiation process. You need to assess whether those changes are reasonable and negotiate prices and deadlines that are acceptable to you both.

Assessing the portfolio

Many crowdsourcers believe that the portfolio is the key element of the application. Indeed, because you're hiring a person to do a specific project, you'll be happy to see that he's done something similar in the past.

As in all forms of hiring, you want to verify that the portfolio actually belongs to the worker. To be certain, check with the organisations that are represented in the portfolio.

Checking the reputation

In crowdsourcing, reputation is crucial. Most macrotaskers try hard to build a strong reputation, hence if you've a worker with a low reputation, you want to be cautious about hiring him.

You may ask questions about the reasons for a low reputation and may find a story that satisfies you. However, if the explanation of a low reputation score becomes long and places the blame on others, walk away from that macrotasker.

Keep in mind that a high reputation score may not be as useful as it appears. Many crowdsourcers know the value of the reputation score and are reluctant to give a low assessment of a worker. To get beyond this problem, contact some of the crowdsourcers who hired the macrotasker before and ask concrete questions:

- ✔ Did the macrotasker complete the task on time?
- ✔ Were there any unexpected complications?
- ✔ Did the macrotasker make any valuable suggestions?
- ✔ Was it always easy to communicate with the macrotasker?

If the answers to these questions are affirmative, you may have found a good worker.

Judging qualifications

Crowdsourcing is more concerned with results than with qualifications. If the macrotasker can demonstrate that he can do the task well, then he can get the job no matter where he went to school or how many degrees he has.

Furthermore, résumés are easier to forge than portfolios. Individuals are always willing to gamble that you won't check their degrees or call the schools they claimed to have attended two or four or ten years ago.

In crowdsourcing, you've three choices:

✔ Decide that qualifications aren't important to you, ignore the résumé, and rely on the portfolio.

✔ Decide that the qualifications are interesting but not the key element in your decision. In that case, you scan the résumé and see whether it's consistent with the work that you see in the portfolio.

✔ Decide that formal credentials are important and take the résumé seriously. In this case, you'd better check to make sure that the qualifications are accurate.

Interviewing

In macrotasking, you deal directly with the macrotasker. Hence it's important to conduct an interview before you make an agreement with the person. In these interviews, you're usually trying to determine whether you're going to be able to work with the macrotasker. In some cases, you may be trying to understand some part of the proposal better or discuss the price or time required to do the job.

Most of the crowdsourcing websites allow you to communicate with the macrotaskers directly without disclosing a private email address, and you'll usually conduct interviews over the phone or via email. Even with such a system, though, you may find email interviews a little bit daunting, especially if you or the macrotasker can't respond to emails instantaneously.

When you conduct an interview over email, start the discussion by sending the macrotasker a note saying that you received the proposal and would like to know a little bit more. Then ask a few questions in order to start the discussion. You have to send at least one, but avoid sending more than four in a single email. When you send more than four, you're asking for a long response that'll take some time to compose. You get a better sense of the macrotasker through an exchange of at least two or three emails.

You can ask, for example, whether the macrotasker sees any problems in the project, whether the project is like anything he's done before, and whether he's working on anything else at this time. Also ask whether there's anything he needs you to tell him.

In the interview, whether you conduct it via email or phone, try to discern three things:

- ✔ **Can you can work with the macrotasker?** Can he take direction? Will he be responsive? Some crowdsourcers may be willing to work with difficult geniuses, but you have to decide whether you'll be able to engage the worker and get a good result.

- ✔ **Do the macrotasker's skills seem to match those demonstrated in the portfolio?** You can ask how he developed some of the products in that portfolio and how he handled problems.

- ✔ **What's a mutually agreeable deadline and cost?** The interview forms part of the negotiation over the project. You need to agree on the deadline for the project and the cost.

Making the selection

You make a choice based on criteria that suit you and your organisation. You're concerned about quality of work, deadlines, cost and the personal qualities of the macrotasker.

You're hiring a macrotasker and hence may be free to take risks that you may not take with a traditional hire. You can choose someone who has more radical ideas about how to do the work, or is willing to work to a tight schedule, or who brings an unusual approach to the project. If that person's approach doesn't work, you can bring the project to a close and look for a new macrotasker.

When you've selected a macrotasker, you're committed to him for the job that you've proposed. If you decide at some point that you no longer want to work with him, you have to pay for the work that he's completed. On some websites, you have to pay for the macrotasker for the entire job. (Check the website's policy before you make a selection.) However, when a job is complete, you're free to choose a new macrotasker for your next job. If you find a worker you like and want to work with him again, you can usually offer him a job directly.

When you've made your selection, you need to notify the site of your choice. The site notifies the worker that he's been accepted and sends messages to the other workers who applied for the job. Finally, it ensures that you're able to pay for the work, though a credit card, a payment service such as PayPal or some other mechanism. With that taken care of, you're ready to start the job.

Managing the work

When the job's ready to go, you communicate with the macrotasker, offering any additional instructions, and begin the job. The macrotask platform keeps track of the number of hours that the worker devotes to the job and pays the worker for each hour. In the meantime, you can track the progress of the job through the website. Some sites give you screenshots of the macrotasker's computer in order to verify the number of hours worked. All of them, though, give you a detailed record of the hours worked and the progress of the project.

As the job progresses, keep in regular contact with the worker. Because most jobs are relatively short, you may want to communicate with the worker at least once a day, or at the start and end of each day. If you're working closely with the macrotasker, you may need to communicate several times a day.

When you communicate with your macrotask worker, you can either use the macrotask website or the common communications tools of email, texting, tweets and Skype. You're generally not required to use the macrotask platform tools. However, you may prefer to use the site's communications tools, because the site usually keeps a complete record of your communications with the worker, which has its uses.

When hiring a macrotasker to work for a company or non-profit organisation, some crowdsourcers invite the worker to remotely participate in team meetings (using Skype or a phone service) or let them be part of discussions. This can be an effective way of engaging a macrotask worker, if such an approach is right for you. Many macrotaskers enjoy working independently and don't need close supervision.

At some point after a job's begun, however, you may find that you develop a bad case of *manager's remorse* – concluding that you hired the wrong macrotasker. If you reach that point, you can terminate your relationship with the worker. To do this, you have to notify that worker of your decision and end the job on the macrotask website. The macrotask platform will ask for your reason, and you owe the worker an explanation, as you do in any working relationship.

If you then want to complete the job on the macrotask site, you're free to do so. You're also able to offer the job to one of the workers who you didn't hire first time around. However, most sites require you to start from scratch, or close to scratch. If you remain satisfied with the job description and the other details of the task, you're able to reuse the material you've already prepared. However, you'll have to open the job on the market, ask for members of the crowd to apply, evaluate the proposals and offer the job to one of the crowd.

You may ask some of the workers that you've already reviewed to apply for the job again, but there are no guarantees for either party. The workers may have already taken on other jobs and be unable to take on yours. After reviewing the new proposals, you may decide that you now have better options. Be civil and polite in making these choices, but you're working with an open job market and such markets can require you to make tough decisions.

Protecting intellectual property

When you're macrotasking, you may have a relationship with the macrotasker that resembles a conventional relationship between an employer and an employee. However, when you employ a macrotasker, you're generally doing what's called 'work for hire'. You're contracting with an individual who'll produce a product (or provide a service) for you. You're expecting full rights to the final product. This is the policy of most crowdsourcing websites.

If you're macrotasking without the protections of one of the macrotasking firms, or if you need different rights to the intellectual property that your macrotasker is producing, consider having an agreement with the macrotasker to clarify those rights. You should clearly state the property rights that you have and the rights that the worker retains.

Ending the Macrotask

Sometimes a macrotask ends with a bang. Sometimes it ends with a whimper. Sometimes it ends at one moment when you receive the final product from the macrotasker, while at other times it ends slowly with a little tweak to this part of the project and small adjustments to that part. In either case, the job ends when you, the crowdsourcer, says it ends. At that point, you accept the work and notify the macrotask website that you'll pay for no further work.

Paying the macrotasker and closing the books

In most cases, you pay the macrotasker as an hourly contract worker. This means that the macrotasker receives a payment each week throughout the project for the number of hours that he's worked. At the end of the project, he expects only a payment for the work that he did for you during that last week.

When you pay a macrotasker by the hour, you pay for the hours he works. You've no guarantee that the work will be of the quality you desire. If the work doesn't seem to be good enough for your job, you can stop the task and pay the worker nothing more. However, you're responsible for all the hours that the macrotasker worked for you up to that point.

In some cases, you may choose to pay the worker a fixed fee for the task. When you pay in that way, review the job at the end, determine whether the work was done properly, and then authorise the payment. Macrotaskers generally don't like this form of payment, though, because of the risk of not being paid when the work's done.

Assessing the experience

When a job's over, macrotasking websites usually ask you to review the quality of the macrotasker's work. These reviews are important to both the macrotasker, who will use the good reviews to get new jobs, and to the crowdsourcers who may next hire the macrotasker. As you review the work, respond to the basic questions that a crowdsourcer may have, such as:

✔ How well did the macrotasker understand the job and do it as you described?

✔ Did the crowdsourcer do the job on time and for the budget offered?

✔ How well did the crowdsourcer work with you? Was the communication good and timely?

✔ Was the crowdsourcer able to bring something to the task that you didn't see? Did he improve on your description?

Considering an Example: Creating an App

Aled runs a specialised publishing house called Moment Upon the Stage that sells play scripts to actors. Actors often need to find a script for an audition at short notice. Because many actors survive on little income, they often lack powerful laptops and broadband connections. However, nearly all have smartphones. Therefore, Aled decides that a good marketing move is to create a smartphone application (app) that allows an actor to order a script and maybe even download that script to his phone.

The smartphone app, if properly done, will add value to Moment Upon the Stage and expand the sales and distribution process. But Moment Upon the Stage doesn't have the expertise to develop such an app. The business has no more sophisticated technology support than Aled's niece, Caitlin, who stops by the office once a week to see whether the computers are running properly, checks that the printers still have toner, and reminds her uncle that he needs to be careful when he hits the 'Reply All' button on an email. So when it comes to creating an app, Aled needs help.

Checking that your task is a macrotask

Aled asks himself four key questions (see the earlier section 'Choosing what's important') to determine whether creating the app is a good candidate for macrotasking:

- ✔ **Is it an independent task?** Yes, the macrotasker can do the job himself, without support from Aled's company.

- ✔ **Is it simple to describe?** The goals of the work can be clearly outlined so that the macrotasker knows the criteria for successful completion.

- ✔ **Does it have a fixed deadline?** Yes. The goal of the project is clear and concrete and should produce a fixed deadline.

- ✔ **Does it require special skills?** The organisation doesn't have the skills to produce an app – so yes, the task does require special skills.

Writing the statement of work

To engage effectively with the crowd, Aled sets about putting together a good statement of work. He covers the following areas:

- ✔ **Job description:** In this case, Aled knows more about what he wants the app to do than how the app should work. Many crowdsourcers are in this kind of circumstance. So, to understand how to write a good description, he goes to a couple of macrotasking websites and looks for similar descriptions. As he writes the description, Aled decides to ask potential applicants to put the job description into their own words. If Aled can understand a potential macrotasker's description of the job, then he believes he'll be able to work with him.

- ✔ **Cost:** By looking at a macrotasking website (such as oDesk or Elance), Aled notes that macrotaskers earn between $10 (£6.30) and $60 (£37.80) per hour for programming apps. Aled knows that he needs someone with experience and someone who can work with a technology novice such has himself, so he decides to offer a wage of $40 (£25.20), which is above the medium wage and should attract some good programmers.

✔ **Delivery date:** Aled wants the app tomorrow but knows that a deadline like that just isn't realistic. Again, he turns to the jobs on a macrotasking website for guidance and decides that similar tasks seem to take about 40 hours, so he uses that figure as his estimate.

✔ **Intermediate milestones:** Initially, Aled can't think of an appropriate intermediate milestone for the job, but he learns from looking at the macrotasking websites that he should ask for a mock-up of the app (sometimes called a wireframe) that allows him to see all the different app screens. Aled decides that he wants to approve such a mock-up before the macrotasker moves to the next stage of work.

✔ **Final requirements:** Aled is cautious about how to test the new app, but his niece, Caitlin, suggests that she be the first person to test it. Her thinking is that because she understands software, she should be able to make the app work. If she can't make it work, then the app will be sent back to the macrotasker for more work.

Caitlin suggests giving the app to Aled next, to see whether he can make it work. As Aled had conceived the app, he should be able to make it work, even though he isn't very good with software. If he can make it work, then they can move on to the final test.

For the final test, Caitlin assembles a dozen of her friends. One's actually an actor, but most are entry-level employees in various New York offices. They all have different phones and different skills with technology. By getting them together, she can see what they're doing and determine whether any aren't able to understand how the app works. If all her friends are able to purchase a script, then the app will pass its final test.

✔ **Additional requirements:** Caitlin suggests that her uncle Aled requires that the macrotasker be available for six months after the end of the job to fix any bugs.

✔ **Specific skills:** Aled lists all the phones that should be able to use the app.

Posting the job

Aled chooses a macrotasking website, creates an account, and follows the instructions to post the job. He identifies the job as 'smart phone app development' and puts it on the site. In addition to the job description, the site asks for the number of hours that he estimates for the job and any deadlines that he has. He enters his estimate of 40 hours and decides to add a note to say that he wants the app within a month. He knows that the macrotasker may be doing multiple jobs, and doesn't want his job pushed behind the others.

As the last step of posting his job, Aled has to enter the hourly wage that he's offering. He'd originally decided he was willing to pay up to $40 ($25.20) in order to keep his costs low, but decides to go with a slightly higher wage of $50 ($31.50) to attract more high-quality workers, to encourage a little competition between them and to allow him to choose one who offers to do the job for his desired price of $40.

With the job on the task market, Aled reviews the profiles of workers who state they're interested in app development jobs. As he scrolls through the list, he sees a couple of people who seem qualified for his job. He sends them a message, inviting them to apply for his job. This is a service offered by the website – a way to bring good workers to jobs that are a good match for them.

Hiring the macrotasker

Within a few days of posting his job, Aled has almost 100 applications. He decides to thin the pool by using the website's reputation score and by looking at the job history of the applicants. He removes any worker who's not achieved a job reputation of eight stars or higher (out of a possible ten). He also removes anyone who's not been able to earn a wage close to the median wage on the site for app programmers. He reasons that anyone who can't earn that figure on the site isn't a top programmer.

Looking at the materials, Aled selects three people who seem to understand the project and have good experience and recommendations, and he conducts email interviews. He always starts by asking the potential macrotasker to describe the project back to him. He then asks the candidates whether they see any problems in the project, whether they have any recommendations, and how they would react if he decided to change the project after seeing the mock-up. One programmer seems especially genial, and so Aled chooses him.

Following the work

Aled decides that he'll ask for updates twice a week from the macrotasker. He can learn the number of hours worked from the macrotasker website, so Aled asks for a description of how much progress has been made on the app. He receives the mock-up after a week and a final version of the app after three weeks.

Ending the macrotask

The macrotask ends after Caitlin held her Saturday-morning test. The group found one problem with the app. The problem's probably not a bug, a mistake in programming, but a detail that Aled hadn't explained well in the original job description. The macrotasker fixes the issue and lets the group test the app one more time. Then Aled closes the project on the website, asks the macrotasker to be available for six more months, and releases the app to his customers.

Chapter 8

Managing with Microtasks

*W*hen you start to *microtask*, looking carefully at a large job and breaking it down into small tasks that the crowd can carry out, you probably won't have to worry about the details of the job. You give your job to a crowdsourcing firm. This firm prepares it for a crowdmarket, places it on that market, and then returns the complete job to you.

Microtasking is both the simplest and most demanding form of crowdsourcing: simple because it produces simple little tasks that should be easy to describe and easy to do; demanding because it's often hard to create those little tasks.

This chapter gives you a full picture of the microtasking process. Even though you personally may not prepare jobs for microtasking, you'll find it useful to see how microtasking is done and how microtasking platforms prepare jobs to be microtasked. Microtasking has the potential to have the greatest impact on businesses and organisations because it expands the scope of work, allowing you to do things you couldn't do before.

Identifying Tasks That You Can Microsource

Microtasking has limitations. Some jobs can't easily be microtasked, and some can't be microtasked at all. You can't easily microtask the design of an annual report, for example, nor can you microtask the work of finding a new way to store food in tropical climates.

In preparing a job for microtasking, you expend a substantial amount of effort, so always begin by checking that the job's suitable for microtasking. Good candidates for microtasking are jobs that tick three boxes:

- ✔ **Volume:** You've a large volume of work to do. If a job involves a small amount of data, you can probably handle the work with macrotasking or maybe even a crowdcontest.

- ✔ **Independence:** You can break the job down into tasks that people can do independently of the whole. If the data can't be handled independently, such as when you're sorting a list, then you may need a more structured organisation to handle your task.

- ✔ **Human judgement:** You need a person doing this, not a machine. If the job doesn't require human judgement, such as the simple application of a formula to a list of numbers, look for a computer program to do the work.

So, if a job requires you to process a large amount of data, and if that data can be processed one unit at a time, and if it requires human intelligence to process that data, it's a good job to microtask.

Emily's the programme director of a non-profit organisation that's engaged in international education. The programme takes teenagers from Eastern Europe and Central Asia to other countries. The students live with a host family and attend school. Emily has to find potential host families for 200 students. From experience, she knows that the easiest way to find hosts is to approach leaders of youth organisations for recommendations. In the past, Emily's been able to find one host family for every two leaders that she contacted. So Emily needs to contact 400 leaders of youth organisations.

This job meets the aforementioned criteria to be a good candidate for microtasking:

- ✔ **Volume:** Emily has to process a lot of data. She needs to sort through a lot of web pages and directories to find the 400 names. If she needed only 40, she may have been able to assign the task to an assistant or to a macrotask worker. However, 400 is beyond the ability of a single person.

- ✔ **Independence:** Each name can be gathered independently of the rest.

- ✔ **Human judgement:** No simple directory of national youth organisations exists. Emily needs to locate a youth organisation, identify the leader of the group, and find the leader's email address or phone number.

This kind of job is often called *list enrichment* or *contact generation*, because it's similar to generating contacts for a salesperson. It's been adapted to microtasking and is offered by a number of crowdsourcing firms such as CrowdFlower (www.crowdflower.com) and BusinessLeads.com (www.businessleads.com).

By using a list-enrichment service, you're completely isolated from the crowd. In the example, Emily describes the information that she's seeking, including the type of youth leader, the countries or areas in which to look, and the required info: name, title, email address and phone number.

Knowing How the Microtasking Process Works

Even though you can microtask through a crowdsourcing company, knowing how to prepare your own microtask is useful. By understanding how to prepare microtasking jobs, you're not only able to do things that aren't standard services, but you're also able to recognise jobs that can be modified to utilise standard crowdsourcing services.

Keeping tasks short and simple

Design your microtasks to be short and simple. Microtask workers try to get the most of out of the crowdmarket and often look for short and simple work. These kinds of jobs allow them to use one of two strategies to get the largest payments:

- ✔ **Intersperse tasks among other work.** Crowdworkers intersperse tasks when they're doing crowdwork at their place of work or are doing something else on the Internet. (Many crowdworkers are already employed by organisations.) They jump back and forth between tasks. Therefore, they're looking for simple tasks that don't require them to review the instructions each time.

- ✔ **Do a long series of the same tasks.** The workers who devote more time to crowdwork realise that they need a little time to understand all the steps of a task fully. Therefore, they want to work on a large number of these tasks, so that they can learn to do them faster and therefore get more money.

If your job has a small number of tasks, offer a slightly higher price for each task than you might think appropriate for the work. If you don't, your job may stall in the crowdmarket. The crowd often avoids jobs with small numbers of tasks. Crowd members conclude that they won't have enough opportunity to learn how to do your job quickly. To encourage them to take the tasks in a small job, offer a little more money.

Creating the basic task

In creating a microtask, you need to determine what you want from the job as a whole and then from each individual task. In most cases, the complete job produces a complex set of data. You assemble this final product from the results of each individual task.

Design your tasks around the idea of doing the same work on different inputs. You supply the crowd with a single set of instructions. The crowd members apply those instructions to different data and give you the results.

In Emily's example (see the earlier 'Identifying Tasks That You Can Microsource' section), her microtasks are the tasks of finding the names of youth leaders and their contact information. She has a common set of instructions for each task. She names a location and asks the crowd to identify a youth leader in that area. She then asks the crowdworkers for specific information about that person.

Finding the basic data

After you create the task, you need to identify the basic data to give to the crowdmarket. I suggest organising the data for microtasks in a spreadsheet – the common tool for preparing microtasks and for communicating with microtask platforms. When designing microtasks in a spreadsheet, use the rows to stand for the microtasks and the columns to stand for the different kinds of information that you're trying to get from the crowd.

In Emily's example (see the earlier 'Identifying Tasks That You Can Microsource' section), she has one basic piece of data at the centre of her microtask: the location where she's trying to identify a youth leader. That location is represented by a US postal code or zip code. She's trying to find a youth leader in that area who might help her find a family to take an exchange student. In order to complete the microtasks, Emily seeks four pieces of information from the crowd: the youth leader's name, employer, title and email address. She organises that information in a spreadsheet as follows:

> ✔ Column 1 contains the postcode data that Emily is giving to the crowd, and is labelled *zip*. This column holds the input data for the microtasks. Emily provides the US zip codes of the areas where she wants to place students. In this dataset, she identifies ten zip codes, and hence has ten microtasks.

The remaining columns contain the information that Emily will receive back from the crowd:

✔ Column 2 is for the leader's name.

✔ Column 3 is for the leader's employer.

✔ Column 4 is for the leader's title.

✔ Column 5 is for the leader's email address.

Figure 8-1 shows a spreadsheet for ten of Emily's microtasks.

To get your microtasking project underway, upload your spreadsheet to a microtasking platform such as Amazon's Mechanical Turk (www.mturk.com) or MobileWorks (www.mobileworks.com). The microtasking platform uses the information in your spreadsheet to create microtasks and offer them to the crowd. The crowdworkers never actually see your spreadsheet. They see just your instructions and the data that you provide in the spreadsheet for each task. The crowdworkers complete their work and enter the results in a field on their screens. When they click a button to finish the task, the platform stores the new information in the appropriate row of its version of the spreadsheet.

When the crowdworkers have completed all your microtasks, the information they've provided fills every row of your spreadsheet. At that point, you can download the completed spreadsheet from the platform so that you can use it. Most platforms also allow you to download it even when only some of the tasks are done.

	Zip	Name	Organisation	Title	Email
1					
2	63131				
3	20002				
4	48037				
5	14609				
6	98105				
7	83201				
8	65801				
9	33602				
10	75202				
11	97058				
12					
13					
14					

Figure 8-1: An example microtask spreadsheet.

Most microtasking platforms upload or download information in a form that's technically known as a *comma-separated values* (.csv) format. When downloading, your spreadsheet program such as Excel, Quattro Pro or Smartsheet will read the .csv file as if it were an ordinary spreadsheet file. You'll never know the difference. When uploading, you may sometimes have to save your microtasks in a .csv format so that you can upload them to the microtask platform. Just go to the Save As menu in your spreadsheet, find the .csv or commaseparated values file type and save your microtasks in that format.

Writing the instructions

Writing instructions for the crowdworker is your next step.

If you skip over to Chapter 11, you can find a detailed discussion of how to write instructions for the crowd. Writing instructions specifically for microtasking, though, has a few special considerations. Microtasks can quickly become complex and confusing, despite your efforts to keep them simple.

In Emily's example (see the earlier 'Identifying Tasks That You Can Microsource' section), Emily writes instructions as follows:

> You're asked to find a youth leader in a specific part of the country. That youth leader can be a scout leader, a church youth leader or any other adult who leads an organisation that provides social services to children between 10 and 16 years of age. You shouldn't include individuals who work with children in the criminal justice system or who work with children who are physically ill, physically handicapped or mentally handicapped.
>
> 1. Above you will find a zip code. Find the name of a Girl Scout troop, Boy Scout troop, 4-H club or similar organisation located in that zip code.
>
> 2. For this organisation, find the name, title and email address of its leader.
>
> 3. Do not use email addresses that go to the organisation. Give only an email address that goes to the leader.

Despite these seemingly clear instructions, a crowdworker may find a youth group in one zip code but whose leader lives in another. For cases such as this, Emily should set out specific instructions that ask the crowd to find a group in that particular zip code and say that where the leader lives doesn't matter.

As a rule, keep microtasking instructions as simple as possible. If you write instructions that are too detailed, you discourage potential workers. You may also increase the number of errors, because the instructions may confuse the workers. For example, using the example of labelling photographs, you may want to include the instruction:

> If the photograph includes both people and landscape, judge which is more prominent, people or landscape, and label the photograph as such.

For some kinds of microtasks, you may want to have an action that catches all microtasks that can't be easily processed by your instructions and tells workers to label them in a way that allows you or an assistant to review all of them:

> If a picture is neither a portrait nor a landscape, label it as neither.

This strategy is most useful when the number of exceptions is likely to be few.

Pricing the tasks

Before you place your microtasks on the task market, you need to set a price for each one of them. The easiest way to set this price is to estimate the amount of time that it takes a crowdworker to do a single task. When you know how long the task should take, you can price the task at a level that gives crowdworkers a specific hourly wage.

The current research into crowdworkers with general skills suggests that these workers are looking to earn between $5 and $12 an hour, or roughly £3 to £8. If you offer a task that takes 4 minutes from accepting the task to submitting the result, the worker can do at most 15 of these tasks an hour. If you want to offer a wage of $6 an hour, you have to offer $6 ÷ 15, or $0.40 (£0.26) per task.

In general, the formula for pricing a microtask is:

> Price per task = Target wage × (Minutes required for each task ÷ 60 minutes)

In microtasking, the crowdmarket doesn't always work in the way that you might expect. If you increase the price that you offer for tasks, the work will likely be done more quickly. However, a higher price doesn't necessarily improve the quality of the work. Higher prices attract bad workers to the tasks as well as good workers.

Training and validating workers

Before you release your microtask to the crowdmarket, prepare a way to train and validate the workers. The easiest approach is to have the crowdworker do a job that you've already completed and hence one that you know the right answer to.

Alena asks the crowdworker to click on a URL that takes her to a video taken from a traffic camera. She asks the worker to count the number of cars in the video. If the crowdworker's number equals the number that Alena counted, Alena allows the worker to start working on real tasks. If the numbers don't match, Alena asks the worker to do a second training step.

Some organisations require crowdworkers to complete a certain number of tasks correctly before they can do microtasks for pay. Many microtasking companies create a YouTube video to show crowdworkers how to do the microtasks.

Checking the results

You need to check the results you receive for accuracy. Depending on the task, you probably accept a degree of error: 5 or 10 per cent, say, but no more.

If you microtask naively by simply posting a request on a crowdmarket without worrying about reviewing the responses you receive, you're likely to find that the bulk of the responses are wrong or unusable.

A student of mine, an ardent hockey fan, wanted to write a paper that required some detailed information that he could only get from professional hockey players. To contact the hockey players, he created microtasks that asked for email addresses for the Washington Capitals players. He placed the tasks one evening and got results the next day. All the results gave the email address for the box office of the Washington Capitals, an address that was no use to him. He rewrote his microtask, explaining that he was trying to get in direct contact with each player or the agent who represented the player. He asked to have each task done by three different people and he raised the price that he was offering for each task, to encourage the microtaskers to spend some time looking for the email address on the web. This time, he got useful information for all but a couple of the players. However, for each player, he still got at least one address that wasn't correct.

In some cases, identifying incorrect work is easy. You see email addresses that lack all proper elements, answers that don't respond to questions or text that has clearly been borrowed from other sources. However, in most cases, identifying mistakes and errors is difficult without actually testing the results. If you're asking for email addresses, for example, you might get email addresses that look plausible but which are actually fake. When you try to use them, the email is returned quickly with the error 'address not known'. You might also get email addresses for people who share the same name as the individual you're trying to contact. The Internet has made the world a small place, and many people are out there have the same names as hockey players, youth leaders, world politicians or even distinguished Broadway actors.

In microtasking, bad results are either intentional or accidental mistakes. *Intentional mistakes* come from members of the crowd who aren't capable of, or not interested in, producing good work. *Accidental mistakes* come from workers who believe they're doing the right thing but are actually creating the wrong result.

You can aim to minimise intentional mistakes by getting the highest quality crowd to work on your tasks. To get the highest quality crowd, you need to qualify the workers. Most people qualify the crowd by giving potential crowdworkers a sample task for which the qualifier already knows the correct answer. When an individual gets the correct answer, the qualifier lets that crowdworker take her microtasks.

Even when you qualify your crowd, though, you can still face problems. Crowdworkers may spend extra time to do the qualifying task but then go on to do a poor job on the work that you give them. To counteract this, some crowdmarkets monitor their workers by slipping qualifying tasks into the workstream. Every now and then, all workers do a qualifying task – a task with a known answer – without knowing that they're doing such a task. They will be paid for it as if it were a real task, but if they fail to do many of these tasks correctly, the crowdmarket excludes them from doing more of your tasks.

On most microtask crowdmarkets, you can exclude specific workers from your tasks who have produced bad work in the past.

Getting a high quality crowd, though, won't remove all errors and bad work. To ensure the best possible results, you have to test the results. One way to do this is to go through and try to use the results as you intended. This process is obviously slow and doesn't work well for jobs that have a large number of microtasks.

A second way to test the results of your microtasks is to ask that each task be done three times. You then compare the results. If the results agree, take the common result. If two results agree and one does not, accept the result from the two that agree. If all three disagree, reject all three answers and ask that the task be done three more times.

Duplicating, triplicating or even quadruplicating tasks doesn't guarantee that you get correct results for your microtasks, even if all the results agree. Crowdworkers can still agree on bad answers. And on top of that, duplicating work increases the cost of the work. If you ask for each task to be done three times, you triple the cost of the job.

You can find more about identifying bad microtasking work in Chapter 16. In that chapter, I look at how to divide work and assemble different kinds of crowds to catch errors and correct them.

As well as the advice I give you in Chapter 16, always bear in mind that you can improve the quality of your microtasks by paying close attention to the fundamentals: writing clear and concise instructions; guiding workers through the task; training workers to do your task as best they can; creating a process to review and test all work; and excluding workers from your tasks who regularly produce bad results.

Assembling the work

The last step of microtasking is to assemble the results from the individual tasks into your final product. In some cases, you have nothing to do. The goal of your job was to produce a database, such as a database of contact information for youth leaders. The crowdmarket sends you that database, usually in spreadsheet form.

In other cases, such as in Alena's example (see the earlier section 'Training and validating workers'), your final product is a statistical analysis of the data you've received. You get the data in some form, usually a spreadsheet, and do the analysis on the results yourself.

But in other cases, you need to assemble a complete product from the results of the crowdmarket. For example, you may decide to translate a large document by breaking it into paragraphs and sending those paragraphs to the crowdmarket for translation. When the tasks are done, you have to put those paragraphs in order to create the final document. You might do this work yourself or you might hire a macrotask worker to do this job.

Most crowdmarkets, including Amazon's Mechanical Turk and CrowdFlower (which also uses Mechanical Turk), have a special system interface, which is known as an application programming interface (API). These APIs allow you to write a program that sends data directly to the crowdmarket and gets the answers back. You can create a program that automatically breaks a large problem into small tasks, send the tasks to the crowdmarket, retrieve the results from those tasks, and assemble the final result. Needless to say, this kind of program requires sophisticated IT staff.

Working through an Example with Mechanical Turk

You don't know nothing about microtasking, to borrow phrasing from Mr Mark Twain, until you've mastered a crowdsourcing platform called Amazon's Mechanical Turk (www.mturk.com). Mechanical Turk is currently the most widely used platform in crowdsourcing and is really a sophisticated *crowdmarket*, a place where crowdsourcers look for workers to do their tasks. It's regularly used by firms that offer crowdsourcing services to the public. (Puzzled about the name? Take a look at Chapter 3, where I explain its origins.)

Throughout this section, I take you through setting up Emily's task (see the earlier section 'Identifying Tasks That You Can Microsource') on Mechanical Turk.

Creating the task

You need to design the form that Mechanical Turk will use to present the task to the crowdworker and to collect the data. To do this, you need to log on to Mechanical Turk as a requester. Here's what to do:

1. **Go to** www.mturk.com.

2. **Click on the Requester (or Get Results) link.**

3. **Log on to Amazon Turk (if you haven't signed up yet, go through the sign-up process).**

4. **Click on Get Started link.**

5. **Click on the type of task you want to create (Data Collection).**

6. **Click on the Get Started button.**

When you complete these steps, Mechanical Turk creates a new data collection project. When it creates the project, Mechanical Turk uses an example that collects data about restaurants. You can modify this example so that it'll do what you want it to. Instead of collecting information about restaurants, Emily wants to collect information about youth leaders.

Describing the basic properties

After you click the Get Started button you see a screen that enables you to describe the basic properties of your project. Here, you give your project a name (which you use to find your project on Mechanical Turk), a title (which is displayed to the crowd), a longer description of the project, and keywords for the project.

The crowdworkers use the name, title, description and keywords to find your microtasks and decide whether they're going to do them. Spend enough time on these elements so that they're accurate and sound engaging.

Changing the qualities of your microtasks

After you describe the basic properties of your microtasks, you move to a screen that asks you for the basic properties of your tasks, or *Human Intelligence Tasks* (HITs), as Mechanical Turk calls them. I provide an example of this screen in Figure 8-2.

For your first job, you can take the values that Mechanical Turk recommends. The only one that you may consider changing is the first value, which sets the amount of time allotted to this task. If the crowdworker doesn't complete the job within this time, Mechanical Turk cancels the task and returns it to the market. This value is more than an estimate of the amount of time required to do the work. It includes the time for bathroom breaks, coffee refills and email responses. You should be generous. The default value, one hour, is fine for short tasks. However, expand it to two or three hours for longer tasks.

Setting up your HIT

Reward per assignment	$ 0.4
	Tip: Consider how long it will take a Worker to complete each task. A 30 second task that pays $0.05 is a $6.00 hourly wage.
Number of assignments per HIT	3
	How many unique Workers do you want to work on each HIT?
Time allotted per assignment	1 (Hours ÷)
	Maximum time a Worker has to work on a single task. Be generous so that Workers are not rushed.
HIT expires in	14 (Days ÷)
	Maximum time your HIT will be available to Workers on Mechanical Turk.
Results are automatically approved in	7 (Days ÷)
	After this time, all unreviewed work is approved and Workers are paid.

Advanced »

Figure 8-2: Setting the qualities of your microtask in Mechanical Turk.

Reproduced with permission from Amazon.com.

Sorting pay, replication and deadline

At the bottom of the screen, you can set the payments for the workers. In case you guess too low or too high, you can change these values later. Figure 8-3 shows this part of the screen.

Figure 8-3:
Worker
payments
screen on
Mechanical
Turk.

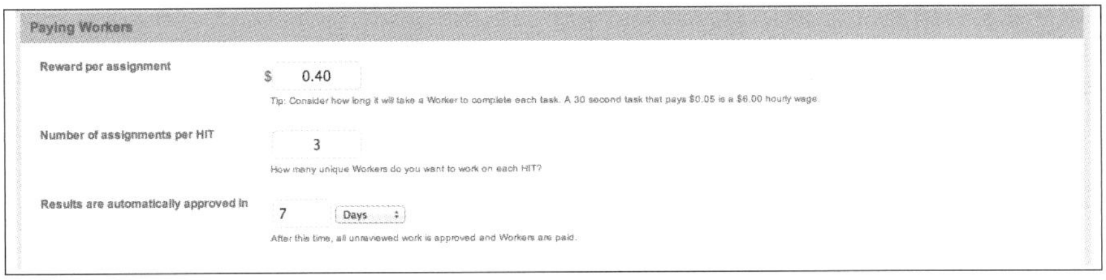

Paying Workers	
Reward per assignment	$ 0.40
	Tip: Consider how long it will take a Worker to complete each task. A 30 second task that pays $0.05 is a $6.00 hourly wage.
Number of assignments per HIT	3
	How many unique Workers do you want to work on each HIT?
Results are automatically approved in	7 Days ‡
	After this time, all unreviewed work is approved and Workers are paid.

You first need to set the price for each task.

A task worker may be able to search the web, identify a youth leader, and copy the information in about three minutes. If she works continuously, she can do 20 tasks an hour. A price of $0.40 would give her a wage of $8 an hour. That value may be a reasonable starting point. Efficient crowdworkers can do a search and copy task in 90 seconds, which produces a wage of $16 an hour.

After setting the price, you need to set the number of assignments or replications. Many times, you replicate the microtasks to check the work and produce the best possible work, with two or three workers doing each task and you then comparing the results. If the workers all produce the same result, you have some confidence that they all did the work correctly.

In Emily's case, she doesn't replicate the microtask to check the results, because each member of the crowd may find a different result for the same task. One member of the crowd may find a Girl Scout troop at a public school, another may find a Girl Scout troop at a Catholic School, a third may find a 4-H Club on the edge of the region, and another may find a Young Achievers' Club, something Emily hadn't considered. Still, even though Emily may not want to replicate each microtask to check the accuracy of the work, she may want to do it to get more information. Her experience has taught her that maybe only one of every two youth leaders is able to help her place a student. Therefore, she may want to do each task three times so that she potentially has three different contacts for each area.

Finally, you need to identify a deadline for accepting the results from the crowdworkers. Normally, Mechanical Turk stores the results. You can review these results and decide which ones to accept and which ones to decline.

However, if you get distracted or forget about your job, you have workers who are going to be getting impatient about being paid. You have to set a date that allows the system to approve any completed task that you've not reviewed. By default, Mechanical Turk sets this date to be seven days after the task is completed.

Crowdworkers normally like to be paid within 24 or 48 hours. If you can keep this deadline short, you get a better reputation among Turkers.

Laying out the work

Your next task, should you choose to accept it, is to prepare a screen for each microtask. The crowdworkers will work from the microtask screen you create. From it, they'll get the basic instructions for the microtask and will enter the information that they find back into it.

To create a microtask screen in Amazon Mechanical Turk, you need to pre-pare a description of what you want in Hypertext Markup Language (HTML) – a computer language for websites and web pages. (You can use HTML to create a web page, set the colour of the background, the size and font of the text, and the location of pictures.) If this first mention of something as alien-sounding as HTML makes you want to run for the hills, don't panic! If you don't know anything about HTML, you may want to take a look at *HTML, XHTML and CSS For Dummies* by Ed Tittel and Jeff Noble (Wiley). But, in truth, you don't need to know much about HTML to set up a microtask screen, because I have the following trick up my sleeve. It may seem tricky at first, but do it once or twice and you'll be a past master in no time.

If you're completely new to HTML, a neat trick for creating a new microtask screen in HTML is to do what programmers have been doing for generations: instead of trying to learn some new piece of technology from the ground up, just look for an existing example that does something similar to what you want to do, copy that example and modify it so that it does what you need. Simple! Fortunately, when Mechanical Turk creates your job, it automatically generates a microtask screen for its example (the one that asks the crowd to find the address of a restaurant's web page). You can modify this screen. In this example, which you can see in Figure 8-4, the screen shows the instruc-tions for the crowdworker in a bulleted list, and the name, address and phone number of the restaurant. After searching for and finding the address of the restaurant's web page, the crowdworker then enters it in the relevant field on the screen. (You can find it by clicking on the Design Layout tab on the Edit Project screen.)

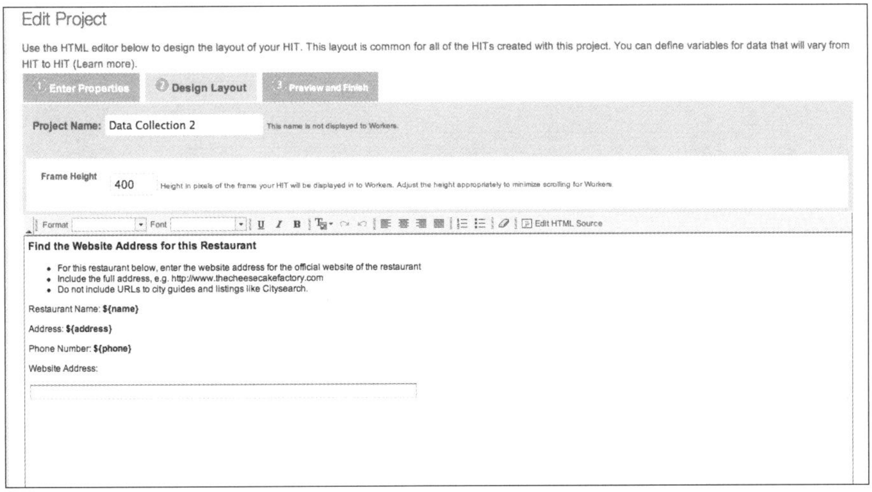

Figure 8-4: A sample microtask screen from Mechanical Turk.

Reproduced with permission from Amazon.com.

Emily needs a screen that's slightly different – a screen that gives the crowd-worker a single piece of information (the zip code) instead of three, and takes four pieces of information in return, instead of one. And the information she needs to obtain is different, too. The way for Emily to create her own screen is to take the screen generated automatically by Mechanical Turk and edit the underlying HTML code. That way, she doesn't have to do it all from scratch.

To edit the underlying HTML code, Emily needs to take these steps:

1. **Click on the button that says Edit HTML Source.**

   This button is on the far right-hand side of the grey task bar that runs through the middle of the screen. After clicking that button, the original HTML source screen appears, as is displayed in Figure 8-5.

   When you first look at the code in Figure 8-5, it may look like a jumble and make no sense. Compare it carefully with the microtask screen in Figure 8-4, though, and it start to makes sense. You start to be able to identify the text that you need to modify in order to generate a micro-task screen that works for you.

2. **Edit the HTML code for the title of your page.**

   When you look at the HTML code, you see text that contains HTML tags. You can identify the HTML code because it's filled with tags. *Tags* are little commands that describe how the text should work. You can identify them because they begin and end with angle brackets, < and >. HTML tags usually come in pairs. One tag tells Mechanical Turk to start doing something and the next one tells it to stop. For example, the `<b>` tag indicates that the text which follows it should be in bold type and the `</b>` tag indicates that the bold text should stop there. Likewise, the

<i> tag indicates that the text which follows it should be italicised and the </i> tag brings the italics to a stop. Any tag containing a forward slash is paired to an earlier tag that is identical but without a slash.

Figure 8-5:
The HTML
source for
microtask-
ing screen.

At the top of the white area in Figure 8-5 is the HTML code <h3>Find the Website Address for this Restaurant</h3> that creates the title at the top of the microtask screen in Figure 8-4. However, you need to change the title of the microtask screen to read <h3>Find the name and email address of the director of a youth organisation</h3>. To make the change, simply erase the information between the two HTML tags (the <h3> and the </h3> tags) and replace it with the new title.

3. **Edit the HTML code that describes your instructions.**

A few lines down, between the <li> and </li> tags, are the three lines of instructions for the sample microtask. The first line of instruction reads <li> For this restaurant below, enter the address of the official website</li>. You need to replace these lines with your own instructions. To do this, delete the text between these two tags and replace them with your own instruction. Your instruction might begin <li> For the zip code below, find the name of an organisation that provides services to children between the ages of 12 and 16</li>. (If you don't need three lines of instructions, you can delete one or two of them. If you need to add an extra line of instruction, just start it with <li> and then type in your instruction, ending the line with </li>.)

4. **Edit the informational HTML codes.**

Currently, the screen gives three pieces of information: name, address and phone number. Again, by looking closely at the code here, you can see that it presents the name of the restaurant with the code <p>Restaurant Name: <b> ${name} </b> </p>. To modify the

HTML code to give the zip code for the region, you simply change that line to read `<p>Zip Code: <b> ${zip} </b> </p>`. (You use `${zip}` to represent the zip code, because zip is the name in the top line of your spreadsheet in Figure 8-1.) You can then delete the next two lines, which present the address and phone number – pieces of information you don't need the crowd to collect.

5. **Create the fields that the crowd will use to enter the information you require from them.**

   Currently, the Mechanical Turk has only one field – Website Address. Because you want the crowd to enter the name, title, employer and email addresses of the youth leaders, you need to create three more fields.

   To do this, you need to work with the HTML code highlighted in grey at the bottom of Figure 8-5. The code here creates fields on the main screen. To create three new fields, you have to copy that code and duplicate it three times.

6. **Modify the fields that the crowd will use so that the fields work the way you want them to.**

   For each of the four fields (name, employer or organisation name, title and email address) you need to modify three elements of the code: the title given to the field, the field ID and the field name. Figure 8-6 identifies those three elements.

Figure 8-6: Changing the Mechanical Turk example.

To modify the first field so that it'll receive the name of one of a youth worker, you simply need to change `<p>Website Address:</p>` to `<p>Name:</p>`. You also change `Q1URL` to `name` in both the field ID and the field name. (You use `name` because that word is in the first row of your spreadsheet (see Figure 8-1).)

After you modify the first field, go ahead and make similar changes to the second to identify it as the field that'll receive the organisation information. You simply change `<p>Website Address:</p>` to `<p>Organisation:</p>`. You also change `Q1URL` to `organisation` in both the field ID and the field name.

Similarly, for the third field, change `<p>Website Address:</p>` to `<p>Title:</p>`. You also change both references to `Q1URL` to `title`.

Finally, for the last field, you change `<p>Website Address:</p>` to `<p>Email Address:</p>`, and change both references to `Q1URL` to `email`.

Congratulations – you've now modified the HTML code and created a microtask screen! You should be able to see the result by clicking on the Preview tab. The final microtask screen should look like Figure 8-7.

Figure 8-7: The microtask screen created for the youth leader example.

> **Edit Project**
>
> Use the HTML editor below to design the layout of your HIT. This layout is common for all of the HITs created with this project. You can define variables for data that will vary from HIT to HIT (Learn more).
>
> 1 Enter Properties · 2 Design Layout · 3 Preview and Finish
>
> **Project Name:** Find Youth Program Directors · This name is not displayed to Workers.
>
> **Frame Height** 400 · Height in pixels of the frame your HIT will be displayed in to Workers. Adjust the height appropriately to minimize scrolling for Workers.
>
> Format Heading 3 ▾ Font ▾ | U *I* **B** | ᵀₐ ⌐ ↻ | ▤ ▦ ▤ ▤ | ▤ ▤ | ⌀ | ▣ Edit HTML Source
>
> **Find the Name and Email Address of the director of a youth organization**
> - Find a Girl Scout Troop, Boy Scout Troop or 4-H CLub located in the zip code given below
> - For this organizaiton, find the name, title, and the email address of its director
> - Do not include emails that go to the organization but not the director.
>
> Zip Code: ${zip}
>
> Name:
>
> Organization:
>
> Title:
>
> Email Address:

Starting with a test run

After describing your tasks and creating your microtask screen, you're ready to start microtasking with a test run. Always start your job with a small test run. Put 10 or 15 tasks to the market to test whether the crowd engages with them and does the work well. You can find story after story of people who sent a job to Mechanical Turk with 10,000 or more microtasks that failed miserably. The problem in these instances was that the instructions were confusing or perhaps the prices they set were wrong. Something went bad.

Be ready to fail with Mechanical Turk, but fail on the cheap. Always do a test run.

The size of the job is determined by the amount of data that you give to Mechanical Turk. To do a small test job, use a small spreadsheet with only ten rows, such as the one I show in Figure 8-1. To have Mechanical Turk read this file, you need to save it in Comma Separated Value format, which is often called .csv format. You can save it in this format within a spreadsheet program.

When you're ready to launch your microtask job, return to the Create Job page, where you'll see a list of the jobs that you've created. To get your job started, click the New Batch button. Mechanical Turk asks you to upload your file of data. It then analyses your data and determines the cost of the job. Start with a short trial run of 15 microtasks (five zip codes, with three contacts per zip code). You're going to offer $0.40 ($0.25) for each microtask, for a total of $6 ($3.75). Mechanical Turk adds a 10 per cent fee, so the grand total will be $6.60 ($4.15). Mechanical Turk requires you to pay the amount in advance, so make sure you have your credit card ready before you start the job.

When you've paid for the microtasks with your credit card, you're ready to go. Click the button marked Publish HITS in the lower right-hand corner and Mechanical Turk will take your microtasks and send them to the crowd.

Don't start jobs that you can't stop. If you need to stop your microtasks in Mechanical Turk, you do so by going to the Manage tab. Click on that tab and you'll see a list of all the jobs, which Mechanical Turk identifies as *batches*, that you've submitted to Mechanical Turk. The list shows how many tasks you submitted and how many have been completed by the crowd. If you hit the Cancel this Batch button, Mechanical Turk will stop your job. If the crowd is still doing some of your tasks, it'll be allowed to complete them. However, the crowd will no longer be able to start new tasks.

Reviewing the work and retrieving the results

After starting the job and giving the crowd time to find and complete the tasks you've set, you need to see how much the crowd has accomplished, review the work done and download the results.

Reviewing your microtasks on Mechanical Turk is easy: just go to the home page and then to the Requester page, where you click on the Manage tab, which takes you to the Manage page. There, you can see how many of your jobs are on the Mechanical Turk market and how many of the tasks are complete.

If you have more than one job on Mechanical Turk, each is described in a little rectangle on the screen. When you're ready to review the results from any job, just click on the Results button in the upper right-hand corner of the rectangle.

The Results screen shows you the results of all the completed microtasks within a job (which Mechanical Turk calls *batches*). You can review each individual task to determine whether it's been properly done. If you think it's been properly done, you can approve it. Approving a task triggers Mechanical Turk to pay the crowdworker who completed the task. If you think a task hasn't been done properly, you can reject it. When you reject a result, Mechanical Turk doesn't pay the crowdworker, and it returns the task to the market so that another crowdworker may attempt it.

When you reject a task, Mechanical Turk asks you the reason for your rejection. Most commonly, task results are rejected because the crowdworker didn't follow the instructions or produce a result that met the crowdsourcer's requirements. Be sure that you have a sound reason when rejecting a task; if you don't, the crowdworker can appeal your rejection.

From the Results screen, you can also download the results of the tasks. In the upper right-hand corner of the screen is a button named Download CSV. When you click on this button, Mechanical Turk downloads the results from your tasks to your computer's hard drive. From there, you can read these results with a spreadsheet program. The spreadsheet looks exactly like your original spreadsheet, except that all of the blank cells are now filled with data.

Congratulations, you've completed your first job on Mechanical Turk!

Reviewing the prices of your microtasks

From the Manage screen, you can review the prices you paid for the microtasks and the hourly wages that the crowdworkers earned by doing your task. In a test run for Emily's example, the workers took about two minutes, on average, to complete a single microtask. At $0.40 ($0.26) per task, they therefore earned an average of $12.30 (about $7.80) an hour.

This average hourly wage enables you to set the prices for your tasks. Setting your prices is important because, ultimately, the market will determine whether your tasks are priced too low or too high. If you price them too low, the crowd won't take them. Price them too high and you may pay too much for each task.

To get the price right, you may find it useful to compare the average hourly wage for your tasks with the minimum hourly wage in your country. In the USA, for example, the minimum wage is $7.25 ($4.60). If the average hourly wage you set for your tasks gets close to that figure, you may find that the crowd tends to avoid your tasks. Of course, however, Mechanical Turk is a global marketplace. The minimum wage for workers in one part of the world is not the same as the minimum wage in other parts of the world.

Chapter 9

Combining the Intelligence of Self-Organised Crowds

*S*ome of the most innovative applications of crowdsourcing are those that use self-organised crowds. *Self-organised crowdsourcing* is similar to crowdcontests in that, to engage a self-organised crowd, you post a goal, something that you would like to accomplish, and you offer a reward for the group of people who are able to accomplish that goal. But instead of telling the crowd how it should work and how it should be organised, you let the crowd answer those questions. You let the crowd decide the best way to work and the best way to organise itself.

Self-organised crowdsourcing is most useful for helping you learn things from the crowd that you can't imagine, such as an idea for a new consumer product that might radically change the market, or a new service that might offer a tremendous improvement to a neighbourhood. If you're looking for something that you can easily imagine and describe, using a conventional public opinion survey may be an easier option. You use a survey, for example, if you want to know whether the public is more likely to vote for a Liberal candidate or a Tory candidate, or to see if they are willing to pay a few more pence to buy a beer that has a better taste but more calories than the most popular brand.

In this chapter I help you discover how you might use a self-organised crowd. I look at how to put a question to the crowd, how to guide the crowd towards your goal, how to work with the leaders of self-organised crowds and, finally, how to use a specialised version of the self-organised crowd – the prediction market.

Getting to Grips with Self-Organised Crowds

Practically speaking, the term *self-organised crowds* isn't the best description of how this kind of crowdsourcing works. The term suggests that the crowd members start working together, slowly start to find some organising principles, and eventually become a unified force. In fact, that isn't the way it usually works. When you post a job for a self-organised crowd, you see a leader emerge who has some idea about how to do your job. That leader begins to recruit other people to help him do the job. Eventually the people form a team and complete the work.

This form of crowdsourcing is referred to as being self-organised because the crowdsourcer isn't organising the crowd. The crowdsourcer is merely posting the job and offering the reward, as he might do in a crowdcontest. The person who's organising the crowd is drawn from the crowd and probably doesn't even know the crowdsourcer.

Self-organised crowds are similar to crowdcontests (see Chapter 5). You put a question to the crowd and ask it to gather information, invent something or make a decision. Self-organised contests are different from crowdcontests, though, because they can't be handled by a single person. They require a team from the crowd. You aren't going to organise that team, though. You're going to let it organise itself. However, you do need to give the crowd guidance about how to organise itself, encourage the members if they have their own ideas and, of course, tell the crowd what you need it to do.

Crowdsourcers commonly use self-organised crowds for many kinds of work, including:

- **Product innovation.** Say you'd like to market a new product. For example, you may want a product that enables you to track your pet and know where it is. You also want to send the animal a signal – a whistle or high-pitched sound – so that you can train it to return home. You can turn to the crowd to design such a product.

- **Disaster relief.** Say a family has been driving into the woods and is lost. The family's car has been found, but the people are missing. Volunteers may know the region far better than professional rescuers, so by turning to the crowd you can do a more thorough search.

- **Data collection.** Say hurricane Anne-Marie has just slammed through your region and you need to know how badly it's damaged the ecosystem. Satellite photos only tell you so much. Instead, you can put a call to the crowd to count species, identify fallen trees or spot changes to the local topography.

The classic example of a self-organised crowd is the DARPA Red Balloon Challenge. In 2010, the Defense Advanced Research Projects Agency (DARPA) in the USA ran a contest to see how well the crowd could organise itself. DARPA anchored ten large weather balloons at various unidentified places around the USA and offered $40,000 to the individual or team who found the balloons first. A group based at the Massachusetts Institute of Technology (MIT) found all ten in just a few hours and won the contest. MIT organised the crowd by using various social media and by promising to divide the prize money among the people who either found a balloon or recruited people who found a balloon.

By their very nature, self-organised crowds give you information. Therefore, consider using self-organised crowds whenever you want to discover something about the crowd. Keep the goal of benefiting from the wisdom of the crowd at the forefront of your project. Although you hope that crowdsourcing will be less expensive than conventional methods of doing work, you're most interested in getting the right material from the right people.

Determining What You Need the Crowd to Do: Information Gathering and Decision Making

When you start working with a self-organised crowd, you need to be sure of what you want the crowd to do. You don't simply turn to the crowd and say 'Tell me what you know.' You have to provide a framework that enables the crowd to work – a set of ideas or directions that guide its efforts. If you don't provide those ideas or directions, you'll have a crowd that won't know what to do.

The first thing you need to do is to decide whether your aim is to gather information or make decisions. Crowds can do either activity well, but they tend to use one method to gather information and another to make decisions. When crowd members gather information, they spread out across the globe and try to enlist other people to help them. They use their social networks to ask friends and friends of friends to help the effort. When the crowd makes a judgement, the members usually spend more time interacting with each other. They may debate, discuss or trade ideas. Sometimes they search for more information, but they spend a greater proportion of their time thinking and processing ideas.

Collective intelligence

The self-organised crowd, like crowdsourcing in general, is an example of a new field called *collective intelligence*. Studies of collective intelligence look at large groups of people and tries to determine how they work together and add their individual contributions to the intelligence of the whole. In crowdsourcing, the crowdmarket is the principal means of combining intelligence. In collective intelligence, the crowd can use other means to combine the contributions of the crowd members, including rules, institutions, coercion, social networks, social ideals and other things.

Many scholars consider collaborative software projects such as those that created the WordPress blogging software or the Linux computer operating system as examples of collective intelligence. In these projects, people collaborate to create software that's freely distributed to the public. While you can consider this work as a form of self-organised crowdsourcing, you can also see social forces that may fall outside the market. People take part in these projects so that they can be part of a community, so that they can gain some status that they may not have otherwise, so that they can use skills that they can't use on their jobs.

Self-organised crowdsourcing is perhaps the trickiest form of crowdsourcing to do well. You increase your chances of a successful outcome if you crowdsource with a group of people who are already interested in your ideas. For example, you improve your likelihood of succeeding with a self-organised project to reorganise the rubbish collection in your town if you connect with the citizens of your town and the institutions that are interested in the welfare of the area. In this case, you might start by talking to local business organisations, school groups and churches. As soon as you're able to convince some of them to volunteer for your project, you can build a site for your project and make a great start in recruiting your crowd.

Gathering information

When you ask the crowd to gather information, you may be asking members to go into the world and collect facts. You can ask them to photograph buildings, find lost children, count wildlife, record prices or do anything that involves finding information. Searching, remembering, creating, collaborating – all are forms of gathering information.

You start a self-organised effort to gather information by posting a request on a social network site, your own web page, a blog or a website where you can attract a crowd. Unlike for other forms of crowdsourcing, you can't find many established websites that encourage a self-organised crowd to gather information. You usually have to create that site yourself, promote your work and draw a crowd to your site. (See Chapter 10 for more about attracting a crowd.)

In your request, you state the information you want and describe how or from where it needs to be collected. You usually need to be fairly specific about what needs to be done, otherwise you find the crowd does what it wants to do and not what you need. If you post a call that says a child is missing in the north of town and that you have an award for the group that finds him, you may discover that you'll be presented with all sorts of children who aren't the ones that you wanted to find.

You can see self-organised crowds being used to gather information in many marketing activities. One common form is the contest that challenges schools or groups to collect cash register receipts from local grocery stores. This kind of contest is usually sponsored by grocery stores or companies that make consumer products. The sponsors offer a prize to the group that collects the largest number of receipts. At the end of the contest, one team takes home a prize, while the sponsor gains a lot of information about how people purchase groceries.

The self-organised crowd can be a powerful means of gathering information. The Society for Disseminating Useful Information (SDUI) publishes a series of English-language periodicals that contain useful information – information that people can use to improve their homes, families and businesses. The periodicals are very popular, and the SDUI has decided it wants to translate these magazines into other languages. For several years, SDUI tried to translate the periodicals itself. The society started by hiring Spanish translators, and quickly found that the process was too expensive and had to stop.

The SDUI then decided it would crowdsource the translation through macrotasking (see Chapter 7). The society found this process faster and more efficient than using the traditional translator, but quickly noticed there were fewer readers in the Spanish-speaking audience than it intended. To better reach a non-English-speaking audience, it decided to try self-organised crowdsourcing.

To this end, SDUI posted a call to translate articles. Members of the crowd could pick any article from an SDUI magazine and translate it. Each article had to be reviewed by at least two other members of the crowd. Everyone involved in the translation would receive free access to the article they translated and free access to one other translated article.

As the work progressed, the self-organising aspect of this crowd taught SDUI which articles had value to readers in other languages and which did not. The members of the crowd translated the articles that had the greatest interest to them. Many articles would be translated into one language and not another. Some would be translated into Spanish and not Afrikaans, and vice versa. Since SDUI was prepared to offer a reward to translate any article, it was surprised to see that some articles were never translated out of English. It learned something from the crowd that it hadn't expected.

Experts are still learning how to use self-organised crowds in disaster relief. In emergency situations, crowds often need additional guidance to focus their attention on the problems at hand or to avoid causing more harm than good. If you're thinking of using self-organised crowds in an emergency situation, you need to make plans and probably have a way that you can bring some leadership to the crowd.

Making a decision

Self-organised crowds do many things. They can gather information for you. They can do work for you. They can even make decisions for you.

The simplest form of decision-making is the vote. You put a question to the crowd members and ask them to select one option. When you've concluded that enough people have participated, you stop the process and count the votes. The result with the largest support is the group decision.

Other approaches are to ask the crowd members to rate an idea on a scale from 1 to 10 and average the results, or to divide the crowd into groups, asking each group to reach a decision through consensus, and then have the groups vote.

You can also create indirect ways to obtain a decision from the crowd, such as through the prediction market. A *prediction market* looks like a simulated stock market or futures market. You can use a prediction market to find out what the crowd thinks about the chances of any event in the future. It can estimate the chances that a politician will win an election, a sports team will win a big tournament or an actor will win an Academy Award. For details of prediction markets, see the later section 'Organising a Prediction Market'.

Gathering and deciding

When you use a self-organised crowd, you usually use it to do multiple things. Commonly, you want it to both gather information for you and make decisions about that information. You want it to tell you which information is important and which is not. To handle both kinds of work, self-organised crowds have to become more complex. They need to have a hierarchy among the crowd so that some members gather information, some make judgements, and some coordinate the work of the others.

Wikipedia is a good example of a self-organised crowd that's engaged in both activities. The bulk of the crowd gather information. They write material and edit material, create new entries, and add pictures and links to the online encyclopaedia.

Researching with a contest

Say that you want to understand better the market for a certain consumer product. To do this, you start a contest to suggest improvements to the product. In defining your contest, you state that you're looking to improve the product and want suggestions for improvements that leave the basic product intact and cost less than $100 (£63).

By themselves, the product improvements tell you something about the crowd. However, they give you information about only part of the crowd – the part that's inventive and intrigued by the idea of working with your product. Not all the people who are interested in your product will make suggestions. The group responding may not even be typical of most of the people who use your product.

When you solicit suggestions, you engage the crowd in information gathering. You engage a larger crowd if you enlist them in making a decision. You can ask the crowd to vote on the different suggestions. From this vote, you can identify the improvement that's the most popular. You should also be able to obtain information about your product. You may be able to determine which element of your product needs the most improvement or which use for your product is the most popular.

For example, if you make a cleaning product and your self-organised crowd decides on the suggestion to give it a mint scent, you may have discovered that people think the product smells terrible, or that the product is used in places where mint smells are appropriate.

You may expand your decision-making process to include a number of votes. You may ask the crowd to decide which suggestion is most useful, most clever, and most efficient.

Wikipedia has a second process that makes decisions about material that's been added to the encyclopaedia. These decisions are made by Wikipedia administrators. These administrators achieve their position through a consensus process. They nominate themselves to the existing administrators. The existing administrators discuss the new nominee and determine whether they've a consensus to accept this person to their ranks. The new administrator can serve for as long as he maintains that consensus. If he starts making decisions that are controversial, he may ultimately lose his role as an administrator.

Designing the Process

When you design a self-organised crowd, you start with three questions:

- **What do I want to find out from the crowd?** For example, you may want to know what people think about your product, and you want to be sure that you're not missing something important.

✔ **What can I get the crowd to do?** For example, you ask the crowd to suggest changes to the product and then you make judgements about those suggestions.

✔ **Where can I find a crowd to do this work?** This last question is crucial. You usually can't find a crowdsourcing platform that offers you a ready self-organised crowd. You have to use websites that may enable you to find a group of people interested in your project and willing to be part of the work.

After you've answered these questions, you can start to think about how to shape a self-organised crowd. The following sections take you through all the considerations for designing your crowdsourcing project with a self-organised crowd.

Finding the crowd

When you use self-organised crowds, you usually can't just go to a simple commercial crowdsourcing platform and find a crowd. You can't find general self-organised crowd platforms either, like Mechanical Turk in microtasking (see Chapter 8), oDesk and Elance in macrotasking (see Chapter 7) or Kickstarter and Indiegogo in crowdfunding (see Chapter 6). The only time that you can regularly find such a site for self-organised crowds is when you undertake innovation crowdsourcing (see Chapter 18). Innovation crowdsourcing, though, isn't the only form of self-organised crowdsourcing.

In the absence of self-organised crowdsourcing platforms, you start the process by identifying a site on the Internet through which you may be able to attract people who are interested in your project. That may be a general social media site like Facebook. If you're working on a community issue such as a problem associated with your town, you might work with a site that's regularly visited by residents of the town. Or, if you're working on a problem that spans geographical areas, such as something that might improve the health of children around the world or help reduce air pollution, you will want to work with a platform that's associated with that issue. Historically, many self-organised crowdsourced projects have been run from blog sites, although you can certainly use a Facebook page to do the same thing.

You start a project by creating the page and educating the public about your problem, and you draw the crowd to that site by using social media, your social network and perhaps the support of people and institutions such as a local police department or community centre that's interested in your work. (Also take a look at Chapter 10 on promoting your project.) When you have a crowd at your chosen site, you can start explaining your project and guiding the crowd to act.

Preparing clear rules

Self-organised crowdsourcing is often presented as a contest or as an activity that appears to be a contest (for more on contests, flick to Chapter 5). The contest involves gathering information and making decisions based on that information. You have to make clear rules to describe both activities. (Visit Chapters 5 and 10 for more helpful pointers on writing rules and task descriptions.)

Sometimes during the course of a project, you discover things in the results that surprise you and make you wish you'd asked a different question of the crowd. Rather than modify your current questions, consider starting a second crowdsourcing activity. That activity may be based on material from the first, but it should offer new rewards to the crowd. In general, crowds are resentful if you change the rules in the middle of an activity. However, they usually welcome a new activity.

Information gathering

Usually, creating rules for this part of the self-organised crowdsourcing is easy. You describe the kind of thing that you're trying to obtain from the crowd – your goal. You describe the crowd is to create the information, how the members can submit it, and the criteria it must meet.

One useful way to obtain information is to engage members in a dialogue. You can select members from the crowd and ask them questions about what they're bringing to the effort, the things they like or dislike about the effort, or the reasons for their vote. You can have a dialogue in many different ways. You can choose members of the crowd at random. You can choose members who have special roles. You can offer a special side contest in order to select people to talk to.

You may find it useful to start your dialogues by addressing the crowd as a whole. You can prepare little videos that describe what you're trying to do or the information you're attempting to gather. These videos can not only help you have better discussions with individual members of the crowd, but they also help the rest of the crowd understand what you're trying to do.

Decision making

The decision-making part of a job is harder to describe to the crowd.

As with all aspects of crowdsourcing, you need to describe the goal to the crowd as clearly as you can. If you were running Wikipedia, for example, you would say that you want to produce a comprehensive general encyclopaedia. However, stating the goal isn't enough. You need to give the crowd principles for making decisions. If you don't give principles, the crowd members can easily make decisions by arguing with each other about whose opinion is better. Such arguments rarely produce anything useful. However, if you give the crowd principles for making decisions, the crowd members will argue about which possible choice best fits which principle. Such arguments are just as noisy as arguments over opinions – indeed, one kind of argument sometimes can't be distinguished from another – but arguments that involve principles or standards usually produce something useful.

The Wikipedia leadership, for example, gives its contributors basic guidelines for encyclopaedia articles. It explains that all contributions should be drawn from secondary sources, clearly written, free from political bias and not pla-giarised. When the community argues over which contributions to accept, it uses these principles as the basis for the discussion.

In the SDUI example in the earlier 'Gathering information' section, the crowd was told to pick the articles that it thinks will be most useful to readers in each language. While that principle leaves the decision to the crowd, it also removes other criteria for making decisions. The crowd doesn't have to con-sider whether the article is important to the English audience, whether it has good illustrations or whether it is prominently featured. The crowd members make their decisions based on their opinion of their own audience.

When you're preparing rules to help organise the crowd, you may also want to recruit a few lieutenants to help and direct the crowd. Your lieutenants may help recruit members of the crowd or help parts of the crowd to focus on their mission. If the crowd is gathering information, these lieutenants may help to organise parts of the crowd and encourage them to look for informa-tion in specific areas. If the crowd is making decisions, these lieutenants may help some parts of the crowd to focus on your question and try to answer it.

Motivating the crowd

When you're creating a self-organised crowd, you need to find a good way to motivate the crowd in order to encourage them to participate. Indeed, much recent academic research on self-organised crowds has suggested that a good plan to motivate the crowd is essential to success.

If you're engaging a simple crowd in which everyone plays the same role, the task of motivating the crowd is fairly easy. You run a contest and reward the winner (pay-one model) or you reward everyone who participates (pay-all).

You usually have simple crowds when you're using them to gather infor-mation. When you're soliciting improvements for a consumer product, for example, you're dealing with a simple crowd. In this case, you can easily use a contest model (see Chapter 5).

You can also find simple crowds when you make decisions. When you're asking a crowd to vote on different alternatives, you usually have a simple crowd. You can draw people to vote by giving them something if they vote or by entering them in a lottery to win a prize.

You have complex crowds when different members of the crowds have different roles. In these crowds, you often ask some members to guide, manage or report on other members of the crowd. In the SDUI example in the earlier section 'Gathering information', the translators have a complex role. They're not only providing information, but they're also disseminating material to others. In such cases, you need a more complex reward, one that reflects the nature of the crowd members' role. They may need both a fixed reward for each article they complete and small rewards that depend on the number of people who use the material.

Rewards to individual members of the crowd should reflect the kind of role that they fill. Many crowdsourcing activities use a star or badge system in which a member receives a silver, gold or platinum badge when he makes sufficient contributions to the project. The badges should reflect the principles that you set for the project – the goals that you think are important.

For more ideas on how to incentivise work, visit Chapter 14.

Looking at the results

You need to look at the results of any self-organised crowd activity carefully. You probably need to spend extra time with the results of self-organised crowds, because you've given the group the freedom to make the decisions. The information that the crowd sends reflects not only the project's goals but also any principles that you gave it, the information that the members have been processing and perhaps other ideas that they've discovered in the course of their work.

For example, many organisations try to use a simple version of Wikipedia's methods to create employee handbooks. They install some wiki software and tell their employees to start entering information. Often, they look at the results a few weeks later and find little that's useful. The wiki will be incomplete. Some entries will be far too detailed, whereas others will describe nothing that's of any use to anyone.

In looking at the results from this kind of project, you need to recognise firstly that you're doing self-organised crowdsourcing. You may be using a private crowd, the crowd of your employees for example, but you're still doing self-organised crowdsourcing for which you should have provided a clear goal, motivation for the crowd and principles for making decisions.

If some of the information you've received isn't useful, revisit your goal. Check that you explained to your crowd what you plan to do with this employee handbook and why you think it's important. If you didn't do so, you allowed the crowd to set the goal for you. Some crowd members may have thought that you are merely being organised, but others will have concluded that you are planning to replace them and that you want to document their jobs. Perhaps some members of the crowd may have become fearful that you're planning on outsourcing the entire office to a small island off the Russian coast. Don't laugh – if you don't explain your goal, you allow the crowd to explain it for you, and you'll see the crowd members' decisions in the work produced.

If the work you receive is incomplete, you've not given the crowd enough motivation to do the work. The crowd members are doing the work as an extra task, as a burden. Some will try to do it quickly and with minimal effort. Others will try to avoid it altogether. So give them a motivation: two hours off on a Friday afternoon of their choice; a free lunch to the author of the best entry. The crowd won't work unless it feels it's getting something out of the deal.

If the entries are of uneven quality, then you've not given good principles for decision making. You need to say at the outset why the results are needed, what information they should contain and, most importantly, what rules the crowd should use in writing the entries. A good way to enforce these principles is to let the crowd members edit the documents, and to give the entire crowd a reward if the work is done by a certain date.

Organising a Prediction Market

Among the many forms of self-organised crowd is the prediction market. *Prediction markets* encourage the crowd to make a judgement about something that may happen. They operate like a stock exchange. A prediction market offers the opportunity to invest in different events that may or may not occur in the future. Each member of the crowd brings money to the market. Sometimes this money is real, sometimes it is a fake currency distributed by the prediction market. The crowd members invest this money, real or fake as the case requires, in some outcome. You learn from the results of these investments.

Prediction markets do only one of the three things that self-organised crowds can do: they make decisions. Using them to gather information or do work isn't easy. You can almost always find something simpler than a prediction market if you're trying to gather data or complete a certain amount of work.

Prediction markets, however, are good as tools for combining the knowledge of the crowd. They're especially useful for combining knowledge that people can't easily articulate. People think that some event is going to happen, but they can't quite say why it's going to happen. All they can say is 'I feel it in my gut' or 'I bet this is going to be the result.' In a prediction market, the crowd members translate these feelings into monetary statements.

Prediction markets operate a little differently from the common forms of crowdsourcing and also from many forms of self-organised crowd. In most forms of crowdsourcing, you use the market as a means of communicating with the crowd and getting useful work from it. In prediction markets, however, you establish a market for the members of the crowd to use.

Running a prediction market is perilously close to running a gambling operation. Before you start a market, check local laws to see whether you can legally run such a market. If you can't, you may discover that you can run a market for a private crowd such as the employees of an organisation. Alternatively, you may try to run a simulated prediction market that uses something other than money as its exchange currency. Just as generations of card players have gambled with cigarettes or chocolate, you may be able to substitute something else for cash.

Even if prediction markets are legal in your jurisdiction, you need to proceed with caution. Many people engage in markets solely to make money and freely do anything they can to manipulate the market in their favour. They can spread rumours or engage in trades that mislead the other participants.

If the prediction market appeals, read on to see how you can organise one.

Finding prediction markets

Because public prediction markets can be considered as something close to a gambling establishment, they aren't common and are usually highly regulated. In the USA, the most sophisticated of these markets is the Iowa Electronic Markets site (`http://tippie.uiowa.edu/iem`), which is run as a research activity by the University of Iowa. The public can participate in the markets that are used for political predictions. The site does run other markets that predict the state of the economy, but these are open only to students and researchers.

In the UK, the gambling establishments offer public political prediction markets that are similar to the political markets of the Iowa Electronic Markets.

You can create private prediction markets by using market software from companies such as Qmarkets (`http://prediction-markets.qmarkets.net`). This software handles all the transactions of the prediction market. You have to design the market, recruit the crowd and analyse the results.

Establishing the rules

You can create many different kinds of prediction market. Two of the simplest, and hence the most common, are the futures market and the pari-mutual market.

Futures markets

In the simplest version of the futures market, you create a set of futures. *Futures* are nothing more than certificates. On a certain date in the future, if a certain event occurs, you will pay the people who own the certificates $1 or the equivalent currency. You will pay nothing if that event doesn't occur. For example, to predict a presidential election, you can offer a set of futures for each different candidate that are worth $1 if that candidate wins.

If you're trying to predict the behaviour of a business competitor, you can offer futures for the time when the competitor announces a new product. You can offer a set of futures that are worth $1 each if the product is released in the first quarter of the year, another set that are worth $1 each if it comes in the second quarter of the year, and so on.

If you're trying to understand the markets for your products, you can also offer a future that's worth $1 if the sales team reaches its quota and is worthless if it doesn't. (You can also offer a future that has a value tied to the quantity of sales. It may be worth $1 for every $500,000 in sales. This kind of future is a more refined tool, but is also more complicated.)

For all the simple $1 futures, the price of the future, when divided by $1, is the crowd's estimate that the event will occur. For example, if the crowd members pay $0.75 for futures that are worth $1 if your company meets its sales projections, then they're 75 per cent certain you will make those projections.

The crowd can never be more than 100 per cent certain about any event in a prediction market, because members will never pay more than $1 for a future that can only be worth $1.

Pari-mutual markets

Pari-mutual markets are like the kinds of betting markets you find at horse tracks. In this style of market, you don't issue futures. Instead, you ask the crowd to invest in one of several possible outcomes. The amount that the crowd bets on any outcome is proportional to the crowd's estimate of the probability that the event will occur. This kind of market is just like bets placed on a football tournament. The bets placed on any team represent the trust that the crowd has in that team.

To use a pari-mutual to compute the crowd's estimate of the chances that an event will occur, you first sum all the investments placed in a market. You then divide the amount invested in each outcome by the total outcome. Figure 9-1 shows how to compute the crowd's estimate of the chances for three candidates in a general election.

Figure 9-1:		Invested	Chances
Pari-mutual	Tory	£375	375/900 = 41.7%
estimates	Liberal Democrat	£75	75/900 = 8.3%
for a general	Labour	£450	450/900 = 50.%
election.	Total Invested	£900	

Laying down the rules

The basic rules for a prediction are simple. A common set of rules is as follows.

You start by giving all members of the crowd a certain amount of fake money and a certain number of futures that say a certain amount of some event will happen. You tell the crowd members that they can buy futures from or sell them to any other member of the crowd in a simple transaction. A *simple transaction* is one that exchanges futures for money with no complications of any other rights. You don't promise to buy options at some later point in the market. You sell rights to futures you don't have.

(Of course, if you have experience of stock markets and want to try more complicated rules, you can, although it isn't clear that more complicated transactions are worth the trouble.)

As you prepare your market, you can consider a couple of other issues:

✓ **Time span:** Be sure to include when the market starts and when the market ends. When you run a prediction market, you need to be conscious of time. First, you need to let the market stay open for an extended period. If you run a market for only 10 or 15 minutes, you're really doing nothing more than taking a poll with money, the crowd merely stating its initial opinion just as if you asked the members to vote on the different alternatives. However, as you keep the market open, the members of the crowd begin to think and to interact with each other. They see what other members have concluded and adjust their opinions. As they make these adjustments, the market begins to reflect the combined intelligence of all individual members.

You want to take several snapshots of the market. You will discover something about the crowd's perceptions by seeing how it revalues the different options at different times. When you open the market, the crowd members will value the different options in one way. An hour later, they will change their values. When you close the market, the crowd may have different opinions. You may find it useful to see how the crowd changes its mind. It may decide quickly on one conclusion and hold it for the entire market. Or it may start with one idea, move to a second and then return to its original conclusion. The crowd may drift through several ideas before it settles on a final choice. Each of these paths tells you something about the crowd members' opinions.

✔ **Stating or not stating the question:** In the rules, be clear about the information you want to gain from the futures market; however, you may not want to give your goals to the crowd. Sometimes, when you tell the crowd the kind of thing that you're trying to obtain from the market, the members adjust their actions to try to give that information to you. But you want the members to follow their natural inclinations. Just give them the rules of the market and let them follow those rules.

As with all forms of crowdsourcing, don't change the rules in the middle of a project.

Assessing the result

After you close the market, you need to assess the results from the activity. This work isn't as straightforward as it may seem. Sometimes prediction markets can seem to be inconsistent. In a futures market for political candidates you may have two similar Tory candidates and you may discover that their options are similarly priced. The crowd may tell you that it believes that one candidate has a 65 per cent chance of winning and the other a 60 per cent chance – a grand total of a 135 per cent chance between them. Here, the market has combined the two candidates into one. The members of the crowd are really purchasing future options on a single kind of Tory candidate.

Prediction markets often deviate from the strict laws of probability. If you sum the chances that all the events will occur, you obtain a probability greater than 100 per cent, which doesn't work with the standard theory of probability and chance. However, you can always judge relative strength from these markets. You may not get a perfect estimate of who'll win, but you can judge that someone is twice as likely to win as someone else.

When you run a prediction market, remember that the crowd is telling you something, but maybe not in a language that's as clear as you'd like.

Part III
Building Skill

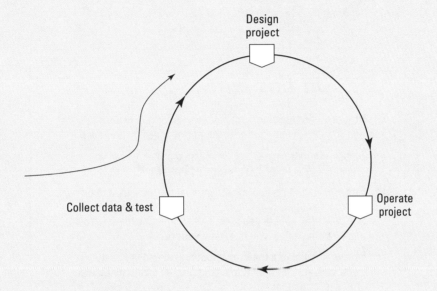

Design
project

Operate
project

Collect data & test

In this part . . .

✔ Attract an enthusiastic group of crowdworkers to your project and keep them engaged with your project as it progresses.

✔ Gather information and give direction to properly brief your crowdworkers, to ensure that you get the results you want.

✔ Find new uses for your favourite social media sites and discover the support that formal crowdsourcing platforms offer. See how they enable you to find and connect with the crowd, and how they allow you to extend your reach.

✔ Fit your activity into the crowdsourcing mould, make the process work and keep on top of your project as it unfolds with effective management.

✔ Learn from your experiences and continuously improve your crowdsourcing activities by considering what you did right, what you did wrong and how you can do it better next time.

Chapter 10

Engaging the Crowd with Your Project

*W*hen you start crowdsourcing, you need an idea, a means of dividing labour, a platform for the work, and, of course, a crowd. If you don't have a crowd or if you're building a self-organised crowd (a group of people given a task and told to solve it in the way they think is best), you have to recruit members. If you're using a commercial market, you may find that the crowd's already gathered at your gates and is waiting to find work. However, even in this case, you may find yourself looking to grow the crowd.

The first steps of building a crowd are very similar to the work of Internet marketing. You're trying to attract a group of workers to your project, so you build a presence on the web via websites, social media pages and blogs, through which you express the goals and ideas of your crowdwork. You can use conventional tools as well, and you can recruit people from organisations such as civic organisations or college alumni networks who may be interested in your project. No matter how you do it, you're trying to get people to come to your project.

You can think of the work of attracting or building a crowd as a form of crowdsourcing – using a small crowd to attract a bigger crowd. You do this by giving your small crowd (call it the *seed crowd*) the task of contacting friends who may be interested in your project. The crowd members can go through their social networks, the organisations they support, their family and their friends.

Using a crowd to attract a crowd is perhaps most useful when you're involved in crowdfunding, but no matter what you're doing with crowdsourcing, you start by building a crowd. And that's exactly what this chapter helps you do.

Getting Started with Crowdbuilding

The following sections provide some of the basics you need to grasp before you dive in to pull together a crowd.

Knowing what motivates the crowd

The first rule of business is: know your market. The rule applies to crowdsourcing; to attract a crowd, you need to understand that crowd.

Chapter 2 explains who the members of the crowd are. The crowd members have all sorts of reasons for being part of the crowd:

✔ **Altruism:** Some give their wages to charity and feel that they're improving the world. Others get involved with crowdfunding to support a cause they believe in.

✔ **A feeling of belonging:** Some are following the lead of others.

✔ **Building skills or experience:** Some crowdworkers are looking to plump up their portfolios – or perhaps use skills they don't get to use in their day jobs.

✔ **Identity:** By engaging in crowdsourcing, they feel they're being identified with something they admire.

✔ **Money:** Some workers are attracted solely by money. For them, crowdworking is the best job they can find, or the best way to use their skills, or the best place for them to work at certain hours or in certain places of the globe. These workers can only be attracted through financials rewards. The higher the price you offer for each task, the more likely you are to get these workers into your crowd.

When you recruit people to join your crowd, you're involved in a transaction. You offer something to the potential members of the crowd and they're free to accept your offer or reject it. You need to be sure to offer something that the crowd wants. For example, the crowdsourcing site Zooniverse offers no money to its crowd, yet has a crowd of over half a million people. It rewards the crowd members by giving them the opportunity to be involved in important scientific research. The crowd members can do work that was once restricted to big universities and important laboratories.

Identifying the talent and resources you need

When you're preparing to recruit a crowd, you should first sit down and identify the skills you need in the members of the crowd. If you require translation, the crowdworkers need to know multiple languages. If your project is about categorisation, the crowdworkers need to be able to recognise the categories. If your project is technical, the crowdworkers need technical skills.

If you need too many skills for your job, you may not have divided the work properly into crowdsourcing tasks. If your plan requires you to have a crowd of Japanese-speaking Java coders who understand something about finance, you haven't broken your work into its component parts. You should be able to break your job into tasks that require one, or at most two, identifiable skills.

Don't overestimate the skills that you need. You may think that your job requires someone with at least a graduate degree, but you may get better results from a crowd with a more common set of skills that you can train in the specific skill that you need. Crowdsourcing can involve teaching as well as working.

Adapting your strategy for public and private crowds

A *private crowd* is made up of people within your network, like employees of your company or users of an organisation's services, whose common expertise, experience or loyalty you want to access. A *public crowd* is made up of all sorts of people with varying levels of skill who show interest in your crowdsourcing.

You can use the techniques for building a crowd to create public or private crowds. However, the two crowds are not quite the same, and so you get a slightly different result when you're building a private crowd from when you're building a public crowd. In the case of public crowds, you recruit from a population of people who're ready to work but may not have the right skills or experience. In the case of private crowds, you're recruiting from people who're more likely to have the right skills but who may not be inclined to do crowdwork.

Use this guidance for each type of crowd:

- **Public:** Attract as many people as you can to your project and then winnow out those who don't have the right skills.

- **Private:** Convince people with the right skills that they should devote some of their time to your crowd. They may be reluctant to join because they don't like to work over the Internet, or because they don't want to spend their time working on your project, or because they think that their boss won't want them to join the crowd.

Inviting People to Join Your Crowd

When you build a crowd, you often start with conventional marketing. You announce an activity and ask people to join in. This is your starting point even if you're going to use the crowd to help you recruit others or try to build a self-organised crowd.

Your first efforts can follow traditional models. You can post a call for a crowd on your web page. You can post it on Facebook. You can send it to community bulletin boards. You can use Twitter. All these are mechanisms for building a crowd.

If you're trying to build a big crowd (and many projects need a large number of workers), you can use many forms of media and tie them back to a single blog, Facebook page or LinkedIn entry through feeds and pingbacks or other mechanisms. That way, you can post a message once but send it to many people through many forms of media.

The following sections provide guidance for seeing the numbers of your crowd swell.

Seeding the crowd

No one likes to be the first person at the party. You stand at the door, talk awkwardly with the host for a moment, and let all the social doubts fly through your head. Perhaps you remembered the wrong time, or date or address. Perhaps the host has such a reputation for bad parties that no one else is willing to come. Perhaps the party is a surprise party and you're about to be embarrassed.

Similarly, you don't to be the first person to join a crowd. You start to wonder about similar issues. Is this crowd legitimate? Will the crowdsourcer actually pay us? Does the rest of the crowd know something that I don't?

Invite a small group of trusted people to start the crowd, before you start inviting the general public. This method not only allows you to complete some of the work before members of the public come to your job, but also allows you to test your tasks with a small, trusted group of people.

If you're building a private crowd, you should certainly start with a small group. You may have a list of most of the potential members. You may take names from the list of company employees, or the membership roll of your organisation, or the directory of residents in a certain neighbourhood. You may even have direct email addresses for all these people and be able to send them individual invitations to join the crowd. They'll be your best advocates for the rest of the organisation. You may even want to bring them into your group, give them a special briefing, and make them feel as if they're part of your inner team.

For a charitable or civic job, you may consider recruiting prominent individuals into the crowd. You then ask them not only to endorse the work but also to actually do some crowd labour. You can publish the number of tasks they've completed and challenge the community to meet and exceed the accomplishments of these individuals. (Of course, this strategy works well only if these prominent individuals actually do the work.)

Engaging on YouTube

Video's a powerful means of attracting people to your project. For some forms of crowdsourcing, such as crowdfunding, you're almost required to have a video. A video gives a lift to your project. It allows you to explain the value of your project directly to the crowd. It can explain a complicated idea in just a few seconds.

You can use YouTube as your video platform. The YouTube site is well indexed in search engines, easily accessible and easy to use. You can film your video with a simple camera or phone and upload the video to YouTube. You can then circulate the video by sending the link through Twitter, by email, on Facebook or through other forms of communication.

When you create a video, make sure your story's simple and clear. Ensure good light, so that you can see people's faces and hear their voices. More importantly, make sure you're explaining your project clearly and that you're emphasising the benefits of the project to the crowd.

When you make a promotional video, send the message 'Join my crowdsourcing project because it will be good for you.' You need to tell the crowd members the benefits that they get from doing the tasks. Tell them that they can gain skills or that they can engage all their talents, that they can help a good cause or that they'll be earning money in the service of a business that's trying to help its community.

Granting bragging rights

Your crowd is usually your best advertisement. The members tell their friends and colleagues of their work. You can encourage the crowd to spread the news of your crowdsourcing project by giving the members bragging rights, by recognising them for their accomplishments, and letting them spread the news of their work.

Bragging rights are crucial to crowdcontests. Unless you have a strong reason to keep the results private, you want to let every winner brag about his success in your contest. The winner gets added compensation by being recognised as accomplished. You get additional attention for your crowdcontest. You may also want to consider some form of recognition for members of the crowd who are finalists or who produced unusually good work.

Fostering Community Spirit

A good crowdsourcing project is about community. You bring a group of people together to do some work, to fund an activity, to build a product, to find information. You may find it useful to let the crowd build a community of its own. You can encourage the members to communicate with each other in a variety of ways. You can use blogs to post messages. You can use Twitter hash tags to do the same thing. You can use a Flickr account to let the members post images of their work. With these kinds of things, you can help your crowd to feel it has a common identity.

When your crowd's established a common identity, you can use that identity to promote your project and encourage other people to join. You can send messages that say that you have a good community that's doing engaging work. You're encouraging others to appreciate that work and join in with it themselves.

Some people are cautious about letting the members of crowd use a blog or Twitter to communicate with each other. Indeed, sometimes a crowd may use such tools to communicate their dissatisfaction with the job or with you as the organiser of the activity. (You may want to read Chapter 14 on managing crowds before you create a blog for your crowdsourcing work.) Still, most crowdsourcing experts believe that blogs and Twitter hash tags are good things. If problems exist, the crowd will find a way to talk. You can be better prepared if you see the messages than if you don't. Running the blog is a good way to catch problems.

The Zooniverse community

The Zooniverse community are a diverse bunch made up of professional scientists, amateur scientists, non-scientists in many forms, a fair number of onlookers and many people who're just plain interested.

Zooniverse uses three sets of tools for building an online presence: blogs, Twitter and a press page. The blogs, at `www.blogs.zooniverse.com`, are updated regularly. They contain postings from the Zooniverse staff and from the scientists who post work at the site. The postings talk about the science that's being supported by the crowdsourcing work, the challenges of using crowds and the accomplishments of the crowd. Zooniverse generally maintains one blog for each project and updates the blogs frequently.

The Twitter feeds are much more dynamic and include comments from scientists, Zooniverse workers and members of the crowd. They talk about the science of the Zooniverse projects, general topics of science, and topics of interest to the workers. Zooniverse maintains a Twitter account for most of the projects as well as a main feed at @The_zooniverse. The owners of these accounts tend to post regularly to Twitter, although the bulk of the postings come from workers.

Finally, Zooniverse maintains a press page on its website, because part of its audience consists of science writers. Many organisations maintain such pages and use them to hold background papers, statistics, links to published papers and other useful information. At Zooniverse, the press page is a simple site that gives the name and email address of a press contact.

Building an online base

If you don't build an online base for your crowd, you're inviting someone else to build it for you. The base can be something as simple as a Facebook page or a community blog. It can also be a multi-topic forum that allows workers to post comments, to chat or to share information. All the major crowdsourcing companies have bases like these – Amazon's Mechanical Turk has mturk forum (`http://mturkforum.com`); Zooniverse has the Zooniverse Blog (`www.blog.zooniverse.org`) (see the sidebar 'The Zooniverse community'); CrowdFlower has a site on the Get Satisfaction platform (`https://getsatisfaction.com/crowdflower`).

Most of these online bases are divided into two sections. The first section is an official blog that's controlled by the crowdsourcer. This blog is a place for news, updates, tips and other information about the project. The second section is usually under the control of the workers, and contains observations about the work, more tips, suggestions about other jobs that can be found on the web, and other information of interest to crowdworkers. For large projects, the workers' forum is often divided into multiple strands: conversations about work, personal chatter, observations and so on.

Showing how tasks contribute to the overall goal

When you start crowdsourcing, you can't expect the crowdworkers to understand the job as you understand it. They'll understand it from the bottom up, and you need to help them understand the big picture by describing how the individual tasks support your goals, and by stating clearly the connection between the two.

Have you heard the story of the woodcutters? A traveller enters a village and finds three people cutting wood. He asks the three workers what they're doing.

'Cutting wood,' says the first.

'Constructing a building,' says the next.

'Building a meeting hall so that the village may gather and prosper,' is the final reply.

The lesson for crowdsourcing and crowdbuilding is that you can encourage the crowd by showing it how their work connects to your goals.

Identifying benefits

Every workplace – no matter how technical, how global, how diverse – is a place to grumble. Workers gather at the water cooler or in the tea room and talk about the things that bother them. To counteract this, in trying to build a community within the crowd, you may need to explain the benefits of the work at your online base. Your workers will quickly see the things that *you* will get out of the work. They need to see what things *they* will get from joining your crowd.

Express your benefits as broadly as you can. Certainly many crowdworkers will respond to the payments that you offer. However, most also look beyond the payments and hope to see something more. Will they be improving a community? Will they gain new skills? Will they add to the world's stock of knowledge? Will they make life a little more comfortable for a child with fewer resources than themselves? Be sure to give as many benefits as you can.

Don't claim benefits that you can't offer. Crowdworkers don't appreciate lies and deceit. You don't want to be known as a crowdsourcer who makes claims that aren't true – that will mean the end of your crowdsourcing.

Updating the crowd on progress

If workers don't see progress, they can easily believe that no progress is being made, even if they complete hundreds or thousands of tasks. So when you try to build a community within the crowd, keep the workers aware of the overall progress of your project.

You can think of these reports of progress as a dialogue with the crowd. Tell the crowd what it's accomplished, what it's done towards completing your job. The crowd can take pride in what it's accomplished and use this information to make decisions about which tasks to take next. If you have a lot of work remaining, the crowd members may decide to invest time to learn your tasks, because they'll have plenty of opportunity to use those skills. In addition, by publically talking about the progress of the task, you may attract new crowd members.

Most crowdsourcing organisations create this dialogue using a blog. (Blogs are now so common that few organisations consider doing any kind of a crowdsourcing effort without one.) You can, however, just as easily use a Facebook page or an email update in which a senior member of the team reports on the status of the work. These posts can also be a way of encouraging the crowd. They can report on individual accomplishments, such as recognising an individual worker who's accomplished an unusual amount of work, or share details of best practices with the crowd.

Dialogue works both ways. Listen to the crowd. On your online base, create room for crowd members to talk to you – commenting on a blog post or Facebook, for example. The crowd give you more loyalty if it perceives you as a human being who's interested in the crowd and is focused on achieving a goal, rather than seeing a faceless web page that gives a brief description of the work. Listening to the crowd also helps you manage it; head over to Chapter 14 for more on managing crowds.

Try using photos to humanise the crowd. If you open a Flickr account or find another way to post images of the crowd at work, you'll find that it becomes a more effective and contented group. By putting a face to every name, you let people visualise their co-workers and understand them as human beings.

Sustaining the Crowd's Interest

You need to keep the crowd interested in your work. Only for certain forms of macrotasking can you ignore the need to refresh your crowd and keep it interested in your work. For microtasking, contests, self-organised crowds, crowdfunding and all the other variations of these basic forms, you need to work to sustain the interest of the crowd.

Crowds are most interested in those who offer a regular supply of work. If you offer different amounts of work from day to day or from week to week, the crowd may start to view you as unreliable and look elsewhere for opportunities.

If you use a commercial crowdsourcing platform, you can be less concerned about offering a steady amount of work. Your jobs will be aggregated with the jobs of others. The crowd is less aware that you may be offering more jobs one week than the next. However, even if you use these services, you're more likely to get greater loyalty from the crowd if you offer a steady amount or at least a predictable amount of work.

You can also boost the loyalty of the crowd by keeping it informed of progress. You usually get the best results when you describe progress in terms of the things that the crowd has accomplished, not the things that you've done. Keep the focus on the crowd and help it see the benefits of what it's done.

Teaching and Training

Teaching and training are an important part of managing crowdsourcing, and they can also be a useful tool for promoting your project. When you create material to show the crowd why a task is important, how it can do the work and what results it can expect, you can also use that material to recruit new workers to the crowd. You can put the training material in a public place on the web and direct potential workers to it. You can tell them that this material explains what they'll do, the skills that they need to join the crowd, and the opportunities they'll get by working in your crowd.

You're more likely to produce vibrant and engaging training material if you also plan to use the material to promote your project. When you produce material to use in this way, you tend to emphasise the final product and the benefits of that project – which is more engaging than a mere description of the task.

Training materials shouldn't be the only form of promotion. However, they can extend and augment the messages that you send to rally a crowd.

Showing the outcome

The crowd likes to know the outcome of the work. It's more likely to engage if it knows what you want – what product you hope to see at the end. When you prepare training materials, make sure that you have a document, podcast or video that shows the results of the crowdsourcing. Depending on the task, show the final product: a completed database, a well-written paragraph, an edited photograph, a transcription for an audio file.

You need to do little, if anything, to adapt this kind of training material to promote your project. You can create a tweet, or a Facebook posting, or even an email with a link to your training material and the words, 'Join our project and you can create this kind of thing.'

Leading the crowd through the tasks

At first, you may conclude that a detailed list of instructions isn't a good tool for recruiting people to your project. Indeed, most people don't find lists of instructions compelling or even interesting. If you think you can post your instructions on a website and that these instructions will draw a crowd to your project, you're mistaken. You should never think that only a list of instructions will bring the crowd to your project.

However, you can use some of your instructions to promote your project when these instructions demonstrate the skills that members of the crowd will learn. Remember that part of the advantage of crowdsourcing is that the crowd gets to acquire new skills. If you can use your instructions or an edited version of your instructions to show the skills that the crowdworkers will gain, you've demonstrated an additional benefit to the workers.

If you were raising a crowd to process graphical images you might promote it by posting a photograph and part of the instructions. For example, 'Can you identify the faces in this photograph? If so, you can help us organise the art collection at the County Museum. You'll help us understand our pictures, tell us what they show and, who knows, maybe find a lost master work.'

You can also use instructions to reduce the concerns of potential crowd members. If you've had trouble getting people to do tasks, and have been unable to get the crowd to respond via increases in payments, then you may be facing a crowd that believes that your task is more complicated than it is. You can illustrate the simplicity by posting your instructions in a public place and directing the crowd to them. Of course, the instructions have to be simple. If they appear complicated, you simply confirm the fears of the crowd.

For the lowdown on writing clear instructions, see Chapter 11.

Engaging on YouTube (again)

YouTube's become an important tool for training crowdworkers. A 90-second video can train a crowd in a way that pages of documents can't. Training videos don't take the place of promotional material, but they can be a useful supplement. They can illustrate the nature of the work that you're offering, especially the social aspects. Many crowdworkers like to engage with other members of the crowd. You can show how they can work together with a simple training video.

Training videos usually supplement promotional materials. You may circulate a link to them with the note, 'For more information, you can look at our training video.'

Chapter 11

Instructing the Crowd

· ·

In This Chapter

▶ Writing a clear statement of work

▶ Putting together easy-to-follow instructions

▶ Taking feedback on board

· ·

*W*hen it comes to management and communication, crowdsourcing requires a careful and thorough approach. Unlike on the traditional shop floor or in an office complex, all your interaction with the crowd passes through information technology, and the process strips away lots of useful knowledge. You can't stop at someone's desk to see how she's doing or observe a work team making its plans. You have to gather all your information and give all your direction through technological means.

Crowds may be intelligent, but they don't always have a direction. And when they do have a direction, they may not be going down the right path for you. Crowdsourcing isn't magical. You can't simply make some vague statement of a goal and expect the crowd to find an elegant and useful solution. From time to time, someone makes a brief communication to a crowd and wonderful things happen. Such events, however, are rare.

So to guide the crowd well, you need to master the skill of communicating with words, of using structure to direct activity, and of supplementing instructions with graphs and pictures. Communication works both ways, and you've also got to get good at hunting down information to see how the crowd is working, how it's engaging with your task, and how you may need to adjust your plans. This chapter gives you a good grounding in managing and communicating with the crowd so you get the best possible results.

Preparing the Fundamental Message: Writing a Statement of Work

The first communication that you generally have with the crowd is the *statement of work*, in which you tell the crowd what you intend to do and how you'll to involve it. The statement explains the goal and is the rallying point for the crowd.

The statement takes different forms in each version of crowdsourcing, as shown in Table 11-1. For more details on running each kind of crowdsourcing project, visit the chapter indicated in the Type column.

Table 11-1	Statements of Work in Different Types of Crowdsourcing	
Type	*Name of Statement*	*Explains*
Crowdcontests (see Chapter 5)	Statement of contest goal	The goal of the contest and how any individual can contribute to the effort
Crowdfunding (see Chapter 6)	Statement of project, case statement or prospectus	What is to be done, how much money is required, how that money is to be used, and the benefits of the project (make sure that you stress these!)
Macrotasking (see Chapter 7)	Statement of work	The task to be done (and nothing more)
Microtasking (see Chapter 8)	Statement of tasks big and small	The overall project (in one document) and the kind of tasks that individual workers will do (in another document)
Innovation crowdsourcing (see Chapter 18)	Statement of problem	The problem that is to be solved

Structuring carefully

A good statement of work shares a common feature with a good joke: a sensible structure. In a joke, a bad structure can completely undermine a funny situation. All the humour, absurdity, wit and cleverness can be completely undermined by a structure that presents the elements of a joke in a way that defuses the punch line. In a statement of work, you can undermine all the ideas and vision with a chaotic structure.

In statement of work, the ideas should generally move from big to small. At each step of the way, the reader should understand how the new ideas fit into the structure that's already been presented. In many cases, the statement starts with an overview of work and then moves into details. Only when asking the crowd to donate its time or resources do you begin the statement of work with the benefits of the proposed project.

This following sections lay down a common structure for a statement of work; follow them chronologically.

Stating the purpose: Explaining what the work is going to do

The statement of work should generally begin by answering the question: 'What is this project going to do?' (However, if you're planning a charitable crowdsourcing activity, see the next section, 'Presenting the benefits, benefits, benefits').

Make the purpose section succinct, rarely longer than a paragraph. In many cases, you can summarise in a single sentence, which is often all the space you have on a crowdsourcing website.

Here are a few examples of purpose statements:

> This project is creating a web page and store for a small firm selling personal care products.

> The workers in this project will be transcribing public health records from non-English-speaking countries.

> This project is identifying new products that will extend the market for our company.

Presenting the benefits, benefits, benefits

In crowdfunding cases, you present the benefits of the project to the prospective donors. These benefits should be both general and personal. They should give the benefits both to the larger world and to the individual who's making the donation. Here are some examples:

> Our project will improve literacy rates in South America and give you an opportunity to be part of a project that helps bring development and stability to an overlooked region.

> The funds will be used to improve safety at a busy intersection and create an elevated bridge that will protect both pedestrians and drivers.

> By contributing to our restaurant, you will allow us to meet a need in our community. You will also get a donor card that will give you far more in benefits at the restaurant than the value of your contribution.

Be honest in stating the benefits of your project. Make sure that you don't inflate the benefits beyond what your audience will find credible. Not every project can save the world. Not every project can end disease. Not every project can bring peace in our time. The crowd can often detect when you're exaggerating and will not engage with your project.

Making sure that they know the requirements

Start your description by identifying the required elements that are needed for the project to be complete. If a member of the crowd isn't interested in or capable of doing these tasks, she can skip to another project. Here's what requirements may look like:

> This project involves creating an annual report that includes pictures portraying company activities, charts showing the firm's economic health, and text describing the plans of each division.

> This project will create 200-word descriptions of our products. Each description will correspond to a picture. Each description has to include physical details of the object and its brand name.

> This project gathers consumer data. The data has to contain price (in US dollars), date, name of store, and location of store (city, street address and zip code.)

Ensuring accuracy with technical specs

The technical specs are an extension of the requirements (see the preceding section) and they require a detailed knowledge of the product or the work process. They're often put into a special section and are more detailed than the standard requirements. For example:

> The system must be programmed in Python and run in the Linux environment.

> The name of the product must always be written in 98-point bold Helvetica.

> The colour of the container must be Pantone PMS 2747.

Establishing your desirables

You can describe things that you'd like to have if at all possible – wishes more than necessities. These qualities often differ from the requirements, because you describe them in less concrete, more general terms.

> The graphic should be bold and strong.

> The English text should be easy to read.

> We would prefer workers with Six Sigma experience.

Drawing the line in the sand: Deal breakers

Tell the crowd about things you won't accept in the work project – the deal breakers:

> The material shouldn't be borrowed from Wikipedia or any other public website.

> You should never contact the owners of these websites, even if you don't understand the text on the front page.

> The list of potential sales contacts should contain no names from outside the Sioux Falls metropolitan area (zip codes 57100–57199).

Warning the crowd away from undesirables

In addition to the deal breakers, you often have undesirable items or actions. You prefer not to see these elements in the final product or activity, but you concede that you may have to accept some of them. For example:

> We prefer to avoid using a spreadsheet for this project.

> We prefer that all purchases for this project be made in Scotland.

> The new container shouldn't resemble the old container for this product.

Summarising acceptance criteria

The last part of a statement of work is usually a special kind of summary. It presents the criteria that you'll use to determine whether the work is acceptable. This section draws heavily on the prior material. Indeed, it shouldn't introduce new ideas. In order to keep the document consistent, you may refer directly to earlier sections without repeating them. Here's an example:

> The video will be accepted if all segments of it are properly used, if all transitions are smooth and professionally done, if the branding follows the instructions in the requirements above and the final form is in the H464 standard as stated in the technical description. The final video should be no less than five minutes in length and no more than six minutes.

Making clarity your goal

Whatever form of crowdsourcing you're using, the better you become at writing the statement of work, the more effective your crowdsourcing becomes.

Using terms of art

Make your statement of work as clear as possible. Use terms that should be familiar to the crowd that you're trying to reach. Many fields have *terms of art* – that is, words that have specific technical meanings. Marketing, for example, uses words such as *exposure*, *preference*, *satisfaction* and *confirmation*, which mean specific things to marketeers. By using terms of art in your statement of work, you can often communicate complex ideas in a straightforward way to the crowd that you're aiming to reach.

When you use terms of art, you may have to introduce them so that you communicate to the crowd that you know exactly what you want. For example, you might write:

> In this project, I'm seeking someone with marketing experience to help me understand customer satisfaction and discomfirmation for our products.

> I am looking for someone skilled in website design who can help us understand how our presentation is context-sensitive and leads users to commit errors.

> We'd like someone who understands quality control to help develop a control chart for our operations and improve our company.

Giving the right amount of detail

One of the great challenges in writing a statement of work is striking the right balance between giving detailed instructions and overloading the crowd. Of course, you want to obtain the product or service that you desire; therefore, you need enough detail. But at the same time, too much detail can overwhelm readers and make a project seem more complicated than it really is. So you need to include enough detail to obtain what you want, but not so much that you stifle the creativity of the crowd. Here are some examples:

- ✔ **Not enough detail:** 'We need someone to prepare spreadsheets for our company.'

  The company may be looking for someone to program marketing models, human resource databases or interactive games for its customers, all of which involve different skills, but this statement doesn't let the crowd members know whether they're capable of preparing the spreadsheets.

- ✔ **Too much detail:** 'We're looking for a worker to help us develop spreadsheets for marketing models. We prefer inverted models with rows and columns reversed, stacked in multiple worksheets with interleaved formulae and pivot charts that link to an external file that presents the results in Geneva, not Helvetica, type.'

> This statement has a lot of detail that suggests you know exactly what you want and aren't going to be satisfied with anything else. It sounds like trouble – if you can understand all the words.
>
> ✔ **Just enough detail:** 'We're looking for someone to program complicated marketing models in a multi-sheet spreadsheet. We have a standard spreadsheet that we've been using for these models, but welcome improvements.'
>
> This statement suggests the complexity of the problem, lets the crowd members know that the company has models they can use, and suggests that the company is open to new ideas.

Getting arty

If space allows, consider including illustrations in your statements of work to clarify the text. Such illustrations are particularly useful when you want the crowd to provide an artistic or technical product.

Finbar, a scientific author, tried to get the crowd to design a cover for his most recent book. As part of his statement of work, he posted a copy of the book's introduction and a few key paragraphs. As a result, he received proposals for covers that had not an ounce of originality. Each proposed cover looked like the cover of any general science book. The covers had a few equations scattered across the cover, a scientific graph and a picture of Albert Einstein.

After reviewing the initial submissions, Finbar spent a little time searching the web and found a few pictures in advertisements that captured some of the ideas for his book. He posted them on the crowdsourcing website alongside this instruction: 'These photos capture the spirit of the book. Do something like them but don't copy them directly.' The next round of submissions were much more creative and got much closer to the spirit of the book.

By themselves, illustrations aren't a complete work statement. They don't tell people what's important and what's not. The description and the illustration should work together.

Looking at an example statement of work

This statement of work for a geography game includes every element that you may need to put in such a statement, as outlined in the preceding sections. Your statements may be considerably simpler.

> I need a programmer to create a geography game to teach students of development studies about South America. The game should be similar to the Africa game at www.exampleurl.com.

The game asks students to identify the names of the countries, their capitals, their populations and their major products. This information can be found at www.anotherexampleurl.com.

The game should look and act like the Africa game. The questions should default to English, but a button should allow the user to switch to Spanish or Portuguese.

The game must be programmed in Java and HTML5. It should operate in any of the three most common web browsers.

It should contain no references to politics, political parties, current leaders or their policies.

I'll accept the game through a four-stage review. A technical committee will review its ability to run on three major websites and be easily fixed or modified. A committee of faculty will review its content and make sure that it doesn't touch on modern political controversies. A committee of students who are skilled at the Africa game will test the program to see whether they can operate it without any new instructions.

Connecting the Kneebone to the Thighbone: Creating Instructions

Sometimes a statement of work is simply not enough. You can't just tell the crowd what you want. You have to tell it how to do it. You most commonly have to do this in microtasking, although you may find that occasionally you have to write instructions for macrotasking and other forms of crowdsourcing.

If you've ever had to assemble a piece of furniture or a complicated toy, you may know one of the basic problems of instructions: instructions that may be clear to the writer are not always clear to the person who's trying to follow them. In crowdsourcing, the final judge of an instruction is the crowd; if the crowd members don't know what the instruction means, then the instruction is simply no good.

To write a good instruction, you need to be careful, clear and organised. You also need feedback from other people. The following sections establish basic principles for creating clear, effective instructions.

Keep in mind that when you write instructions for microtaskers, you often need to add additional material to help them complete the task. Generally, best practice is to separate that material from the instructions. Keep the instructions succinct and clear. Put the additional material in a separate section.

Thinking about who does what to what

The best instructions contain these three elements:

- ✔ **Subject:** The person performing the task – the crowdworker
- ✔ **Action:** The action that the crowdworker is to perform
- ✔ **Object:** The thing or idea that the crowdworker is working on

Here are some examples:

> You should click on the URL and review the images on the page.
>
> You should paste your translation into the field at the bottom of the page.
>
> You should verify all the information in the grey box, including name, title, email address and phone number.

Addressing the subject

When you write instructions, you address the crowdworkers and show them how to do the job. You have two choices:

- ✔ **Personal address:** You write 'You should do this' or 'You will do that' or 'You should be moving'.
- ✔ **Impersonal address:** You substitute 'the worker' or its synonyms as the subject: 'The worker should do this' or 'The crowdworker will do that' or 'The worker should be moving'.

Both forms of address have advantages and disadvantages. When you use personal address, you can make the instructions sound more individual, more connected to the worker. However, if you're not careful, you can sound as if you're bossing the crowd with harsh commands.

At the same time, when you use an impersonal form, you put a little distance between yourself and the crowd. You don't sound as if you're giving commands to the worker, but you may sound as if you're talking to someone else, someone who's not in the crowd.

Describing the action

Whenever possible, describe actions with positive words. Avoid negatives, which can be confusing and actually encourage workers to do the very things that you want them to shun. Rather than telling crowdworkers *not* to do something, tell them to do a positive action.

Identifying objects

Sometimes you can simply describe the object: 'the field in the middle of the screen', 'the image in the upper right hand corner', 'the data from the pop-up window'.

If something is complicated to describe, or if it's used many times by the worker, you may want to give it a special name. 'We will call the data in red font *the red data*'. Such names can greatly simplify the descriptions. For example, you may write:

> On your screen, you will see one image on the left, which we will call the target image, and four images on the right, which we will call the sample images. The sample images are numbered from one to four.

> Compare the target image with the four sample images. If the target image matches any one of the sample images, then put the number of that sample image in the box at the bottom of the screen. If the sample image matches none of the sample images, put the number 0 in the box at the bottom.

Notice that the following description is a much simpler one that doesn't give a name to the target image:

> Compare the image on the left of the screen to the images on the right of the screen. If the image on the left matches any of the images on the right, then write the number of the image on the right in the little box below the image on the left.

These two descriptions illustrate the advantages and disadvantages of identifying objects with special names. If you give objects special names, you can clearly identify the objects that the crowd has to manipulate. However, you may also produce instructions that are much longer. If you rely on general names to describe objects, you may be able to produce shorter descriptions, but these descriptions may not be as clear.

Don't get too carried away coming up with special names. You can quickly make a description confusing by giving each object a shorthand name. If you give too many things names, the worker has to take the time and effort to learn all the names.

Deciding the order of instructions

Usually, you write instructions in order: one, two, three. First you do this. Then you do that. Finally, you do the last thing. If any hard-and-fast rule exists for instructions, it's this: keep your instructions in order.

For microtasking, you want to follow this rule to the letter. The simplest instructions are those that follow a rigid temporal order.

Getting Feedback on Your Guidance

When you're preparing a statement of work and/or a list of instructions, give it to friends or colleagues and ask them to try to understand the job or follow the instructions. If they're having trouble with them, the crowd isn't likely to do any better.

Feedback from the crowd is also essential. Having its feedback early can save you trouble later. If the crowd reviews the instructions, you're less likely to discover that it can't understand the task.

Put the statement of work and/or instructions on a crowdsourcing website. Do a small test run. Ask five or six members of the crowd to do the work and then give you a review of the instructions. Their feedback can help you refine your instructions.

Be open to messages from the crowd about the project, too. Working with the crowd involves a dialogue. You offer a statement. You give the crowd a set of instructions. It responds to you. You listen.

You may, however, discover that the crowd doesn't always communicate with words. You've written a statement of work and posted instructions on the crowdsourcing site and you're waiting for an email message from the crowd or a post on your crowdsourcing blog to tell you that the instructions are good or that they're bad. However, the crowd may not be talking to you through email or through a blog. It may be trying to communicate with you through the market.

The crowd sends two messages through the market. It tells you that it likes your jobs or that it doesn't like your jobs. It can like your job because it has a big payment or because the job is easy to do. It can dislike your job because it offers only a low payment, because the job is hard or because understanding what you want is difficult.

For microtasking, the market often provides the only information about how the crowd is thinking and how it's engaging with your tasks.

If your job isn't attracting much attention from the crowd, you may be getting a message from the crowdworkers about your statement of work or instructions. The crowd may be telling you that your statement of work is too complicated or your instructions are too hard to follow.

When the crowd doesn't take your tasks, especially your microtasks, first review your statement of work and instructions. If they're complicated or confusing, revise them. If the crowd still doesn't take your tasks after you've revised the statement of work and instructions, consider adjusting the wage that you're offering.

Chapter 12

Crowdsourcing with Social Media

In This Chapter

▶ Seeing what social media can do for your crowdsourcing

▶ Gathering a private crowd

▶ Reaching the crowd with simple social media strategies

▶ Using a crowdsourcing tool to extend your reach

*I*f you're familiar with social media – websites that you can use to organise your social interaction – and make use of it in your business, you may wonder whether you can use it for crowdsourcing. The good news is that using social media is closely connected to crowdsourcing, and social media platforms can be useful for supporting crowdsourcing. Twitter, LinkedIn, Facebook, Flickr, YouTube, Pinterest, and even the WordPress blog on your website – you can use them all to recruit crowds, to engage crowds and to promote the work of crowdsourcing. In some cases, you can even conduct elementary crowdsourcing with nothing more than ordinary social media platforms.

In this chapter, I show you the principles for using social media to conduct your crowdsourcing projects. Because some of the more established forms of social media such as Facebook, Twitter and blogs are so well known, I focus on these, but you can use the same techniques on other platforms too.

Knowing the Benefits and the Limitations of Social Media Crowdsourcing

You can find several benefits of crowdsourcing with social media platforms:

✔ You may be more familiar with social media than with any specialised crowdsourcing platforms. Because you aren't learning to work with a new platform, you can concentrate on the steps of crowdsourcing and doing them properly.

✔ Social media often gives you access to large crowds of people who have a connection to you. Such crowds may be especially useful in crowd-funding.

✔ Social media platforms are far better known than most of the crowd-sourcing platforms and can be a natural place to promote your work.

However, social media is designed for certain kinds of social activity and not for crowdsourcing, so crowdsourcing on social media also has its downsides:

✔ Even with the most sophisticated *plugins* (that is, additional software that you can *plug into* an application to customise what it can do), social media can usually handle only the most simple forms of crowdsourc-ing: a simple crowdcontest or elementary macrotasking. Social media doesn't easily lend itself to microtasking or complicated forms of work-flow (see Chapter 16).

✔ Social media doesn't handle your relations with the workers like a crowdsourcing platform does. Instead of a crowdsourcing platform han-dling these responsibilities for you, with social media you are respon-sible for payments and tax paperwork.

✔ Social media provides you only with connections to your friends, but not to the right crowd. While you may live in a world with only six degrees of separation and can find any individual by chasing connections of con-nections, you may easily have to wade through a lot of friends of friends to find the specific skills that you need.

Don't try to crowdsource via social media simply because you already under-stand this medium and conclude that it may be easier to make crowdsourcing work on Twitter or Facebook than to learn how to use a crowdsourcing tool. This conclusion is a classic technological mistake, and many an individual has found out that using the wrong tool to do a job can be costly – a cost that you pay more in time and effort than in money. You start with a social plat-form because you know it and then discover that you have to learn a crowd-sourcing plugin. You learn the crowdsourcing plugin and then discover that you don't have the right crowd. However, since you invested in learning the plugin, you start to recruit your own crowd. This chain can continue for every step of the work. Each time, you decide that you've invested too much to stop, but you still have to do one more piece of hard work: complete the tax paperwork, check answers by hand or guide the work through each step of the process.

When you choose your tool at the outset, check that it's sufficient for your job. While you may be able to open a bottle of beer with a pair of pliers or drive a nail with a crescent wrench, you also know that you can find better tools for both of these jobs. Use the right tools for the right job.

Building a Private Crowd with Social Media

Social media isn't just a means for staying in touch with friends; it can be a crowd-management tool that enables people to manage their contact with other people. Of course, people have been able to manage human contact for generations with technologies no more sophisticated than a sheet of paper and a pen filled with blue-black ink. However, social media brings to this activity all the power of automation and enables you to:

✔ Engage a large group of people

✔ Engage people more quickly and at a greater distance

✔ Reduce the cost of sharing certain kinds of information such as photographs, documents and personal news

In all, these qualities of social media make it a good tool for managing a crowd. Social media is especially good for managing a *private crowd*, one that's united by a common interest, common value, common skill or common employment.

Private crowds are very important in crowdsourcing. They enable you to achieve some of the benefits of crowdsourcing without all of the drawbacks. Private crowds are most commonly found within companies, where employers use the employees as the crowd. When you crowdsource with company employees, you can be more confident that the information you give the crowd won't go to people who might use it against you.

Private crowds can give you:

✔ A group of people that you can trust, because they share common ideas, goals, backgrounds or employers

✔ Workers who understand the kinds of work that you're doing, because they're already involved with it

✔ Workers with a known background or skills that have already been checked by other people

Of course, private crowds have some drawbacks as well:

✔ A private crowd may not have people with the skills you need. You may need to look outside your organisation for these skills.

✔ A private crowd may not be big enough. When you put a question to it, you may not have enough people to answer it.

✔ A private crowd may not be able to give you a new point of view, because the crowd is familiar only with the ideas and concepts that you already know.

Building a private crowd with social media is much like trying to expand your personal circle of friends. You need to put effort into the work, and you soon discover that a few basic activities help you form relationships. Here are a few pointers to help you create and maintain a helpful and positive private crowd:

- ✔ **Create a clear statement of the purpose and values of the crowd.** This activity is much like the first step you take to build any kind of organisation. You want a web page or other presence on the Internet that explains what your crowd is, what it does, and the benefits of being part of it.

  People want to know the value that they'll obtain by being part of this work, so shout about the benefits of belonging to the crowd. You can describe the work all you want, but if you can't communicate the value, you're only going to drum up a few members.

- ✔ **Recruit a group of friends, employees or another social group to start with.** Building a group is easier when you already have a few members.

- ✔ **Ask the crowd members to invite their friends to join the crowd.** People always find it easier to join when they've been invited personally.

- ✔ **Have a means for chasing connections.** When someone joins your crowd, ask for a list of his friends and then invite the ones that seem appropriate to join your crowd. If you do this, however, be mindful of the spam problem. People receive a lot of unwanted email. Ask them to join your crowd only if you think they can help you.

- ✔ **Communicate with the crowd.** Make sure that the crowd members feel they're part of a living and productive organisation. Give them updates about the progress of the work. Let them know that their contribution is valued.

- ✔ **Give crowd members something to do.** Crowds need to be active. If crowd members aren't working, they can slowly drift apart and stop being a crowd. If the crowdsourcing site has no work, the crowd members have no reason to check that site regularly. If they stop checking the site, they will do other things with their time. Some crowdsourcers have found that they can keep a private crowd engaged with various puzzles, challenges and contests, although that strategy may not be the best. If people expect to work but have no jobs, they tend to become annoyed and leave.

- ✔ **Let crowd members talk to each other.** If your crowd doesn't talk in your presence, it's certainly talking in your absence! Let your crowd members share experiences, gossip, and talk over social media. You may start to understand how they think and have a few ideas that improve your crowdsourcing.

- ✔ **Let the crowd see what it's done.** Use social media to show the results of the crowdsourcing project so that all may see it, including the crowd itself.

Doing Simple Crowdsourcing with Social Media

If you know how to use some form of social media, and you think that you want to use that social media for crowdsourcing, ask yourself two questions:

- ✔ Will I be doing this job a second time?
- ✔ Does this job involve payments to more than one member of the crowd?

If the answer to either of these questions is 'yes', you probably want to use one of the crowdsourcing tools that works with social media. In that case, jump to the next section, 'Turning the Process Upside Down: Using a Crowdsourcing Tool', which deals with such tools.

However, if you have a simple task to do and you know how to use social media platforms, then feel free to use these platforms to crowdsource.

All social media platforms have policies about the use of their sites. Before you attempt any form of crowdsourcing on social media, review the site's policies on crowdsourcing and make sure that your task conforms to these policies.

Crowdfunding: Fundraising with Facebook

Facebook (www.facebook.com) has become a common site for fundraising. Most organisations that try to raise money through Facebook use a fundraising app such as FundRazr (see the later section 'Crowdfunding: Fundraising with FundRazr'), or have a customised site that makes it easy to contribute funds. However, you can do elementary crowdfunding on Facebook with nothing more than a simple page that describes your needs.

Create a page on Facebook that explains why you need funds and how much you're looking to raise. Emphasise the benefits of donating these funds. As with all crowdfunding, you need to emphasise the benefits to both the donor and to the cause. (See Chapter 6 more for more ideas about crowdfunding.)

When creating the Facebook page, add a photo or a graphic that illustrates the need for funds. If you're doing a fundraiser for medical funds, you might include a picture of a person who'd benefit from the money. If you're raising money for an artistic endeavour, perhaps you can have a sketch of the proposed work or an example of prior work.

Make sure that you clearly indicate on the page how people can give money. You may direct people to an organisation's home page if it has a donation link, or to a PayPal account. You may even suggest that people send a cheque to an address.

You need to help potential donors determine that your campaign is legitimate. If you're raising money within a small circle of friends, you can probably achieve this aim by letting people contact you if they have any questions. If you're working with a larger crowd, direct the crowd to a well-known website or use an accredited fundraising tool (see the later section 'Crowdfunding: Going fundraising').

After you establish your campaign, you need to engage your crowd. Here are some pointers:

✔ Start this process by sending messages to your friends and encourage them to donate.

✔ Ask the growing crowd to spread the word on Facebook; the members can 'share' details of your campaign to their news feed. The more that you can build on the network of the crowd, the more likely your campaign is to be successful.

✔ Make a donation yourself – actions speak louder than words.

✔ Use the Wall on your Facebook page to give reports on the progress of the campaign and talk about the recipients of the funds.

✔ When you receive a donation, send a receipt and thank-you note.

When you design your fundraising campaign, review not only the policies of Facebook but also legislation in your country. In some areas, you have responsibilities that go beyond those that Facebook requires. For example, you may be required to keep a list of all donations and to be able to prove that the funds were actually used for the purposes stated.

For more on crowdfunding, head to Chapter 6.

Macrotasking: Looking for freelancers with LinkedIn

LinkedIn (`www.linkedin.com`) presents itself as a tool for managing business connections. It has a search tool that enables you to find people with specific skills among both your direct connections and your extended network – your colleagues, the colleagues of your colleagues, the colleagues of the colleagues of your colleagues, and so on. Many people use this search tool to help them recruit new employees. With this facility, LinkedIn can be a platform for macrotasking. Macrotasking (see Chapter 7) is a form of contract employment, and hence it fits easily into the LinkedIn framework. LinkedIn enables you to post contract jobs on its site and then recruit applicants from people who have entries within the LinkedIn database.

LinkedIn has a standard form for posting a job on its site. In this form, you have to describe the job. As with all forms of macrotasking, the better you are able to state the requirements of the job, the more likely you are to find a contractor who can do your job. You also have to determine whether you'll paying the contractor by the hour or by the job, and clearly state the kind of skills you're seeking.

Unlike most macrotasking sites, LinkedIn charges you a fee to post a job. This fee may make LinkedIn less attractive than commercial macrotasking sites which don't require a fee to post a job. However, on the plus side, you find people on LinkedIn with a much broader set of skills than those generally found on macrotasking sites.

After you post your job, you can use LinkedIn to talk to the crowd. LinkedIn publicises the job to its members. You can send notices of your job to people that you know. You can also communicate with the crowd in ways that you can't on a traditional macrotasking site. If you've a higher grade of membership in LinkedIn, you can send messages to connections. If you don't, you can offer a referral bonus to anyone who can connect you with the right contractor. Recent research has shown that referral bonuses or similar kinds of payments can help a crowd solve a problem, even if your problem is that you need help to find the right contractor.

Crowdcontests: Turning to Twitter

Crowdcontests, in which people compete for a prize (see Chapter 5), are a simple form of crowdsourcing that you can conduct on any form of social media. Certain forms of such contests work nicely with Twitter (http://twitter.com), which gives you the ability to reach a large community but restricts your communications to 140 characters or fewer.

Twitter is especially useful for the most elementary form of the crowdcontest, the form that's really an extension of an Internet search. In this form of crowdcontest, you're looking for some key piece of information. You've looked at all the major search engines and found nothing useful. You've looked at some of the big information databases and hit a brick wall. Twitter allows you to put a question to a large crowd.

Belinda is looking for the Chinese restaurant where she celebrated after her wedding 20 years ago. She's forgotten the name, although she vaguely recalls that it was something popular such as the 'Golden Dragon'. Even the neighbourhood is now somewhat vague. All she has is a picture of the wedding party with the restaurant owner, somewhat dark and dingy. Belinda runs a contest on Twitter to find an answer to her question. She tweets '£3 reward for name and address of Chinese restaurant near Norwich in 1992' and includes a link to the photo. An hour later, Belinda's got a name, an address and a table booking to celebrate her 20th wedding anniversary with her husband at, you guessed it, the Golden Dragon.

Twitter is commonly used for marketing contests, which are similar to crowd-contests. Firms use Twitter for sweepstakes, to obtain creative photographs or to elicit unusual suggestions from customers on how to use the firm's products. Because of these regular contests, Twitter has a well-developed set of policies on contests that you should review before you start your own contest.

If you're running a contest that's more complicated than simply finding a piece of data, you may need to develop your own web page to support the contest. If you're running many simple contests, you may find that a basic web page combined with Twitter adequately supports all your work.

Microtasking: Translating via a blog

Microtasking is one of the complicated forms of crowdsourcing, because it requires you to divide a large job into small tasks, distribute those tasks to the crowd and then assemble the results of that work into a unified whole. (For details of microtasking, take a look at Chapter 8.) You need specialised tools for many microtasking jobs, but you can handle basic microtasks with tools as simple as a blog or a spreadsheet. You can use these tools to do a simple crowd data collection or a crowd translation.

Aarav has a short article that he wants translated from English into Kannada. Aarav runs each paragraph through a translation program to obtain a starting translation. Then he creates a spreadsheet – in one column is the English original, and in the next is the program's translation – and publishes the spreadsheet on his blog. He provides instructions for the microtaskers on his blog: they claim a paragraph by putting their name and the date next to it; they email the translated paragraph back to him with the paragraph number in the subject line; and so on. Aarav then advertises the microtask to his crowd. If he has enough readers of his blog, he may have to do no additional advertising. If he needs to reach more people, he can tweet, post a notice on Facebook or do any of the usual things to draw attention to the work.

Aarav gets a good response, and soon all the paragraphs are out being translated. He hires someone to assemble the paragraphs into a complete text and someone else to read and verify the final translation. Job done.

Turning the Process Upside Down: Using a Crowdsourcing Tool

Social media is a great tool for communicating with crowds. You can publicise your job, give instructions, listen to ideas and promote accomplishments. If you restrict yourself to social media, you can do the simplest crowdsourcing jobs and, in the process, you may be able to teach yourself all the details of crowdsourcing. However, you will likely be able to accomplish more if you start with a crowdsourcing platform and learn how to use it.

A number of vendors have created crowdsourcing tools that work with social media, and I explore the main ones in this section. These tools are plugins, links or other forms of software that give you an environment within the social media platform that's similar to that of a full-service crowdsourcing platform.

Usually, the social media platform (such as Facebook or YouTube) has a link to one or more of these crowdsourcing tools, and you use these crowdsourcing tools on a website. To be able to use the tools, you first need to design your crowdsourcing job and then go to the site which hosts the crowdsourcing tool. Here, you enter the details of your job – the description, instructions, reward and so on. When you've done that, the crowdsourcing tool heads back to the social media site and uses the details you entered to recruit the crowd. The tool will contact your friends, the friends of your friends, and other people to build a crowd.

Many crowdsourcing tools work with different forms of social media. The tools work with Facebook, so you can, if you want, restrict yourself to Facebook. If you want to raise your crowd through Twitter, that's fine; the tools work with Twitter. Some even enable you to connect to the address book of your email account and use the names in it to raise a crowd.

Crowdfunding: Going fundraising

Fundraising is easier within Facebook or other forms of social media if you use a system that handles the detailed work, including the collection of funds, correspondence with the crowd, issuing receipts, and creating letters of appreciation. An example of such a system is FundRazr (`http://fundrazr.com`). It lets you work within the Facebook environment, but makes it easy to plan and manage a crowdfunding campaign.

When you use a system such as FundRazr, you can see how crowdfunding and crowdsourcing can be divided across many systems. FundRazr uses Facebook to communicate with the crowd. It also uses the online payment site PayPal (`www.paypal.com`) to handle payments, transfers of funds and accounting. You then manage the campaign through FundRazr. You log on to FundRazr and define the campaign and add your Facebook and PayPal accounts. FundRazr then handles the necessary correspondence with those accounts.

FundRazr can manage a crowdfunding campaign for an individual or a non-profit organisation. The screen for the personal campaign allows you to define the basic elements of the campaign: a short title, a statement of the reason for the campaign, and the financial goal of the campaign. (At the time of writing, FundRazr uses the incremental fundraising model only. The goal is merely a target. The cause receives any amount collected by the site, even if the total falls far short of the goal. FundRazr doesn't currently offer an all-or-nothing model.)

After you create your campaign, you can then promote it to the crowd through Facebook. FundRazr gives you the tools for promoting the campaign in a variety of ways, such as through your own Wall, the Walls of pages that you control, and even FundRazr's own crowdfunding page. You can also take direct control of the correspondence and promote the campaign to anyone you choose.

Facebook, FundRazr and PayPal all have policies for crowdfunding campaigns. Review these policies before you start your campaign. At the moment, FundRazr doesn't handle equity crowdfunding. (For details of equity crowdfunding, visit Chapter 6.)

Crowdcontests: Modifying marketing methods

Many of the crowdcontest applications that have been developed for Facebook and other forms of social media are designed to help solve marketing problems. Companies run contests in order to bring attention to their products and services rather than do useful work. A company may ask for pictures of the different ways that customers use one of its products. It asks people to vote on these pictures and then rewards the picture that receives the most votes.

You can't use commercial crowdcontest systems for all forms of crowdcontest, but they do work for certain kinds of contests. For example, you can easily use commercial crowdcontest applications for a crowdcontest that creates a logo or similar design to represent your company. If you run such a contest within Facebook, you may not contact the range and quality of designers that you can find at a site dedicated to design contests. Still, you may want the kind of designer that you believe you can find only on Facebook.

Top Tab (`http://toptabapp.com`) is an example of a crowdcontest system that works within Facebook. You can best understand it as a system that handles communication within Facebook. You define your contest on your own web page and then give Top Tab a link to that contest page. You describe the contest for the Top Tab system and provide a picture to help promote the contest. Top Tab then makes your contest available within Facebook.

Like most forms of crowdsourcing within social media, Top Tab makes you responsible for driving the crowd to the competition. You may find that this approach to crowdsourcing is appropriate for your work. You may want to run a crowdcontest within your circle of friends or within your company. In such a case, social media such as Facebook makes it easy for you to reach your intended audience.

Microtasking and crowdsurveys: Asking for Opinions on Facebook

Many organisations find the greatest value in crowdsourcing to be the ideas that the crowd can provide about products and marketing. They view crowdsourcing as a way of extracting information from the crowd, and they deploy surveys and polls to the crowd in order to collect this information.

Crowdsurveys, like crowdfunding, have become a specialised division of crowdsourcing, even though they're a form of microtasking. You ask for each member of the crowd to give you a little bit of information, and then you combine those bits of information into a large picture about the state of the market.

When you run a crowdsurvey within social media, you attempt to find out the ideas of a group of people who are directly connected to you or are part of your greater social network. Within Facebook, you can conduct such polling in a simple manner by posting a question on your Wall and asking people to respond to you. 'How should I approach this problem?' you may ask, and then you give the crowd three possible responses. You then collect the responses and summarise them.

Of course, you may find it easier to run a crowdsurvey if you've an app or system that manages a poll within Facebook. One such application is Polldaddy (`http://polldaddy.com`), a crowdsourcing application that uses Facebook, blogs and other forms of social media to recruit crowds.

After you create an account with Polldaddy, you can define sophisticated questionnaires. You can ask most kinds of questions: yes/no, multiple choice, and Likert scale responses (questions that ask the subject to answer on a scale of 1–5, where 1 represents a good feeling, 5 stands for a bad feeling, and 3 stands for a response that's neither good nor bad but is firmly neutral).

With the poll created, you can use Polldaddy to post it to your Wall within Facebook, to other pages that you control, or even to a Polldaddy page. Then you have the responsibility for encouraging the crowd to come to your poll. You post messages. You ask your friends to send their friends. You invite everyone that you want to come to the poll.

A crowdsourced survey or poll isn't the same thing as a carefully designed market survey. A market survey is designed to capture the ideas of your current market or your potential market. A crowdsourced survey always draws upon the population of people who are active online and who are interested in you or your organisation. This group may be rather different to any other market that you care to engage.

Microtasking: Reading the tweet leaves

You can find out a great deal from social media, including from messages that weren't intended for you. You can find out what the crowd is saying about a topic, how it feels about it or what it would like to do about it. You can look at a collection of texts, Wall postings, tweets or even conventional emails and judge what each message is saying. This kind of work is called *sentiment analysis*.

Google (`www.google.com`), for example, uses the techniques of sentiment analysis to track the incidence of influenza. Instead of looking at tweets or messages, it looks at the terms that people enter into its search engine. While Google may not be a form of social media, the search terms are communications from the crowd. In this case, the crowd is everyone who uses the Google search engine. The messages that we send to Google are the things that interest us. From those messages, Google tries to estimate how many people are ill with the flu.

The way that Google estimates the number of people with the flu is by counting the number of times that people enter the term 'flu' in their search engine. People tend to search for information about an illness when they (or someone they know) are sick, or when they're afraid of becoming sick. Hence the number of searches for the word 'flu' should closely follow the incidence rate of the disease (see www.google.org/flutrends/us/#US).

Sentiment analysis works in a manner that's similar to the Google flu project but looks at more complicated messages and tries to extract more sophisticated ideas.

As an example, suppose you attend a concert in a huge arena. Fifty thousand people are in the audience and hundreds of them are tweeting about the event minute by minute. They tweet about the music, the singers, their friends, the smoke in the building and the beer that someone's accidentally poured on their shirt. Sentiment analysis would aim to combine all the information in the tweets and determine whether the concert is any good, and whether the audience is happy or is about to riot and storm the stage.

If you change this situation slightly to imagine all the people gathered at a political rally in a large city-centre square, you can determine whether the situation is about to turn violent.

Sentiment analysis analyses large collections of information and tries to determine the feelings – the sentiment – of the writers. You collect a group of tweets with hash tags that indicate the tweets are coming from a common event, and then you try to determine the emotions or the sentiment of the writers. Unlike the Google flu example, for sentiment analysis you can't simply write a program to search for a single word. Instead, you need people to examine each message and try to identify what emotion the writer's communicating. If you have a lot of messages, you can't just use a few people – you have to use the crowd.

Sentiment analysis, which is also called *message catagorisation*, is a common crowdsourced task. You can easily do it on Amazon's Mechanical Turk (www.mturk.com) website.

If you perform sentiment analysis on a group of tweets in Mechanical Turk, you put all your tweets in the first column of a spreadsheet and send that sheet to Mechanical Turk. You then devise a simple check box that asks the question 'Do you think this tweet is happy, sad, angry, confused or something else?' You release your tasks and receive back a spreadsheet that contains the information about how the crowd views those tweets. You can then analyse that information to understand the collective sentiment of those tweets. (See Chapter 8 for more information about working with Mechanical Turk.)

Several other firms offer crowdsourced sentiment analysis, such as CrowdFlower's Senti service (http://crowdflower.com). Senti engages a crowd to categorise each message. The crowd determines whether each message relates to a certain question, ranks its relevance, and answers any questions that you pose. Figure 12-1 shows a summary of a Senti review of 5,000 tweets that mention a store identified as 'Brand X'.

The crowdsourced analysis suggests that only about 40 per cent of the tweets are relevant to Brand X – only 1,998 out of 5,000. As a whole, these tweets suggest that their authors have a fairly neutral view of the product. Only a few have a particularly positive or negative feeling about it.

Figure 12-1: Crowd-sourced review of tweets.

Recognising the Difference between Social Media and Social Research

Crowdsourcing is closely related to social research fields such as market research or public opinion polling. In these fields, you try to obtain information from a group of people (the population sample) and turn that information into useful ideas.

If you're working with a population sample, you believe that your it represents a larger group of individuals such as car owners, mobile phone users or voters in the UK. You hope that you can make conclusions about the larger group of people that your sample represents. In both market research and opinion polling, you go to great efforts to make sure that your sample is a representative sample.

In crowdsourcing, the crowd is the crowd. It doesn't represent anybody but itself. If you try to draw conclusions from the crowd about people who aren't in that crowd, you may easily be wrong. You may believe that the crowd represents a bigger population, but that belief doesn't help you unless you can find a way of showing that the belief is true.

However, you often don't care whether the crowd represents public opinion. You're looking for good ideas and you believe that the crowd can give them to you.

Crowdsourcing is closest to market research when you work with a crowd of people who you hope you can turn into customers. You often try to do this when you crowdsource via social media.

'Contacts into friends and friends into customers' is a common phrase that marketing professionals use to describe their work on the web. If you're attempting to engage a crowd and encourage the people to use your products or services, then you may benefit substantially by using a crowdsurvey within social media, even if your crowd doesn't represent any larger market.

Chapter 13

Picking Your Platform

· ·

In This Chapter

▶ Knowing how a platform helps you

▶ Seeing which platform works for your project

▶ Considering a platform's crowds, support and policies

▶ Looking at different platforms' offerings

· ·

You think that you're ready to start crowdsourcing. You have an idea and a plan. For your next step, you need to choose a platform. The *platform* is a website, a crowdmarket and an organisation of people who can help you to crowdsource. When you use a crowdsourcing platform, you're not alone. You have a group of people who understand crowdsourcing and who are ready and waiting to help you.

A crowdsourcing platform isn't absolutely essential in order to crowdsource. Chapter 12 shows how you can crowdsource with social media, and you can crowdsource from a private web page if you like. If you have a desire to do things from first principles, you can even crowdsource from a busy street corner with nothing more than a clipboard and a booming voice. In some cases, crowdsourcing without using a formal crowdsourcing platform makes sense. You can search for macrotaskers on craigslist, for example, or publicise a fundraising campaign on Facebook.

In many cases, however, the assistance and support that a formal crowdsourcing platform can give you is invaluable. Crowdsourcing can involve a lot of details. You have to make a formal agreement with a macrotasker or qualify all the microtaskers, and you have to file tax information for your fundraising. You can easily forget some of these details or simply make a mistake. Crowdfunding platforms help you handle all those details and make sure that you're crowdsourcing well.

By any reasonable count, the number of crowdsourcing platforms is in the thousands and is growing rapidly. Crowdsourcing platforms aren't interchangeable. Each does a better job supporting certain kinds of work, and a poorer job of handling others. Just as you can't do all your home repairs with a screwdriver, so you can't do every kind of crowdsourcing on a single platform. So, in this chapter I give plenty of guidance on how to choose a platform, covering all the areas you need to consider.

Getting the Benefits of a Platform

When you use a crowdsourcing platform, you're not merely buying access to a crowdmarket or engaging an intermediary between you and the crowd. You're gaining the benefits of expertise, an expertise that will simplify your crowdsourcing.

Crowdsourcing platforms generally give you five benefits:

- ✔ Means to raise a crowd
- ✔ Access to crowdsourcing expertise
- ✔ Ability to use standard forms of crowdsourcing
- ✔ Help with bookkeeping
- ✔ Reduced risk of failure

Of course, crowdsourcing platforms aren't universal solutions to all problems, and they have their drawbacks:

- ✔ They can lock you into a fixed form of crowdsourcing. You start the job thinking you're doing one form of crowdsourcing, and realise that you should've done it another way.
- ✔ They may direct you towards a crowd that doesn't have the expertise you need.
- ✔ They may not be able to handle all the labour issues that are present in your country or jurisdiction.
- ✔ They add an additional expense to crowdsourcing.

 Some people resist using a crowdsourcing platform, because of the additional cost. In many, many cases, such crowdsourcers are being penny-wise and pound-foolish. The costs of a crowdsourcing platform are usually small compared with the benefits. Just as few individuals would create their own word-processing program in order to write a book, so very few people should crowdsource without the support of a strong crowdsourcing platform.

Raising the crowd

Without a platform, the hardest part of crowdsourcing is raising the right crowd. You turn to crowdsourcing because you need some additional skill and you usually don't have an easy way to get that skill. If you're in an organisation, you have no one in your group who possesses that skill. If you're an individual, you have no idea where you might find someone who has the skills you need.

Crowdsourcing platforms, though, come with crowds. Since crowdsourcing platforms handle the work of many crowdsourcers, they have many jobs to offer. Hence they offer steady work for the crowd and attract a group of workers who like the jobs on the platform. So when you choose a crowdsourcing platform, you're also choosing a ready-made crowd.

Of course, the crowd at the crowdsourcing platform may not be sufficient for your work. You may have to supplement the crowd with people you recruit through social media (see Chapter 12), your employees or your friends. Most commonly, supplementing the crowd of the crowdsourcing platform is done in crowdfunding, where you almost always know people who can contribute to your cause or encourage others to contribute. You'll want to bring these people to your crowd. (See Chapter 6 for more on crowdfunding.) Even in situations where you do have to supplement the crowd, the crowdsourcing platform still gives you a crowd with which to start your project. After all, it's better to start with some kind of a crowd than with no crowd at all.

Knowing what other people know

Experience brings skill. Crowdsourcing may be easy to do, but each crowdsourcer – especially a newbie – has lessons to learn. When you work with a crowdsourcing platform, you generally have access to people who've done crowdsourcing before and can help you avoid basic mistakes.

First, most platforms have staff that help you prepare your job and post it on the platform. You usually reach the staff through a customer relations button on the platform. Sometimes, the staff contact you as soon as you create an account. On crowdfunding platforms, the staff show you how to present your project in the best possible light. On macrotasking platforms, they show you how to organise your job, how to assign a price to the work and how to choose a well-qualified worker.

Often, you can contact other crowdsourcers who've used the site and want to share their experience. Sometimes, you talk with these crowdsourcers through forums or blogs supported by the crowdsourcing platform. In many cases, you can read case studies by these crowdsourcers and contact the crowdsourcers directly. In some cases, you can contact crowdworkers through forms or blogs. The crowdworkers can tell which jobs are good and which aren't, which ideas work and which don't.

Using standardised crowdsourced services

Sometimes you want to do the kinds of things that crowdsourcing can do, but you don't want to crowdsource. Perhaps you want someone to clean your data or tag photographs, transcribe records or test a mobile app, but you certainly don't want to design a task, write a description of the work, find a platform or raise a crowd. What you want, then, is a *standardised crowd-sourced service*, which does those things for you, rather than a crowdsourcing platform, where you do them yourself.

Many companies offer standardised crowdsourced services, although they may not explicitly advertise them as being crowdsourcing. Whereas in the past, people searched for standardised crowdsourced services by conducting an Internet search for 'crowdsourcing', you now search for the specific service you require. Indeed, you may never be told that the service is actually a form of crowdsourcing.

Here are some examples of standardised services. (Most standardised crowdsourcing services are applications of microtasking (see Chapter 8), although a few are forms of macrotasking (see Chapter 7).)

- ✔ Microtasking-based:

  - Transcription services, including the transcription of medical records

  - Sales contact generation and similar activities

  - Translation services

  - Search engine optimisation of websites

  - Tagging and photographic description

- ✔ Macrotasking-based:

  - All kinds of general office work

  - Website development

  - Mobile app development

  - Software testing

If you're especially interested in trying crowdsourced-based versions of these services, you can find a list of them in the Crowd Labor section of the directory at crowdsourcing.org (`www.crowdsourcing.org/directory`).

If you're doing a crowdsourcing task that fits neatly into one of these standard services, using one of the standardised crowdsourcing platforms is easier than doing the job of crowdsourcing yourself. And, importantly, you're more likely to succeed if you fit your work into a standardised form of crowdsourcing than if you try to develop an entirely new form. When you use a standardised form of crowdsourcing, you know that it's been tested and that the crowd generally already understands how the process works.

Using a standardised crowdsourcing service usually leaves you with little to do. You give your job description and details of any data you need to the appropriate crowdsourcing platform. The platform then takes your job, makes any adjustments that are needed, gives the job to its crowd, and returns the results to you.

For example, say you have a large database that has duplicate records, missing information and, in some cases, contradictory information, and you need to have it cleaned. To do this job, you identify a crowdsourcing data cleaning service, give it the web address of your database and details of the work that you need done on the data. The service then prepares the crowdsourcing job and gives you a cleaned database.

Standardised crowdsourcing services tend to be a little more expensive than standard crowdsourcing platforms that require you to prepare the job and review the results. Still, they're usually much less expensive than the conventional ways of performing these services, ways that may involve big organisations and full-time employees. Many of the platforms that provide standardised services don't actually advertise that they undertake crowdsourcing jobs. They just emphasise the services that they provide and how the services are less expensive than other ways of doing the work.

You can find standard forms of any form of crowdsourcing. Standard ways have developed of doing microtasking, macrotasking, crowdfunding and crowdcontests. You even have standard ways of managing self-organised crowds for innovation. Before you start to plan a crowdsourcing job, do a little research to see whether an organisation offers a standardised service that can do the work that you need.

Getting a helping hand with bookkeeping

You can easily forget that crowdsourcing involves a substantial amount of bookkeeping. You can't merely raise a crowd, ask it to do a job, and then disperse the members at the end of the day with the promise of milk and biscuits. You need to track each individual member of the crowd, know how much work that individual did and pay her, after completing all the appropriate paperwork and taxes.

As a crowdsourcer, you must keep the same kind of records that any other business keeps. Even though you're using a new form of management, you're still responsible for keeping records of your labour expenses. If the Internal Revenue Service or Her Majesty's Revenue and Customs asks you to explain the amounts that you paid for crowdsourced work, you need to be able to produce enough evidence to show that you actually paid the crowd for its work. If you don't know what records you need to keep, talk with a business school or an organisation such as the Better Business Bureau (www.bbb.org). (You can also find out more about the requirements of payrolls in Chapter 14.)

The bookkeeping services of the crowdsourcing platforms may actually be the greatest benefit of using them. These services enable you to focus on the work that you need to do. You don't need to worry about the details of how to monitor the workers, keep records or file reports with tax agencies. You can concentrate on the details of the crowdsourcing job.

Cutting the risk factor

The first four benefits of crowdsourcing platforms add up to the final benefit of crowdsourcing platforms: they cut the risk of doing this kind of work.

Crowdsourcing isn't an especially risky activity. Certainly, you shouldn't feel that you're likely to bankrupt yourself, destroy your reputation or foment revolution merely because you crowdsource. However, you do take a little risk when you crowdsource. You take the risk that you prepare a crowdsourcing job and no crowd comes to do it. You take the risk that the crowdworkers might not do the job properly. You take the risk that you might lose the money you budgeted for the crowdsourcing job, and more. You take the risk that you might gain a reputation as a bad crowdsourcer and never recover from it.

By working with a crowdsourcing platform, you reduce the risk of failing. You work in an environment that's produced good crowdsourcing jobs in the past. You have a good crowd. You're able to rely on the expertise of others. You follow best practices. And you don't have to worry about many of the details of running a crowdsourcing job.

The more that you can reduce the risk of crowdsourcing, the more likely you are to be able to complete your crowdsourcing job and obtain a result you can use. Some crowdsourcing platforms are so confident in their own ability to do your job successfully that they offer a full refund if your job fails to produce a useful result. (You will, or course, want to check the conditions for this kind of refund.)

Finding the Right Crowd

When you've found a platform you like the look of, you need to review the crowd to see whether its members have the right skills and experience to be able to do your work.

Crowdsourcing attracts many kinds of workers. First, it attracts traditional workers who are trying to find a new market for their skill. Often, these workers are looking to earn some additional money, work non-standard hours, find new kinds of tasks or find more regular work by being part of a global market. Crowdsourcing also attracts workers who've gained their skills in non-traditional ways. They may not have formal training but they can do the work and find a market for their services with the crowd.

Crowdsourcing is concerned with accomplishment, not formal training. For all kinds of workers, those with traditional training and those who've learned on their own, their accomplishments are more important than their backgrounds. Accomplishments demonstrate what workers can actually do. Some platforms let you review the education and training of individual workers, but be sure to focus on accomplishments.

Reviewing products

Because crowdsourcing involves the work of the crowd, you usually find it best to start by reviewing accomplishments platform-wide rather than at the level of individual members. Most platforms display a gallery of recent projects that includes the original description of the project, the final work, and the cost of the project. In some cases, the platform also identifies the individual workers who contributed to the work.

Crowds are more important than individual workers. You may not be able to hire the workers who are promoted on the platform. However, if those workers are doing the kinds of work that you're seeking, you know that you're likely to find others like them in the crowd.

In reviewing products, pay careful attention to the prices of individual work projects. Crowds often divide, quite naturally, into two tiers:

- ✔ **Top tier:** Experienced workers who've demonstrated their skills. They do consistently good work and get top payments for their labour.

- ✔ **Bottom tier:** A much less consistent group of workers. Most have little experience and are trying to build a portfolio to show what they can do. Sometimes they do well. Sometimes they don't. They're generally paid less than the top-tier workers.

Make sure you price your job so that you get the kind of workers you want.

Checking out individual portfolios

In some kinds of crowdsourcing, notably macrotasking and certain crowd-contests, you can review the portfolios of individual workers. If you're negotiating with a worker to do a task for you, this review is especially valuable, because you know the capabilities of the worker. However, you don't always get to hire the worker you want, so look at portfolios as examples of the kinds of work that the crowd can do.

Most crowdsourcing platforms build the portfolios of clients and workers from their databases, hence the portfolios represent actual work by actual workers. However, you'd be naïve to assume that portfolio fraud never happens. If the work doesn't seem consistent, contact the platform and ask for clarification, or look to other crowds.

In microtasking, you rarely have the opportunity to review the skills of any individual worker. At best, you may be able to see the portfolio of a worker that the platform has identified as outstanding. You make most of your judgements about the skills of the crowd by reviewing the products that the crowd has produced or by seeing how other organisations use the platform.

Looking for the Right Support

Crowdsourcing may be one of the trends that encourages do-it-yourself projects, but it's still an activity that requires skill and discipline. You don't sign up to a crowdsourcing platform and buy crowdsourcing labour in the way that you go into a convenience store and purchase a snack. To get the best results, you have to know what you're doing, prepare your job, manage the work carefully, and review the results.

Many platforms provide an assistant to help with your project. For some platforms, these assistants are available to anyone who opens an account. On others, you have to pay an additional fee for this help. Generally, these assistants can help you with three activities:

✔ Designing and managing your project

✔ Mediating between you and the crowd over problems

✔ Helping with intellectual property issues

Guiding your project

If you're doing a crowdsourced project for the first time, you may receive a great deal of help from the assistants who work for the platform. Remember, each platform is a market with its own rules, procedures and quirks. You're not merely creating a job. You're placing that job on the market, managing it, and then trying to use the results in your own work or in your own organisation. The assistants can help you fit these tasks into the platform's frameworks.

 Listen to the advice of the assistants carefully and decide whether it's sound. The assistants often try to fit you and your job into an existing mould. They try to make your work look like tasks they've handled before. This situation can be good or bad. If your work actually fits into the old pattern, the advice is great. You know that your work is similar to a job that's been done successfully before. But if your job doesn't match the models and ideas of prior jobs, you may face trouble. Your job may be forced into a shape that it doesn't really fit. If this happens, you're likely to have problems as you try to complete the job.

Acting as mediator

Most platforms have individuals who mediate between you and the crowd over any problems that emerge. Crowdsourcing places work in the context of a market; problems are generally claims and counterclaims about payments. The workers claim that they did the job properly and weren't paid. As the crowdsourcer, you might claim that the work wasn't done properly and hence you're not prepared to pay the crowd. A mediator can help resolve the problem.

 If a platform offers no mediator for problems between the crowdsourcer and the crowd, think carefully before using it. In such situations, you're responsible for handling any disagreements that occur between you and the crowd.

In most cases, a disagreement between you and a crowdworker is likely to damage your reputation and produce a spate of bad publicity for you. Bad publicity can be quite damaging, and a crowdworker with a good social network can disrupt your ability to do many kinds of business. Furthermore, although in many crowdsourcing jobs the payments are too small to be accepted by most courts as a legitimate claim, some crowdsourcing jobs do involve substantial amounts of money and could be the basis for a court case. Indeed, some crowdworkers have filed court cases against companies when they thought they were underpaid.

The case of the misplaced decimal

The value of good mediation is seen in the case of a crowdsourcer who mistyped the payment on a microtasked job that was submitted to a crowdsourcing platform. The crowdsourcer intended to pay $0.10 (£0.063) for each microtask, but somehow submitted the figure $10 (£6.30). The error was substantial, because the project incorporated several thousand tasks. The crowd, always looking for profitable jobs, grabbed these tasks and completed them quickly.

The crowdsourcer then contacted a representative of the platform and asked for mediation with the crowd. The crowdsourcer was indeed liable for the mistake and hoped to reduce the cost of the mistake. The representative started a negotiation with the crowd. She explained the problem, admitted that the crowdsourcer was liable for the full cost of the tasks, and asked each worker to take a lower payment. Some demanded the full $10 per task, but most were willing to take a lower payment, which transformed the consequences of the mistake from a financial disaster to an expensive embarrassment.

If you're microtasking, you certainly want a platform with a mediator. If you get into trouble with a microtask crowd, you may find yourself handling hundreds or thousands of complaints. If the disagreement becomes serious enough, you may find yourself with a *class action suit* – a legal case that combines the interests of all the members of the crowd.

Protecting intellectual property

Make sure that the platform offers assistance with disputes over intellectual property. After disputes about payment, the second most common form of problem involves intellectual property. Often, these issues involve intellectual property that isn't used, such as material that was submitted to a crowdcontest but didn't win the prize, or the work of a macrotasker that was judged insufficient. In such cases, the crowdworkers may want to reuse such material in some form, but you might want to prevent such reuse because the material might identify your products or brands.

Good crowdsourcing platforms have detailed policies about intellectual property. However, you may need help understanding how such policies work and how they apply in cases of a disagreement. You may want help from a representative who can interpret the policies or serve as a mediator.

If you're concerned about disputed intellectual property, ask the representative how the platform's resolved disagreements in the past. The details of such cases may be confidential, but if not, such details can help you understand how to protect yourself.

If a crowdsourcing platform doesn't have a policy regarding intellectual property, you can use this platform with the risk that you and the crowd will get into an argument about who owns the rights for the final work product.

Deciding How Much You Want to Do

You need to consider how deeply you want to be involved in the details of crowdsourcing. You may want to roll up your sleeves and get stuck in with the process and use it to radically transform your work or your organisation. On the other hand, you might just want a simple service and not care whether that service is provided by a crowd, a permanent employee or a pack of well-trained seals.

What kind of technical sophistication are you willing to bring to the project? You have a choice between two types of platform:

✔ **The simple, does-it-for-you platform:** You need almost no technical skill for this type of platform. You give the platform the description of the job and the data. The platform returns the finished work.

Some crowdsourced platforms are little more than markets. They handle the details of each transaction with the worker but they do little to help you design your job and interact with your organisation. They require more effort on your part. At the same time, they're generally less expensive than platforms that provide full organised services.

✔ **The expect-you-to-be-a-techie platform:** These platforms, which are often those involved with microtasking, offer *application programming interfaces* (APIs). APIs enable you to use the crowdsourcing platform as part of your own work or even as part of that of a bigger organisation. With an API, you can write programs that guide jobs in and out of the crowd, a process known as *controlled workflow* (see Chapter 16).

Crowdsourcers use controlled workflow when they do photographic tagging, for example, creating tiny tasks that ask different members of the crowd to do different things. The workflow passes a picture to one member of the crowd and asks her to identify the location of the photograph. The photograph then goes to another member of the crowd to determine whether the picture includes any people. Finally it passes to a third worker with a request for more information.

You can also use APIs to bring the crowd into traditional organisations. You can, for example, create for a company a piece of software that helps guide work through the organisation. It can pass the work from employee to employee and then call on the crowd for certain tasks.

Crowdsourcing APIs are an advanced topic. You need considerable expertise in Internet programming to use them well. (You can get more information about APIs in Chapter 16.)

As you review different crowdsourcing platforms, you find that they offer a trade-off between effort and cost. They more you have to do, the lower your cost. You need to decide how much effort you want to give to designing and managing your crowdsourcing project and how much money you're willing to pay someone else to do that work for you.

If you're new to crowdsourcing, you probably want the platform that gives you the greatest amount of support. You might want to make use of a standard service or the expertise of its staff. If you already have some crowdsourcing experience under your belt, don't automatically assume that you need to move to a different platform. Many people keep working with the first platform they use, particularly if they've found a good and reliable crowd at that platform. Crowdsourcers tend to switch platforms when they seek a new crowd – a new group of people who'll do a better job with their work – or if they want to develop a new kind of crowdsourcing service.

At some point, you might decide that you want to reorganise your crowdsourcing job. Perhaps instead of following the steps available on your current platform, you want the workers to handle the steps of your job in a different order or you want to engage them in a way that your current platform doesn't allow. In such a case, you may be ready to move towards one of the platforms that encourages you to take charge of the job or even offers you an API so you can write a program to control the tasks.

Don't think you have to be loyal to a single platform. Not all platforms do all things equally well. You may have different kinds of projects that work on different platforms. So, you may want to choose one platform for certain tasks and other platforms for others. But the more platforms you use, the more procedures and policies you have to know, so use as few platforms as possible to meet your needs.

Reading the Fine Print

Before you give your credit card number to a platform and start your crowdsourced job, you need to carefully review the policies for the platform. They form part of your agreement with the platform. Most platforms allow you to read their policies when you visit the platform. Some require you to open an account before you can see all the policies. However, all platforms allow you to read their policies before you submit the job.

Understanding the cost

As you review the platforms, you need to know the full cost of your job, which includes the cost of labour, the fees charged by the platform, and charges for additional services such as helping to set up the job or getting a more prominent placement for your job on the platform.

All crowdsourcing platforms charge for their services beyond the payments that you make to the crowd. You pay the cost of the job in one of two ways:

- ✔ **A surcharge:** You pay an amount on top of the payments to the workers. Amazon's Mechanical Turk, for example, adds an additional 10 per cent on top of labour costs.

- ✔ **A fixed fee:** You pay a fee that covers both the costs of using the platform and the money that goes to the crowd. 99designs and many of the other crowdcontest sites often charge a fixed fee.

Most crowdsourcing platforms charge a comprehensive fee for their services. However, you need to verify that they don't have other fees that aren't obvious, such as fees for uploading data, for getting results to you in a certain format, or for publicising the endeavour.

Expecting a refund

Some platforms advertise that you receive a complete refund if you're not satisfied with their services. You need to review the terms and conditions of such refunds. Crowdsourcing platforms are intermediaries and may only guarantee the quality of their own work, not that of the crowd. Review the policies to see whether the platform is indeed guaranteeing that it'll provide a crowd that can do your work properly (a few do). To obtain a refund in such cases, you probably need to show that the failure of the crowd wasn't caused by any mistake of yours. You're likely to be responsible for communicating your needs to the crowd, for setting your price correctly, and for judging the work in a way that corresponds to your descriptions.

Knowing your responsibilities

When you give a job to a crowdsourcing platform, you're a manager, not a consumer. You have the rights and responsibilities of someone who oversees some aspect of work. You should know how the platform expects you to describe your job and to state the criteria that you'll use to judge the work and the means by which you will pay the workers.

Most crowdsourcing platforms have a lengthy set of policies. You should at least know the procedure that the platform uses to judge the work. You want to avoid the problem of having a task judged as being done correctly and hence requiring a payment even though you decide that the task doesn't meet your requirements.

Doing a Little Comparison Shopping

The preceding sections give you pointers on choosing a platform. Now you can explore. Type 'crowdsourcing' into an Internet search engine together with a term that describes the task you want to do, and survey the results. Take a look at the Crowdsourcing.org website at `http://crowdsourcing.org`, too. This platform has the most current list of crowdsourcing platforms, organised as follows:

- ✔ **Cloud labour:** Both macrotasking and microtasking
- ✔ **Crowd creativity:** Crowdcontests for artists and similar activities
- ✔ **Crowdfunding:** Both equity and non-equity crowdfunding
- ✔ **Distributed knowledge:** Wikis, idea markets and other forms of collaboration; often a form of self-organised crowd
- ✔ **Open innovation:** Crowdcontests and self-organised crowds for generating new ideas (see Chapters 9 and 18)

Also consider the crowdsourcing platforms I mention in the following sections and compare the different capabilities, policies and prices of each.

Often the easiest way to start crowdsourcing is to find someone who's run a similar crowdsourcing job to the one you have in mind and copy what they've done. If you don't know anyone among your friends or social network who's crowdsourced before, you can turn to the crowdsourcing platforms. Most of them list projects that have been successfully run on their platforms. You can study these projects, see how they work and even contact the individuals who organised them.

Do be a little cautious when you read example projects on crowdsourcing websites. These websites like to post jobs that are successful rather than those that fail. Often, however, you learn more by reading about the failures than the successes. Just don't expect many stories of failure on the commercial sites.

Good places to head to for stories of failure are the Crowdsourcing news sites, such as Daily Crowdsource (`www.dailycrowdsource.com`), crowdsourcing,org (`www.crowdsourcing.org`), Crowdsourcing Gazette UK (`www.crowdsource-gazette.com`) or crowdsourcingblog.de (`www.crowdsourcingblog.de`) in Germany. By making time to check on at some of these websites, you can get a better sense of problems that past crowdsourcers have encountered.

Checking out the contest providers

An early application of crowdcontests was graphic design. You can find dozens of platforms that offer design services for logos, business cards, brochures, web platforms and other products. Two such platforms are 99designs (www.99designs.co.uk) and crowdSPRING (www.crowdspring.com). The two platforms are similar but not identical. They offer similar design services that they organise into three levels. The different levels – inexpensive, moderately priced and expensive – engage different crowds and offer different services.

A related application of crowdcontests is the production of video commercials. Among the firms that offer crowdcontests for video production are Poptent (www.poptent.net) and GeniusRocket (www.geniusrocket.com). Both platforms allow you to run open contests that accept submissions from anyone and closed contests that are limited to individuals who've provided their skills. And the platforms offer portfolios of work that they've managed through their contests.

Connecting with the macrotaskers

Two of the larger and more active general macrotasking platforms are oDesk (www.odesk.com) and Elance (www.elance.com). Both platforms offer macrotasking for web development, software app development, accounting services, and a variety of technical, business and other tasks. They have similar crowds and similar pricing policies. However, oDesk has more sophisticated technology for tracking work and hence has different procedures and different policies for managing macrotasking.

You can find many specialised macrotasking platforms, including two that deal exclusively with software development: uTest (www.utest.com) and TopCoder (www.topcoder.com). The two platforms deal with slightly different kinds of services and hence have different crowds, different interfaces, different policies and different pricing schemes. uTest provides a software testing service, and TopCoder offers a wide range of software development services.

Looking at options for microtasking

Microtasking platforms tend to be divided according to the services they provide. If you're looking to do photographic tagging, you go to one of four or five different platforms. If you're going to be carrying out a transcription, you look at a second group of platforms. If you're translating a text from one language into another, you go to a third group of platforms.

The only exception among microtasking platforms is Amazon's Mechanical Turk (www.mturk.com), which is a general-purpose microtasking marketplace. Mechanical Turk has developed a large crowd of general-skill workers that can handle well-established tasks such as transcription or data cleaning, or it can be used as a place to develop new microtasks.

You may find that you need a certain sophistication to use Mechanical Turk. You can, however, use Mechanical Turk through other microtasking platforms that serve as simplified interfaces for certain kinds of jobs. For example, Smartsheet (www.smartsheet.com) connects Mechanical Turk to the cells of a spreadsheet.

Many microtasking platforms use Mechanical Turk as a general crowdmarket. They give you access to the large crowd supported by Mechanical Turk and yet make it easier to prepare jobs for that crowd. They also manage the crowd, so that you don't have to deal with any disagreements between yourself and the crowd.

Among the list of microtasking platforms that utilise Mechanical Turk are the following:

- **Microtask (**www.microtask.com**):** Offers transcription services. It takes handwritten documents and puts them into machine-readable form. It's developed a sophisticated process that uses Mechanical Turk as its source of labour. This process ensures that the work is done accurately and that the information remains confidential.

- **CrowdFlower (**http://crowdflower.com**):** Offers a much larger collection of services including data cleaning, tagging, sentiment analysis, data collection and surveys. Each of these services has its own process and manager. CrowdFlower not only uses Mechanical Turk as a microtask labour source but also engages other labour markets.

- **Tagasauris (**www.tagasauris.com**):** Provides secure tagging services. You provide it with pictures or other forms of data, and it gets the crowd to provide descriptions and keywords for that input. Like the other platforms, it's developed a process that utilises Mechanical Turk as a labour source. However, Tagasauris is built on a sophisticated technology that you can reconfigure to handle different kinds of microtask service.

For more on Mechanical Turk, visit Chapter 3.

Finding the best funders

Crowdfunding platforms tend to be more localised than the other forms of crowdsourcing. When you crowdfund, you need to tap into a crowd that knows your needs, understands your goals, and believes in what you're doing. Furthermore, crowdfunding is governed by local laws, whether it involves doing charity work, non-equity funding or equity crowdfunding. Still, several large regional platforms exist. Among them are two based in the USA: Kickstarter (www.kickstarter.com) and WhenYouWish (www.when youwish.com).

The two platforms have much in common but differ on a key policy. Kickstarter supports *all-or-nothing* crowdfunding. You have to raise pledges for the entire sum or you get nothing. By contrast, WhenYouWish attempts to collect all the pledges for your project even if you haven't reached the goal that you set.

Because crowdfunding is often controlled by local laws, you may have to search for platforms that are based near you or your organisation. In Europe, you can find booomerang.dk (www.booomerang.dk) in Denmark and Crowdcube (www.crowdcube.com) in the UK.

Chapter 14

Managing Your Crowd

Crowdsourcing can be deceiving. After you understand the basic forms of crowdsourcing, you may quickly conclude that crowdsourcing is a simple activity. Identify a problem. Choose a platform. Write instructions. Listen to your crowd, in case it has something to say. Then the crowd solves your problem.

Indeed, crowdsourcing is a simple process. But like many simple processes, it requires a good manager, someone who can fit a complicated activity into the crowdsourcing mould and make the process work.

In this chapter, I look at how to manage and lead your crowd – how to guide the members towards your goals, how to detect problems before they occur, how to respect the crowd's rights and how to deal with members of the crowd who are displeased with their work.

Starting with the Right Balance of Skills

Crowdsourcing management requires you to develop two sets of skills:

✔ **Analytical skills:** These skills are for the parts of crowdsourcing that you can express in words, numbers or symbols. You identify your problem, shape it into a job that can be crowdsourced, describe it in a way that your crowd can understand, set the price, and release the job to the market. You can find more about these analytic skills in Chapters 10, 11, 12, 13, 14 and 16. If you don't have these skills, you can't even start to crowdsource.

✓ **Personal skills:** Using these skills, you address the concerns of your co-workers who think that crowdsourcing's a waste of time. You find a way of attracting a crowd to your project and convince the members to donate time, money or effort to your work or the work of your organisation. You calm the crowd when the tasks seem too hard, the deadline too short or the payment too low. Most importantly, you protect the reputation of your organisation and ensure that the crowd sees it as a good place to work. Without human skills, you may be able to start a crowdsourcing job, but you may not be able to finish it.

You need both analytical and personal skills to be a good manager of crowdsourcing. For example, you need to know the right steps for the job (analytical). But you also need to appreciate why some crowd members find the steps hard or illogical, and create a way to help those individuals learn the proper procedure (human).

To prepare to be a crowdsourcer, a manager of crowds, consider how to manage a volunteer activity such as a day-long project to clean a local park.

Start with the analytical skills you need for this clean-up project. Your analytical skills will help you set the basic plan for the project. You can identify the steps that the crowd needs to follow and the resources that it needs. Start by looking at the overall goal – cleaning the park – and by dividing that goal into tasks. These tasks are the things that the crowd needs to do in order to clean the park. Finally, link these tasks together to form a plan for the day.

If you don't have the analytical skills to do these things, you get nothing done. A crowd of volunteers arrives at the park. The volunteers stand in a group gossiping and wondering who's in charge. Eventually, everyone slopes off to the local café for a hot beverage and a pastry.

Even if you have a plan for cleaning the park, you still have to teach that plan to the group, which requires personal skill in addition to analytical skill. You have to show some people how to use a rake. You have to explain your method for collecting rubbish. You may even have to teach people how to cooperate. Sometimes you teach with words. Sometime you teach by demonstrating the right method. Sometimes you have to work alongside people for a while so that they can follow your example.

Finally, you have to spend much of the day handling the individual problems that would otherwise undermine the effort. You address the volunteer who's refusing to work and shamelessly flirting with your assistant. You tame the complainer, who believes that the whole effort's a waste of time. You gently redirect the officious volunteer who keeps bossing others. Finally, you make sure that all volunteers receive the compensation they want, whether that's the gratitude of your organisation, a sense of doing good, a free lunch, or a chance to spend time with friends and neighbours.

You can see how you need both analytical and human skills to successfully manage a crowd. But the challenge of crowdsourcing is that you don't have the advantage of being physically present with your crowd. You manage it at a distance using computer communication. That makes the human side of management trickier. You have to convey emotion and gauge the attitudes of the workers via online interactions. In addition, workers can feel isolated, not part of a team, not getting the attention that they need from their manager. To overcome this problem, you need to learn from your crowd (see Chapter 15).

You sometimes hear managers say that a worker started a job on the wrong foot, or workers claim that managers didn't know what they wanted when they posted a job. Both of these statements show that good management needs to start at the beginning of a job. You're on the short road to failure if you don't have good analytical and human skills at the start. For example, you need to have a good description of your macrotask, or clear instructions for your microtasks, or a well-crafted statement for your crowdfunding campaign, or the appropriate criteria for your crowdcontest. (Chapter 11 contains all the info you need to prepare materials for guiding the crowd.)

Choosing the Right People

You demonstrate your skill as a manager when you make a good choice. If you're uncomfortable choosing between workers, then you're unlikely to be a good manager of crowds.

In both macrotasking and crowdcontests, you have to choose your workers. If you don't attract people with the right skills, you won't achieve the right result. Look at the accomplishments of the workers rather than just résumés of training, and hold a dialogue with those people who seem promising. You can give them an example and say 'I need something like this' or point to something that they've done and say 'It should be something like that, only slightly different.'

In microtasking, the selection process is a little less important, because you're free to reject the work of any individual. Still, you can easily find that you're regularly getting wrong results from the same person. You can send that worker a friendly note saying that he may want to stop trying to do your tasks and find work elsewhere.

When selecting members of your crowd, you're looking for people with the right skills. Don't be tempted to accept low quality because you've not mastered the skills yourself! Crowdsourcing should expand the skills that you have at your disposal. For example, you may have a project that needs a database. Because you don't understand databases, you decide to ask for a spreadsheet, which is a technology you better understand. At the end, you may still have a project that met at least some of your goals. However, the result was limited by you, not by the crowd.

When you're preparing a job for macrotasking or a crowdcontest that you don't completely understand, engage the crowd through questions that help educate you. Ask:

- ✔ Do you see any problems with this project?
- ✔ Is there anything that'll keep you from meeting the deadline?
- ✔ Is there anything that'll keep you from meeting the budget?
- ✔ Is there a simpler way to do this project?
- ✔ What are the benefits of your way instead of the simpler way?

Managing the Crowd Through the Project

You've chosen a crowd and you've made a commitment to the project. If you stop now, you have to admit that something was wrong, that the project didn't work. Sometimes, you want to accept that conclusion and quit. However, you generally try to manage the project to a successful conclusion. Here's how.

Using a consistent voice

In any form of project management, you generally want to have a single manager. Nothing causes your project to fail faster than two, three or four voices giving directions about the project and confusing the crowd. The workers become frustrated because they don't know what to do. You become frustrated because the crowd isn't making progress.

Crowdsourcing management is a little different from traditional project management. In traditional project management, you identify a single person as the manager. In crowdsourcing, where most of the directions are given through electronic communications, you're looking for a single, consistent voice. You can have many people giving commands, but they need to speak with one voice.

If you're using a crowdsourcing platform, you have an electronic record of all communications with the crowd. If you're the only manager, you can use that record to make sure that your own communications are consistent. (Or if you need to change your mind, you can explain why you're making the change.) If many people are managing the crowd, they can use that record to make sure they speak with one voice.

In crowdfunding, you often achieve substantial benefits from having multiple people handling the project. All managers can pull their friends and social networks into the crowd. However, this core of managers should give consistent messages to the crowd. Because you can keep an electronic record of their correspondence, you can avoid the problem of having one leader claiming that you're raising money to save the whales, another stating that you're saving penguins, and a third alleging that neither whales nor penguins are the issue and that you're protecting polar bears instead. (Chapter 6 will help you understand how to communicate for crowdfunding.)

Keeping in touch

Regularly correspond with your crowd. If you don't, you're apt to find that your original ideas have drifted substantially and that the crowd's working towards something that's quite different from what you believe you're getting. You can ask for updates, look at intermediate results, let the group know what you're thinking, and solicit feedback.

If you start a regular pattern of communicating with the crowd, you're better able to control the crowd members' anxiety should things start to fall apart. If you have a history of communicating with the crowd, the members are less likely to be bothered by thinking that you're checking up on them. Members will be used to you communicating with them and so won't feel concerned by any questions you ask seeking information about how the job is going or by you wanting to look at their intermediate results.

Communicating across cultures

When you crowdsource, you can usually limit your crowd to people from your own culture. You can have a Portuguese crowd if you live in Brazil, a German crowd if you live in Germany, an English crowd if you live in the UK. However, you may get more skills, more points of view or more work if you have an international crowd.

When crowdsourcing fails, you usually find failed communications at the heart of it. If you're working with an international crowd, it's better to be complete than be concise. Don't assume that the crowd understands the underlying assumptions of the work. Don't assume that the crowd will fill in the gap between steps in your instructions. If you have any doubts, write down your ideas in complete detail. You're more likely to create a successful project if you have too many words than if you have too few.

If you're not sure whether the crowd understands your descriptions, ask the members to put the instructions into their words. (This procedure works best for macrotasking and crowdcontests.) If the workers just return your words, you should take that as a sign that you're in trouble. If they can't produce a good restatement of what you want, consider ending the project.

Giving feedback

Build trust with the crowd by giving concrete feedback:

- **Positive feedback:** Tell them 'This work is great! Keep up the good work,' not something long-winded and less concrete in tone like 'I've been reviewing the work from the past few days and comparing it with what you've done before, and comparing it with the original description that I posted six months ago, and have concluded that the work is good.' Give positive feedback promptly.

- **Negative feedback:** Don't dive in. Wait a while to give the workers a chance to brace themselves for bad news (if they get bad news too quickly, they're likely to reject it out of hand). Don't say anything sharp or too pointed, such as, 'What were you thinking? Your work was rubbish. Begone and never darken my crowdsourcing door again.' Word your comments to soften the blow: 'I've been reviewing the work from the past few days and comparing it with what you've done before, and comparing it with the original description that I posted six months ago. I've concluded that a quality problem exists, but it's one that you should be able to fix for the future.' Then go on to give concrete details of the issue and the fix required.

Tracking milestones

When you work in crowdsourcing, you soon find that *milestones* – intermediate goals – are useful both to you and to the crowd. However, the crowdsourcer and the crowd tend to use milestones in slightly different ways.

As a crowdsourcer, you use milestones as a way of checking your plans. Each time your project approaches an intermediate goal, you can check to see whether the work's going well, whether you have enough resources to complete the task, or whether you need to make new plans for the job.

When you set milestones for the crowd, however, you use them as a means of motivating the workers, and of getting the crowd to concentrate on the overall goal of the job and on the value of each individual contribution.

You can clearly see how to use intermediate goals to motivate the crowd by looking at a crowdfunding example. (See Chapter 6 for more information about crowdfunding.) At the outset of a crowdfunding campaign, the crowd can believe that it has plenty of time to meet the goals. For example, if you're trying to raise $12,000 (£7,560) in eight weeks, you're likely to face a crowd that isn't particularly motivated to contribute a share. Individual members of the crowd will look at the final deadline and conclude that it's a long time in the future and that you don't really need their contributions, at least not yet.

If you examine how contributions are usually made in a crowdfunding drive, you'll find that they don't come in a neat, orderly fashion. Instead, you'll see that one-eighth are contributed by the end of the first week, one-quarter by the end of the second week, half by the end of the fourth, and three-quarters by the end of the sixth. People tend to give money in a rush just before deadlines arrive.

To motivate the crowd throughout the course of an eight-week crowdfunding campaign, you can easily set three obvious intermediate goals: to raise one-quarter of the funds at two weeks, a half at four, and three-quarters at six weeks. At each of the intermediate goals, you remind the crowd of the campaign's goal and of how to contribute to the project. 'We need to raise $6,000 by the end of this week,' you tell them. 'On average, we have to raise $215 each day.' At the end, you tell each member of crowd that his contribution was important and that it'll make a difference.

The lesson you can learn from such a campaign can apply to every form of crowdsourcing: you set intermediate goals not only to give you an idea of how the work is progressing, but also to remind the crowd members that every individual effort is important and to encourage them to work on the job. You can easily use this technique when you microtask (see Chapter 10 for ways to promote your project, and Chapter 16 for more ideas about workflows), and you can also find ways of using intermediate goals to encourage the crowd in other forms of crowdsourcing, too.

Giving the crowd space to work

Although you generally find that you do a better job of managing the crowd by communicating with the crowd, you want to avoid being a hovering boss, a manager who's not giving the crowd the opportunity to work on its own. You may find it difficult to distinguish between when you're merely paying attention to an important project and when you're probing too deeply into the process and making the crowd resentful.

Of course, each crowd has its qualities, and each manager is unique. Still, a few ideas can help you find the right balance between being a responsible manager and hovering boss:

- ✔ Ask for information at regular intervals (such as weekly) or at natural intervals in the project.

- ✔ Let some of your messages be merely social: 'Saw that you were working on the project today, and thought I'd say hello.'

- ✔ Ask the crowd for information rather than demanding it: 'Saw that you were working today. Any news?'

Respecting Workers' Rights

In dealing with your workers, you can prevent much trouble by remembering that they're human beings and they have rights. Professional crowdsourcing companies offer their workers a statement of rights. Most of these statements cover common points:

- ✔ **Respectful treatment:** Be prompt in answering any correspondence from workers. Treat all workers equally. Focus only on issues involving work, not issues involving personal background or personal opinion, even if the worker raises such issues. Make correspondence with workers dispassionate, even if your lack of passion makes the letter seem a little less personal.

- ✔ **Prompt payment:** Establish a payment policy for the workers and display that policy on your site. (Usually, you link to this kind of policy statement from a page that describes your activity, such as the 'About Us' page and from the page you use to recruit members of the crowd.) The statement should say how you review work, how much time it'll take for work to be accepted, and the maximum amount of time required for payments to be processed. Workers don't like uncertainty. They prefer jobs that give a clear timeline for payments. They also like crowdsourcers who make payments quickly. (See the following section for more about paying workers.)

- ✔ **Transparent judgements when work is rejected:** Every worker expects rejection from time to time. These rejections are common points of dispute between workers and the crowdsourcer. You can eliminate most of these disputes and simplify the others if you have a policy that all jobs are judged in an open way and that when you reject jobs, you give a clear reason that's directly connected to the description of the job or the job instructions.

✔ **Right to appeal:** If a worker has a job rejected, he has the right to appeal that decision. In general, you may find it worthwhile to have an independent person, an ombudsman, handle the appeal. If you're working with a large crowdsourcing service, you may find that it has an ombudsman who can take appeals. In an open appeal system, you restate the reason why the work was rejected or the person banned, and ask the worker to address that reason. Usually, any appeal judgement is final.

A well-designed appeal system helps uncover problems in the work, such as poorly written instructions or a badly conceived goal. When you receive an appeal, start by asking yourself, 'How will this help me make my crowdsourcing better?' This question usually helps you approach the appeal with a more open mind and often makes the appeal process less contentious.

Keeping on Top of the Details: Payroll and Accounting

Behind many of the fundamental rights of workers are the practices of good accounting. Workers should be able to review the records that track how much they work and how much they've been paid.

In most countries, you're required to report the earnings of the crowd to the national taxation authority, such as Her Majesty's Revenue and Customs in the UK or the Internal Revenue Service in the USA. To support the figures that you give the tax authorities, you need to keep track of the number of jobs or hours worked by each member of the crowd. In some cases, you may be responsible for paying certain kinds of taxes, such as payroll taxes. If you use a crowdsourcing platform (see Chapter 12), however, you'll find that it usually provides payroll, record and taxation services.

If you're unfamiliar with the requirements in your country, consult with someone who's able to advise you properly, such as a Certified Public Accountant in the USA or a Chartered Accountant in the UK. In both countries, you can find payroll specialists who understand the legal and technical issues of payrolls. In the USA, they're called Certified Payroll Professionals. In the UK, they're Payroll Professionals.

Unless you crowdsource for an organisation that operates a payroll operation, using a payroll service to pay your workers is a good idea. These services keep records, report income to the appropriate offices and help you pay any taxes that you need to pay. You can use almost any payroll service that caters for small businesses. Many of the major crowdsourcing platforms have payroll services that you can use even if you don't use their platform for crowdsourcing.

Incentivising to Build Quality

You can use money to attract workers to the market, but you can't always use it to encourage the crowd to work well. A higher reward may encourage better submissions for crowdcontests, but it doesn't necessarily give a macrotasker more skill or encourage a microtasker to spend more time on the job and devote more effort to checking the product. To improve the quality of work, you can reward best practice and be inspired by *gamification* – creating a fun, challenging game out of crowdsourcing.

You can reward best practices and use gamification incentives in all forms of crowdsourcing, but they're often associated with microtasking.

Rewarding best practices

You can often improve the quality of your work by putting it in the hands of workers. The workers often identify the strategies that complete the job in the least amount of time and produce the fewest problems. You can discover these strategies by encouraging your workers to blog about their approach to work. (Think of the blog as an online suggestions box.) You can review the blog, test ideas, reward the best ones and encourage other workers to adopt the good practice through a page that identifies workers who submit good ideas. You might award a badge each month to the best contributors (see the 'Awarding badges' section later in this chapter) or even offer a cash award for the for the best suggestion for each job.

To test an idea, you use it to modify the instructions or training material for your job and then allow only part of the crowd to complete the job with the new materials. When this part of the crowd has competed its tasks, you compare the work with the tasks completed using the old methods. You can then see whether the new materials helped the workers complete the work more quickly or with fewer problems.

You can't always require workers to do the work in a specific way. However, the ideas from a good blog help you improve the quality of your crowdsourcing. You can promote best practices, incorporate them into your training materials, and use them in your instructions. For more on improving your crowdsourcing, head to Chapter 15.

Taking inspiration from gamification

Many crowdsourcers have attempted to turn their crowdsourcing platforms into systems that resemble video games. They call this process *gamification*. The crowdsourcers claim that they'll someday produce a system in which transcribing a business record will be as much fun as navigating through a maze, finding organisational data will be as engaging as finding hidden treasures, and categorising tweets will have all the excitement of killing enemy soldiers.

At the moment, no one has produced a crowdsourcing platform that's as entertaining as a video game. A few have created games that are similar to the educational programs we give to children. These platforms may present crowdsourcing in slightly more interesting ways, but they can never completely hide the fact that the activity's a form of work. Still, even if you can't turn crowdsourcing into a game, you can at least use some of the incentives that games use.

Awarding badges

You can identify and reward through the use of badges or honorary titles. These badges are both symbolic and practical. They make a worker feel accomplished and appreciated. They also can be incorporated into the worker's reputation. A worker can quickly summarise his accomplishments by reporting that he's earned a silver badge on one job, two gold stars on another, and a rare platinum badge on a third.

The Old Weather Project on the Zooniverse crowdsourcing platform gives badges to workers who've completed a certain amount of work. These badges are named after the ranks in the British Navy. You start as a cadet. You get a lieutenant's badge when you've transcribed 30 records. The top badge is that of captain, which is given to the person who's transcribed the most records for a single ship.

You can also use badges to reward quality of work. These badges tend to be more subjective than badges awarded for the quantity of work. You can make them concrete and more effective by tying them to quantity. In a crowdcontest, for example, you can offer a silver star to the submission that you judge to be the best submission you've seen in ten contests. In microtasking, you may award a gold star to someone who's completed 50 tasks with at least 45 of them being done correctly.

Encourage the workers to take your badges seriously by offering a small financial reward for each. Most workers view the badges as an honour, and they see the financial reward as representing that honour.

You can use the badges to identify workers who are more efficient, more reliable or more skilled. In addition to giving them recognition or cash rewards, you give them access to special classes of jobs, jobs that may be more sophisticated or offer higher compensation.

Posting to the leaderboard

In addition to badges, you can use a leaderboard – a computer screen that shows the identities of the top ten workers. Generally, you use a leaderboard to reward quantity, so you show the identities of workers who've completed the largest number of tasks today, this week, this month, or on this job.

Leaderboards can encourage competition within a certain group of the workers. Some workers review the leaderboard and do the work that keeps them on the board or at the top of the board. You may also give the best results if you offer small cash prizes to the workers who are at the top of the leaderboard. You can offer a prize to those who are at the top of the board at the end of the day, the end of the week, or the end of the project (or another reasonable period).

Leaderboards are especially useful for large jobs, because they encourage competition within the crowd. As deadlines draw near, you can publicise the board and even offer a special reward for those people who do the most work.

As with badges, you can use a leaderboard to identify workers who've done the highest quality of work. In microtasking, you can recognise the people who've completed tasks with the least number of errors. To encourage workers to do more tasks, you can set the minimum number of tasks required for workers to be on the board. Each week, you can raise the number to encourage the best workers to add their effort to the job.

Recognising Trouble

Everyone makes mistakes. You start a project that quickly becomes an adventure that you didn't anticipate. The work is too hard. It takes too long. The results aren't those that you want. You can redouble your efforts and try to get the best that you can from the job, or you can go back to the beginning and start the work in a different way. As you manage your crowdsourced project, you need to keep assessing the situation and asking whether you should continue the job or stop the work and resort to a different approach.

Knowing your options

When you're doing an important job, one that's crucial to your success or that has to be done by an immovable deadline, you should always review other methods that you might use to do the work and ask whether those methods may not be easier or less risky. Consider whether you'd be more likely to get a good result if you hired a full-time employee to do the job or contracted with a conventional firm to do it. As a good manager and a good crowdsourcer, you owe it to yourself to make the best decision.

Say that you're trying to design a smartphone app through macrotasking. As the job starts, you begin to sense trouble. You start to think that your worker may not be creating the kind of program you want. If you look at your options, you may conclude that you can:

- ✔ **Correspond with the worker to see whether you can clarify the work.** You should correspond if you believe that your job may be going astray. You have little additional cost and are likely to see improvement or get a better understanding of your worker's ability to complete the job as you intended.

- ✔ **Stop the project, revise the job description, and then give it to your current worker.** In talking with your worker, you may conclude that you need to stop the project and rewrite the description. If you do that, you're admitting that the project was flawed at the start and that you bear some of the responsibility. You certainly have to pay the worker for the work done. You also need to work out whether you want to continue with your current worker or return to the crowdmarket and get a worker who's a better fit for your job.

- ✔ **Stop the project, go back to the crowdmarket, and give the job to another worker.** You've decided that the problems lie with the crowd-worker. But will a change of worker justify the cost of the switch? You probably have to pay the first worker for the work already done, because you chose to hire that individual. (You can withhold payment only if the worker doesn't seem to have the skills suggested in his portfolio or if your crowdsourcing platform has a policy that allows you to withhold payment for mediocre work.) In addition, you have to take the time to review the portfolios of other workers, choose a new worker, and develop a new relationship with that worker.

  If you return to the crowdmarket, set a higher price for your job to make it more attractive and engage a higher skilled worker who can get it done more quickly.

- ✔ **Stop the project and give it to a full-time worker.** Taking this route may be easier or harder, cheaper or more costly, depending on the people who may be available for you to hire. If you've no one who can do that work, you have to hire someone, train him and get him involved in your project. In that case, you'll find this alternative quite expensive. You should choose it only if you feel that you have no alternative.

Computing the price of failure

For many jobs, you base your decision to stop or continue on the cost of failure rather than the cost of change. If the cost of failure is high, and if it'll result in lost revenue or lost alternatives, make sure that you've as many alternatives as possible. You generally have such alternatives in a conventional organisation, although you don't always see them. If a conventional employee is unable to complete a job, you usually have the alternatives of reassigning the work to others, bringing in temporary workers or asking for help from other divisions.

If you're crowdsourcing a critical job, you may want to plan to have extra alternatives from the start: you crowdsource the same job to multiple workers or teams, or you keep part of a conventional staff ready to pick up the work.

Treating the cause, not the symptom

As you review your options, you want to determine the root cause of the problem.

Say you notice that your crowdworker isn't spending much time on his macro-tasking job. You conclude that you have the wrong worker, and ditch him. But changing workers doesn't solve the issue. The next worker doesn't do much work either. You quiz the second worker and discover that not only does he not really understand the job, but he thinks you've underpriced the work. Ah ha! Now you know the actual issues.

Sometimes, you find that the root cause is a fundamental flaw in the job. The job doesn't neatly fit into a crowdsourcing framework because it can't be split between multiple workers, or it requires more knowledge than a single worker may have, or it requires a history with your organisation that can't be found in any independent individual. In such cases, you have only one option: stop the job and reconsider your plans.

Stopping a Project

The decision to quit a crowdsourcing job isn't an easy one to take, especially if you're new to the field and are still learning how to handle the crowd. My advice is that when you realise that you need to halt a project, get moving. If you delay or drift, you're unlikely to make the situation any better.

Exiting firmly and gracefully

Act firmly. Notify the crowdsourcing platform of your decision and ask about any consequences. You may be responsible for payments for the time already spent on the job. You may also have to notify the crowd.

When you notify the crowd, follow the kinds of rules you use for dealing with personnel issues. Be clear. Be polite. Stick to the facts. Say only what you need to say. Avoid emotion. Remember, you may need to start a new crowd-sourced job and you don't want to do anything that unnecessarily damages your reputation.

Protecting your intellectual property

When you stop a job, think about any intellectual property that the crowd may have created for you, such as sketches of designs, code for an app, and the storyboard for a video.

Commercial crowdsourcing platforms generally have a policy that you have to follow (you agree to this when you sign up – so check it before you start a job!). Depending on the policy, you have four options:

✔ Keep all the intellectual property and use it as you see fit.

✔ Keep all the intellectual property but don't use it in public.

✔ The crowdworkers keep any property they created but can't use it publically in any way that's connected to you.

✔ The crowdworkers keep any property and can reuse it in any way.

If you keep the intellectual property, you usually have to pay for the work done. If you don't keep the material, you may or may not have to pay for the partial work.

Be concerned about the reuse of intellectual property only if the material can be traced to your organisation or if you want to base further work on the ideas. In creative crowdsourcing, the crowd often wants to try to reuse ideas that weren't acceptable to a client. The workers won't want you to use ideas that they've created if they think they've not been fully compensated for these ideas.

When Crowds Attack: Dealing with Angry Crowds

Crowdsourcing jobs, like any other form of human relationship, can end badly. When you let a crowdworker go from your project, or you end a project prematurely, he may feel angry or wronged. As a result, he may want to hurt you or your organisation. Just as fired workers may try to disrupt the office they're leaving, terminated crowdworkers may try to attack your organisation in the arena where they work: the Internet.

Most commonly, crowds express their anger by posting claims about your alleged misdeeds and maltreatment to blogs and Twitter accounts and other forms of social media. In most cases, the crowd quickly loses interest and lets the issue fade into the deep recesses of cyberspace.

In other cases, the crowd members pursue their perceived grievances further, and you need to take action. In the most extreme cases, the workers may try to mount a cyber-attack against your computer systems or even attack you physically. (One commercial crowdsourcing platform, which I'll call CrowdCorp.net, reported that it had to briefly guard its offices when a fired crowdworker threatened to come to the company's office and do bodily harm to the officers and managers.)

Assessing the situation

When crowds attack, first assess the situation. Review the case to be sure that you understand the circumstances that have led the crowd to attack. Commonly, you find that the problem's based on the grievances of a single individual. Start with that assumption, look for the event that caused the attack, and try to address it.

Make sure that the case doesn't point to a bigger problem in your crowdsourcing effort. Instead of addressing a single worker who's angry over his experience, you may be facing the first person who's willing to talk about a problem that affects many of your workers. Even if you find that the problem starts with a single worker, check with other workers to see whether they've the same kind of experience.

If you suspect that you may have a bigger problem, have an online town meeting or other activity that allows you to address a large group of workers. Be prepared that the first reaction of the workers may not be pleasant. Often town meetings follow a pattern that builds to an emotional climax before the group calms, starts to express itself rationally, and gives you useful information.

Handling a discontented worker

If the uprising is caused by a single worker, you can usually identify the individual. You often find a chain of emails or tweets pointing to that person.

Even if you can't identify the single worker who started the attack, perhaps because he's hidden behind an alias, try to reach that individual through a mass email or tweet or some other form of communication. You may get responses from more than one person, but you may also get the chance to listen to the crowd and bring the incident under control.

Addressing the individual

Meetings with discontented individuals can often be tense or emotional. They can be especially challenging when conducted over the Internet, where you're not face to face. However, you may need to hold such a meeting to try to resolve the situation.

Always approach such meetings calmly. Keep focused on the key issue: removing an objection that's interfering with your organisation's ability to crowdsource. Don't take any remark personally. (Harder said than done, to be sure, but you have to try.) Always identify the problem and ask the worker, 'What can we do to fix this problem?'

Some problems seem trivial. Individuals identify tiny slights that are of symbolic importance to them – for example, payment delays of a day or two. Indeed, payment complaints are common. But, generally, as long as payments are consistent with the market, they usually aren't the central problem. Usually, the key problem is a perception of management. The worker feels that he's not been treated well.

Determine whether the problem's with your crowdsourcing work or merely an event with one individual. If something's wrong with your crowdsourcing, address it, but be careful about promising that the problem will never happen again, as workers sometimes request. At best, you can promise to be open to the workers and ready to fix problems as they occur.

If you have any concern about who (other than you and the crowdworker) may be following the discussion or who may also be able to read emails or postings, conduct the meeting over the phone. In meetings with angry personnel, you may say things to try to address the problem that may easily be read out of context and by other people in ways that you didn't intend.

If you do try to address the problem over email or another text-based form of communication, write as if your emails will eventually become public. Always treat the other person respectfully. Never threaten or make promises that you don't intend to keep.

If the problem looks as if it's going to expand – or worse, if the problem's expanding already – seek professional advice. Because your relationship with the crowd involves human workers, you may find that you can't say some things publically. You may also find that you have legal means of addressing the problem.

Protecting your crowdsourcing

When you're dealing with a disgruntled individual, always remember that you're trying to protect your crowdsourcing project and your ability to crowdsource. You don't want a solution that hurts that process, even if that solution proves that you acted properly in the design and management of your crowdsourcing.

From time to time, you may face an attack that's driven by an unjustified complaint. For example, a worker claims that he was fired from the project without a good cause and starts a campaign against you on the Internet. You know that this individual submitted completely fraudulent work, or work stolen from others, or nothing at all. You may even have the evidence to show the poor quality of the work. You need to look for a way to bring the problem to a close, stop the attack, and cause the worker to go away.

If the worker has evidence that may be interpreted as showing bad management on your part, you may have to negotiate a solution that gives a partial payment to the worker in exchange for an end to the attack. You certainly don't want to start your discussions with this option, but you may want to consider it as you talk with the worker.

If you have to negotiate a solution, you may want to insist that neither you nor the worker admit fault. You may also want a lawyer to draft a formal agreement.

Recognising structural problems

In assessing the situation, you may find a number of structural problems, problems that have developed because of the way in which you organised the crowd. The most common problems are rooted in communications issues. You may find that the instructions were misleading or confusing. However, you can also find a number of other problems that may have caused the worker to start the attack. These problems can include:

- ✔ Delayed payments
- ✔ Inappropriate communications to the crowd
- ✔ Inappropriate or changed deadlines

✔ Inappropriate tools (software or file formats) for the job

✔ Misleading promotional material for the project

✔ Modifications to the project

To help identify structural problems, start by reviewing the other chapters in this part of the book, notably Chapters 10, 13 and 14. These chapters describe what you need to do to communicate with the crowd and guide its actions.

When you find a structural problem, you usually have two options. You can either try to fix the problem and continue with the work, or stop the job and restart it from the beginning. In either case, you're likely to have to pay for work that's been done improperly. In the first case, when you're trying to finish a partially complete job, you usually have to accept the blame for the problem. You don't need to beat yourself up in public, but you do need to say 'The problem seems to have been in the way I organised the job. I've attempted to correct the mistake, and I hope that we can get the job done quickly.'

Managing the public relations problem

When it comes to crowdsourcing, reputation matters. If crowdworkers conclude that you're crowdsourcing in ways that are difficult for them or that put them at a disadvantage, they'll seek work elsewhere and may even seek higher payments for your jobs.

If the attack looks like nothing more than an isolated email to you or tweet to the world at large, you may choose to be patient, review the case, and let the storm pass. However, if the crowd looks as if it intends to keep the attack going, you need to take action.

Follow these three fundamental rules of public relations:

✔ **Keep ahead of the story.** If someone's spreading stories about you or your organisation on the Internet, you want your side of the story presented clearly and accurately. You don't want others to define the issues, the conflict or the facts. Make sure that your perspective is visible to those who are attacking you and to their audience. Make them respond to you rather than you to them.

✔ **Don't let bad news dribble into the public domain.** Make sure that you know the full story of the situation, including details of all events or communications that may reflect badly on you or your organisation. Once you know the facts, get them on your website, and handle them.

You don't want to face a publication relations problem in which bad facts are dribbling onto the Internet. Bad news leaking out over time suggests that there actually is a story behind the problem that reflects badly on you. Let the bad news get to the public quickly.

✔ **Separate ego from business.** Even if you're completely without fault, you can never convince everyone that you're in the right. Of course, do the best you can to present your side of the story, but remember that your first goal is to protect your organisation and allow it to work effectively in the future.

Chapter 15

Learning on the Job

. . . .

In This Chapter

▶ Aiming for continuous improvement

▶ Knowing how to handle common issues

▶ Expecting the unexpected

▶ Doing a pilot run to iron out problems

▶ Rejigging a crowdfunding campaign

. . . .

So you've posted the job description, recruited the crowd, accepted the results and paid your workers. You've finished your first crowdsourcing job. You may wonder what to do next. Well, if you're never going to do another crowdsourcing job in your life, you can close this book, return it to the shelf and forget about it until your aunt holds a garage sale and asks whether you have anything that you'd like to donate.

But if you're thinking about another crowdsourcing job – either soon or in the distant future – you may want to read this chapter, which is all about learning from what you've done. Each time you do a crowdsourcing job, aim to take all the information gathered from your experience with crowdsourcing and ask what you did right, what you did wrong and how you can do it better next time.

This chapter gives you the information you need about how to learn from your crowdsourcing jobs and how to improve the way in which you run those jobs.

Following the Cycle of Continuous Improvement

When you try to learn from your results to plan for your next crowdsourcing job, you're taking part in the cycle of continuous improvement. The *cycle of continuous improvement* is a management technique which assumes that you can always make your work better, because nothing's ever perfect. You do a task, look at the results, see what you can learn, and then do another task and repeat the cycle.

This technique is something that you can use to manage your projects. It gives you a systematic framework through which you can collect data, and a disciplined way to make adjustments to your plans. Figure 15-1 shows a simple version of the cycle, and the following sections outline each part of the cycle in turn.

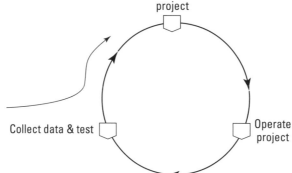

Figure 15-1: The cycle of continuous improvement.

This version of the cycle of improvement has three steps:

1. **Design your crowdsourcing project.** You identify a task that needs to be macrotasked, or you design a crowdfunding project, or you prepare a microtasking job, or you organise a crowdcontest.

   In designing your project, you need to anticipate the kinds of problems you may face. You may be concerned that the project may take too long, or that you may not receive enough entries for your contest, or that the microtasks may contain too many errors. As you think about the problems you may face, you can start to think about the kinds of information or data you may want to collect that can allow you to address any of these potential problems.

2. **Run your project.** You send the project to the crowdmarket and wait for results.

3. **Gather and analyse data from the results of your project.** The data can be simple or complex. You can count the number of people who enter your contest. You can look at all the work that's submitted to your macrotask and ask how much of it really meets your standard. You can count the number of errors in microtasks. You can record how long it took to get the job done. Collect information that helps you assess the quality of your project.

   With your information, you can look at your project and decide which things went well and which did not. As you make decisions, you can begin to think about the changes you may make in your crowdsourcing to improve the results.

After Step 3, you return to the start of the cycle. This time, you can incorporate what you've discovered.

In the cycle of continuous improvement, you never stop improving. You're always looking for something that you may do better, always gathering information to help you understand different aspects of your project, and always evaluating that data.

Note that in the cycle of continuous improvement, you change your plans in a systematic way. Except in an emergency (and such things occasionally happen), you don't make changes in the middle of a project. If you make undisciplined changes, you're likely to get undisciplined results. (Most crowdsourcing sites help you to be disciplined, because they limit the changes that you can make in the middle of a project.)

Apply the cycle of continuous improvement to all your work, even if you're just doing a simple project that's never to be repeated. Sometimes, you want to break a project into smaller steps and run each step through the cycle. Sometimes, especially when you microtask, you want to do a test version of the project. Always, you want to assess each project in order to build your skill with crowdsourcing.

You can find the cycle of continuous improvement in many books about project management. Each presentation seems slightly different. In some places, the cycle has three steps. In others, it has four, or five, or seven, or eleven. You needn't worry about the number of steps. The cycle can have as many steps as you want. The important thing to remember is that when you go through a cycle of continuous improvement, you always try to learn from what you've done and improve your task the next time.

Managing improvement:
Walter Shewhart and his cycle

The cycle of continuous improvement is generally credited to Walter Shewhart, an engineer at the American Telegraph and Telephone Company during the 1920s and 1930s. He devised the cycle as a means of handling uncertainty and managing change for production processes.

Shewhart argued that you can never know everything about a project, no matter how much data you collect. (He lived in the era when mechanical punched-card machines were new and seemed to be able to process massive amounts of data.) He also recognised that if you modify your production process in an undisciplined way, you get undisciplined results.

Shewhart argued that the cycle of continuous improvement allows you to gather data in a way that answers specific questions about your project and anticipate the results of any changes you may make. He also recognised, as have those that followed him, that a process can always be improved.

Don't wait until your project's over to start using the cycle of continuous improvement. You don't start learning from your results when the project's over. You start learning at the very beginning; if you don't, you won't know how to interpret your results. You may find yourself looking at a project that's gone badly wrong and not knowing what caused the problem. Worse, you may think that you know the problem when you really don't. In either case, you won't be able to learn from your project and you'll be unable to fix any problem.

Using the Cycle in Crowdsourcing

As the name suggests, with the cycle of continuous improvement, you don't wait until the end of a project before thinking about making improvements to your work. You work with a cycle of improvement that's part of your crowdsourcing from the very start. You start to think about what you might learn from your job and how you might use those lessons to make your project better from the outset – as you plan the job. As the job unfolds, you might get more information that enables you to improve your crowdsourcing still further.

However, the first lesson of the cycle of continuous improvement is the lesson of managed change, of treating problems that arise in a systematic way. In other words, don't react to every problem and immediately rush to try to fix it. Instead, gather data, determine what needs to be adjusted and fix your job at the right time.

Anticipating trouble

By using the cycle of continuous improvement from the very start of a project, you start thinking about potential problems in a new way. Instead of thinking that they indicate failure, you look at them as telling you something about your job.

To benefit from using the cycle, you need to determine what the nature of a particular problem may be telling you. For example, suppose you put a macrotasking job on a crowdsourcing platform and no one takes the job. You wait a week and you get no bids. Workers look at the job and then put it back and move to another job. From this situation, you can speculate that your job may be:

- **Underpriced.** The crowd believes that you're not offering enough money or allocating enough time to the job.

- **Too confusing.** The crowd reads the statement of work, doesn't understand it and puts the job back.

- **On the wrong platform.** The crowdsourcing site you choose may not have enough people in its crowd with the right skills for your job. When people look at the job, they realise they can't do it.

To determine which of these problems may be affecting your job, you need to do some research. However, you'll be a better crowdsourcer if you anticipate problems as you plan your project and know what further information you may need to prevent them. You don't need to expect the worst, but you do need to be prepared to think ahead and learn from anything that may go wrong with your job.

Problems are never about you. They're about the process. The moment you think you're fixing a mistake you made or defending a process you designed, you're no longer an effective manager. Treat your project as if someone else designed it and you're merely trying to correct any shortcomings. Have no pride of authorship and no guilt of failure. You should only think, 'We're going to improve this. We're going to make it better.'

Keeping an eye out for stumbling blocks

When you start designing your project, think about what may go wrong.

Some problems are relatively straightforward and easy to detect. In a macrotasking project, you may have hired a crowdworker who doesn't have the right skills for the job. In a microtasking job, you may not have released your tasks to the market. In a crowdfunding campaign, you may not have notified anyone who's interested in your project. In a crowdcontest, you may have set the deadline to the wrong date.

When you consider more complicated problems, you discover that they're not as easy to detect or as easy to solve. In macrotasking, you receive material that isn't quite right, no matter what you tell the crowdworker. In microtasking, you find that your tasks aren't attracting crowdworkers and that some of the tasks are done wrongly. In crowdfunding, you receive contributions are that small, appear at erratic intervals, and come with strange comments. In a crowdcontest, you receive submissions that seem to have little to do with what you requested.

The following sections help you identify some of the stumbling blocks that crowdsourcers commonly encounter.

Test your project before you start a full-scale operation. It's always less painful to find problems in a preliminary test or in a discussion among colleagues than when you're trying to complete a real project to a deadline.

Rooting out poor instructions

Many problems can be traced to poorly written instructions. When you have ambiguous or confusing instructions, you receive information that suggests the crowd doesn't understand what you want. If your instructions are at fault, you may find that:

- ✔ Microtasks sit in the crowdmarket for a long time.
- ✔ Microtasks are first accepted by the crowd but are eventually returned incomplete.
- ✔ Microtasks are returned with results that have little to do with your request.
- ✔ Many people visit your crowdfunding site, but few donate.
- ✔ Comments on your crowdfunding site seem odd.
- ✔ A macrotask worker repeatedly asks for clarification or doesn't seem to understand what you want.
- ✔ A macrotask request doesn't elicit the number of proposals you anticipate.
- ✔ Crowdcontests don't get the number of responses you expect.

If you're experiencing any of these problems in your crowdsourcing, then your instructions may not be as clear as you'd like. Chapter 11 contains lots of helpful guidance on writing clear instructions. Here's what to look for with each type of crowdfunding:

- ✔ **Microtasking:** Ask members of the crowd to review the instructions and give you feedback. Put the instructions on the market and ask the crowd to critique them. You can ask the crowd members to put them in their own language or identify problems with them. You should probably ask for 10 or 12 responses, to get different points of view. (If you do this, you'll probably want to add the restriction that you'll pay each crowd-worker only once for doing this task.)

✔ **Macrotasking:** You can often catch this problem before you hire a crowdworker. Ask any potential crowdworker to review your instructions and to put those instructions into her own words. You may want to ask the crowdworker a string of related questions to make sure she understands the instructions. You can ask her to paraphrase the instructions, describe problems that she sees in the specifications, and give examples of similar instructions she's seen.

Testing your instructions before you hire a worker is much easier than testing them after a macrotask is complete. In the latter situation you may get into a dispute with the crowdworker over the results of the task. If you're in a dispute with a crowdworker over your instructions, you may want a neutral third party to test those instructions with the worker.

✔ **Crowdcontests:** You often have the opportunity to adjust your instructions during the contest or after the participants have completed an initial stage. If you're refining the instructions in the middle of a contest, ask the remaining contestants how their submissions meet your new criteria or how they fall short.

If you're running a crowdcontest for a creative project, you may find that the participants can better communicate using their artistic skills than using words. They may be able to describe what they understand from your words, but they'll probably find it easier to demonstrate what they understand in their art.

✔ **Crowdfunding:** You can't easily separate the problem of poorly written descriptions from the problem that your project appeals only to a small crowd. All you know is that the crowd has read your description and isn't engaged by your project. If a large number of people visit your crowdfunding project's page but only a few offer money, then your problem may be found in your description of the project.

If you seem to be having trouble with your instructions or descriptions, you may want to restrict your job to a specific region or culture. Crowdsourcing's a global activity, but most markets allow you to restrict your crowd to individuals who live in a certain area or have certain skills.

Addressing issues with the division of labour

Usually, you find problems with the division of labour only in macrotasking or microtasking. If you find that a lot of people look at your task but only a few complete it, you may have divided your work in a way that's awkward. You may have created tasks that require too many different skills. The workers can complete the first part of the task but are unable to complete the remainder of the task.

In microtasking, if you're getting a large number of incomplete tasks returned, you may not have divided the task into natural units. You may see the same phenomenon if you have poor instructions, if you price the task incorrectly, or if you have unworkable market rules.

In macrotasking, you can often discover a poor division of labour during the first stage of the process. If you don't receive a large number of proposals for your project, you may have designed it poorly. You should be able to learn more about this problem during the interview stage. You can also send a task to a worker that you'd like to hire and ask her whether the project has any problems.

Seeing how rules can hinder the project

When you have problems with markets, you see your project stop dead. You see the crowd review your project but it submits nothing.

Perhaps the crowd members see that the deadline's too soon and they don't have time to do the work. Alternatively, they may see that the deadline's far in the future and conclude that you want a more complicated submission then the one they want to offer.

The crowd may dislike some of the details of your crowdsourcing activity. They may not like the format in which you want the work submitted, or they may not want to agree to your restrictions on intellectual property. So if you're getting no submissions for your crowdsourcing, you may want to check the market rules you're using.

Identifying workflow hiccups

You have workflow problems when your crowdsourcing job involves multiple workers and has multiple tasks and stops before all of the tasks are done. The job starts well but it stalls after a few steps. The product of one worker, or one crowd, cannot easily be used by the next worker (or crowd).

Workflow problems are most commonly found in complex microtask jobs. Sometimes, you find a workflow problem in a macrotask. However, you usually have more control over the interactions of crowdworkers in macrotasking, and directly oversee them. You can usually identify situations when the product of one macrotasker isn't right for the next worker.

You can suspect a workflow problem if your jobs involve a complicated workflow and start well but fail to conclude. If this is the case, in future, you really need to test your workflow in a preliminary run (see the later section 'Lowering the Stakes with a Pilot Run').

Reading the signs from the crowd

You need to carefully interpret the responses of the crowd, otherwise you may be tempted to treat the symptom and not the underlying cause of an issue. In general, you obtain four kinds of information from your results:

- ✔ **Size and nature of the crowd:** In all forms of crowdsourcing, you can usually identify a great deal about the size and nature of the crowd. You can find out how many people visited your project on a crowdsourcing platform. You can see where they're located, how many engaged with your job and how many completed it.

- ✔ **Number of completed tasks:** You always know the number of completed tasks. In microtasking, you receive the results of each task. In crowdfunding, you obtain equivalent information in the number of people who donate to your campaign. In macrotasking, you have the number of people who apply for your job. In crowdcontests, you know the number of submissions.

- ✔ **Time required to finish task:** Most crowdsourcing sites give you detailed information about the time that workers require to complete a task. In microtasking, you can often see the time the day when a worker accepted a task and the time when she returned it to the crowdsourcing site. In other forms of crowdsourcing, you can often obtain similar forms of information. In crowdcontests, you may be able to find out how much time an individual required between the moment when she first visited your contest description and when she submitted an entry.

- ✔ **Nature of results:** You find some of the most useful information in the work itself. You can tell whether the work closely conforms to your descriptions or deviates in a common way from your ideas.

Sometimes you can elicit comments from the crowd. In crowdfunding, for example, you can solicit remarks from those who donate money. Often such remarks are nothing more than nondescript encouragements for your activities. However, comments may also contain repeated messages that suggest that donors fail to understand your project or support only one aspect of it.

Handling the Unexpected

No matter how well you plan your project and how dutifully you follow the cycle of continuous improvement, you may still find yourself facing a completely unexpected event. You carefully make plans. You follow all the guidelines when you release your project to the crowd. You monitor the work diligently. But when you receive the results, something you didn't anticipate has occurred, and you need to make a decision. Read on for guidance on how to cope when crowdsourcing throws you a curve ball.

Accepting bad results

You can face two kinds of unexpected event: complete and utter disasters, and weird results that you can somehow adapt to your purposes. For the latter type, look for ways to accept the unusual result.

For example, suppose you've carefully planned a marketing project and have macrotasked the data analysis. You wrote a careful description of the analysis and the methods that workers should use. You interviewed several crowdworkers and selected one who understood the project and seemed to know the methods that you needed. Still, when you receive the report, you find that the analysis has been performed using a method that's radically different from the one you specified.

When the worker has used a different method from the one you specified, you may find that you can make use of the material, especially if you're facing a deadline and can't afford the time'd be required to repost the job and interview more crowdworkers. Your best solution may be to accept the work on the condition that the crowdworker explains the new method and shows how the analysis answers the questions that you were hoping to answer. Take comfort from the thought that crowdsourcing transfers knowledge as well as labour. You may have an opportunity to learn something new.

Stopping, revising and restarting

When the unexpected occurs, you may stop the process, revise the job and restart the work. In such circumstances, you're applying the continuous improvement cycle many times during a single job. You design the job, run it, gather information from partial results, and decide what to do next. If you let the job continue, you obtain more partial results and make another decision.

If you decide to stop a job in the middle and revise it, act as if you're terminating a bad start to the job and begin anew. Rarely can you combine material from the initial version of your project with that from the revised version.

Revising jobs in microtasking is quite easy because most platforms let you review the results in small batches. (If you're getting the results in a single batch, you're probably doing a small job. In that case, simply trash the results and start again.)

If your first batch of microtasks produce unexpected results, then you really have three choices, not two. You can keep things as they are: you stop the tasks, revise them, and then restart. Or you can let the crowd do a few more tasks and then see whether the result changes. If you take this last path, put a limit on the number of tasks, so that the crowd doesn't produce a large number of results that you may not be able to use.

Demanding a refund

Many crowdsourcing platforms advertise a complete refund policy. As with all such claims, examine the details closely. Don't base your plans on the idea that you'll get a complete refund if your crowdsourcing job goes badly. Indeed, most crowdsourcing platforms start their refund policy with a statement saying that you're guaranteed to have to pay only for work that's actually done by the workers, but you've no guarantee that the work will be done well. Nonetheless, you may find circumstances in which you can demand at least a partial refund.

You can't expect a refund if your job hasn't been done properly. Only when you do fixed-cost macrotasking can you expect an unconditional refund for badly done work. Usually, you can expect a refund only if the crowdsourcing platform has broken its agreement with you.

When you're involved in a transaction in crowdsourcing, you're part of a two-sided agreement. You, as crowdsourcer, agree to provide a description of a job, work with the crowdsourcing platform in the way that it has organised, and pay for the job when complete. The crowdsourcing platform, as the representative of the crowdworkers, agrees to place your job on a market, oversee the work on the job, and deliver the results in a certain form.

Most crowdsourcing platforms present a lengthy set of terms when you create an account. You have to accept these terms before you can start your job. These terms vary from platform to platform, but they may allow refunds for four kinds of circumstances:

- ✔ **You've offered a job for a fixed price on a macrotask platform.** Some macrotask platforms allow you to offer a job for a fixed amount – an amount that you'll pay no matter how long the job takes. When the crowd's completed the job, you can review it and accept or reject it. If you accept it, you get the final product and pay the fixed price no matter how much or how little time the worker put into it. If you reject it, you are refunded the money you paid to the worker (minus any fees that you owe to the platform) and you get no product at all. Most crowdsourcing jobs aren't done this way, and crowdworkers don't like such jobs because they bear the risk that they may not get paid at all. Because of this risk that you won't like the results of their work, crowdworkers tend to offer slightly higher bids for fixed price bids.

- ✔ **The platform failed to manage the job properly.** Uncommon, but it does happen from time to time. You submit a job and it becomes lost in the system or is assigned to the wrong worker or is handled in the wrong way. You can determine that you had a job in this category if you look at the workflow and discover that it simply doesn't make sense. You submitted a job as a web design and it came back as a logo design. You asked for translation and you received editing services. If you have a job in this category, you're well within your rights to ask for a refund.

✔ **You made a mistake using the system that the platform should have caught.** Pretty common, but you'll have a hard time proving your case. You're arguing that you submitted the wrong kind of job because the crowdsourcing platform is confusing. You can make the strongest argument if you can show that you did things that were logical and obvious for your job but took you to the wrong part of the crowdsourcing platform.

This kind of problem is especially common with crowdcontests and crowdfunding campaigns. Often, a platform offers so many versions of either activity that the user can't make a good choice. If you have any questions about the kind of crowdsourcing activity that you're doing, contact the platform before you start the job. If you've started the job and suspect you've made a mistake, contact the platform immediately.

✔ **The crowdworkers wilfully misunderstood your job or did it incorrectly.** A more-common problem than crowdsourcing platforms like to admit, and more responsibility exists on both sides than the crowdsourcer tends to acknowledge. If you face this kind of problem, you need to show that any reasonable person would have interpreted your job description correctly and done the work in the proper way.

Even if the crowdsourcing platform made a mistake and now owes you a refund, you generally get the best response if you identify the problem early and give those running the platform a chance to correct it. Manage your project. Follow its progress.

Paying and trashing

In most cases, you can recover from a bad crowdsourcing job with the loss of only a little time, a modest amount of money and a slightly bruised ego. Because crowdsourcing breaks jobs into small parts, you aren't in a situation where you can lose much.

However, do consider stopping the job, paying the fees and walking away when you have one kind of difficult situation: a situation in which you're trying to crowdsource a job that really shouldn't be crowdsourced. Some jobs simply can't easily be crowdsourced. They require too much management, too much history, and too broad a base of knowledge to fit easily into the crowdsourcing model. If you're reading the information from the crowd and it tells you that you've made a mistake, then walk away. Don't spend more time trying to make the job work.

Lowering the Stakes with a Pilot Run

If you're doing a crowdsourcing job for the first time, do a pilot run. Run the job with a small crowd or for a limited period of time to ensure that all the details are right.

Crowdsourcing has few universal truths beyond the wisdom of the pilot run. In microtasking, you do a pilot run when you offer 20 tasks instead of 20,000. In crowdcontests, you do a pilot run when you run a two-stage contest and offer a small prize for contestants who offer interesting preliminary designs. In macrotasking, you do a pilot run when you ask for a storyboard of a video rather than a full production. In crowdfunding, you do a pilot run when you try to fund a small project instead of your full idea.

If you do a pilot run, you can test all aspects of your job without putting a large amount of money at risk. You can also engage the crowd to help refine your ideas. Here are some areas to consider:

- ✔ **Finding the price point:** One of the most compelling reasons for doing a pilot run of your crowdsourcing project is to work out the right price at which to offer for the full job. You want to set the price in a way that attracts a crowd with the right skills and gets the job done quickly.

  If you're microtasking, you almost always want to do a pilot study. Offer 25 tasks and see how much time the crowd takes to complete them. If the tasks are handled quickly and correctly, you probably don't need to increase the payments. If the tasks sit in the market for a long time, you may need to set a higher price to attract the crowd.

  You may need to offer at least 25 or even 50 tasks for a pilot run of microtasking. Sometimes, the crowd doesn't like to do a microtask job that offers only a few tasks. The crowd members believe that by repeating the task they can do it quickly and hence earn more money.

- ✔ **Engaging the crowd and improving the work:** In many forms of crowdsourcing, you get better results if you engage the crowd during the pilot run and learn about the kind of work that the crowd members want or how they think your job should be organised.

  In macrotasking, for example, you can provide small pilot jobs and ask the crowdworkers for their opinions about the work or their ideas about how to organise the work in a different manner. Because you're only dealing with a small part of the job, you can easily reorganise the work if the workers have an interesting idea.

You can obtain a similar kind of benefit in crowdcontests. Crowdcontests are single activities, so you can often make a mistake by asking for the kind of product that the crowd doesn't want to provide. In a crowdcontest, your pilot run may be much broader than the final contest and solicit as many ideas as possible. You then identify the most promising ideas and start a second round of the contest.

✔ **Revising the instructions:** Nothing is more important to crowdsourcing than clear instructions (see Chapter 11), so test them in your pilot. Not only can you see how well the crowd handles your ideas, but you can also ask it to provide feedback. Ask the members whether they understood what you wrote, whether they'd phrase the instructions in another way, whether they have any ideas about how you can guide the crowd.

✔ **Redirecting the workflow:** If you're doing a complicated workflow in crowdsourcing (see Chapter 16), do many pilot studies to refine your design and make sure that each step works. Test each step individually. Make sure that each set of instructions produces the right results in the right time for the right price. When you're sure that each individual step works, connect the steps together to make sure that the entire process works properly.

Adapting a Crowdfunding Campaign According to Results

When you're doing crowdfunding, you have an inflexible goal but a flexible crowd. When you've identified your project and posted it to a crowdmarket, you really can't change your *idea*. If you do, you may have to explain to those members of the crowd who made an early contribution that you plan to use their money for something other than the idea you originally proposed.

However, in crowdfunding you can change *crowds* in the middle of the campaign. If your original crowd isn't providing you with the funds, you can look elsewhere.

In non-equity crowdfunding, you can usually refine or make small additions to your original statement. However, in equity crowdfunding, when you're trying to sell part of your company, you can't change your original ideas and original plan for the company without stopping the campaign, reorganising your company and starting again.

For more on crowdfunding, flick to Chapter 6. The following sections help your modify your crowdfunding crowd according to results.

Changing the means and the message

If you're not getting enough interest in your crowdfunding campaign, you may need to change the means that you're using to draw the crowd. Even with modern social media, you can easily find yourself trapped in a little community that's sending messages to its own members and to no one else.

If you're not seeing much traffic at your site even though you're sending out multiple messages, you may want to change the way in which you promote your campaign, perhaps by describing the project in a new way and developing a new strategy for circulating that description. You can change the medium that you're using and move to other forms of social media. You may also want to recruit a new inner core of people who'll start sending messages to a new group of people. For more on building a crowd, see Chapter 10.

Changing your platform

If you've changed the message and haven't seen an increase in the number and value of donations, you may want to change the crowdfunding platform you use. While you generally have to recruit your own crowd for a crowdfunding campaign, you may also find that your crowd prefers one platform over the other. After you've received feedback from the crowd, you may choose to switch platforms.

Changing the goal

If you simply aren't getting sufficient interest in your campaign, you may eventually conclude that you're running the wrong campaign. Your project is ill-conceived, your description doesn't engage the crowd, or your core members aren't as interested as they claimed to be. In such a case, you may want to change the goal. If you change the goal, you need to stop the campaign and start anew.

If you're doing all-or-nothing crowdfunding (see Chapter 6), you lose all the initial funds that you've collected. However, if you haven't collected much towards your goal, you may conclude that you're more likely to succeed by starting afresh than by expanding your current campaign.

Making continuous checks and improvements

United Amalgamated Microtasks, commonly known as UAM, is a crowdsourcing firm that accepts large jobs from clients and breaks them into microtasks. Typically, these jobs are activities such as cleaning databases, finding the names of sales contacts and looking at web pages to determine whether they're good places in which to advertise. UAM uses the cycle of continuous improvement on a daily basis to manage its crowdsourcing jobs.

From its experience in the microtasking field, UAM estimates how many microtasks will be done on its market each day. Each morning, the microtask manager, Akiko, reviews the progress of each job and compares the number of tasks that were completed the day before with the number that she estimated would be done. If the crowd doesn't complete the estimated number of tasks for two days in a row, the manager adjusts the job to try to improve it.

In most cases, Akiko can do one of two things. She can either change the description and instructions for the job, or she can increase the wage that UAW is offering for each task. First, she'll look at the description and instructions. If she thinks she can improve them, she'll rewrite the description and instructions immediately and post them on the market. If Akiko decides that the price for each task is too low, she'll stop the job and wait two hours to make sure that no tasks are in the hands of the workers. She'll then increase the price for each task.

Part IV
Getting All You Can Get from the Crowd

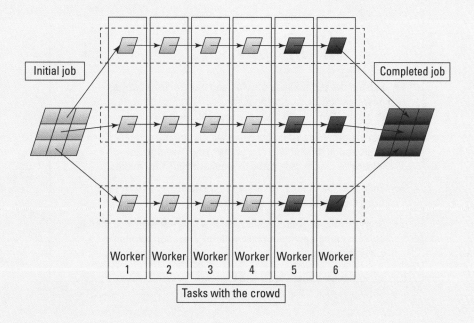

Initial job

Completed job

Worker 1 Worker 2 Worker 3 Worker 4 Worker 5 Worker 6

Tasks with the crowd

In this part . . .

- ✔ Expand the possibilities of what you can achieve through microtasking by employing workflow. Get microtasking to do things that you might not have thought were possible.

- ✔ Deploy crowdsourcing across a wide area and arrange it at short notice so that you can gather, organise and interpret information from the crowd to monitor significant events.

- ✔ Embrace innovation crowdsourcing and stay energised with fresh ideas and new perspectives.

- ✔ Start to think of your organisation in a different way and plan to bring exciting new talent into your organisation through crowdsourcing.

Chapter 16

Combining Microtasks and Preparing Workflow

*M*icrotasking takes some effort, there's no doubt about it. You have to design your tasks, upload them to a microtask market, let the crowd do its work, check the results and then download the work that meets your standards. (See Chapter 8 for a discussion of how to microtask.) With all this to do, you could be forgiven for wanting to keep your microtasking job as simple as possible. After all, why would you want to make it more complicated? Well, of course you should keep your microtasks as simple as possible, but sometimes the very simplest microtasks aren't the best. Simple microtasks may be easy to design and easy to start, but they can only do simple things.

Checking the results of microtasks can take real effort. You have to review each task to be sure that the work's done properly. When you've uploaded a large number of tasks, you quickly learn that checking the results of each microtask takes a lot of time and isn't always feasible. Microtasks have a way of expanding. You start by doing 10, but soon you're doing 100 tasks, and before you know it you're doing 1,000. You can probably check 10 microtasks and maybe even check 100, but when you're running 1,000, you can't check them all.

To check for errors in microtasks or to get microtasks to do complicated things, you need a process called *workflow*, where the work flows from one task to the next. Workflow is a very powerful tool. With it, you can get microtasks to do things that you might not have imagined were possible (see the sidebar, 'Using microtasks to see the big picture').

Using microtasks to see the big picture

The crowdsourcing company Tagasauris came from a simple idea, an idea that originally didn't involve workflow. The founders of Tagasauris wanted to use crowdsourcing to write descriptions of photographs. However, the company founders knew that naïve approaches to the problem wouldn't work. 'You can't assume that the crowd will always produce useful results,' explains Todd Carter, CEO of the firm. 'And you can't duplicate the work, because the way one member of the crowd describes an image can be very different from the way another member of the crowd describes the same image.'

In the end, the company developed a complex workflow to prepare descriptions. 'We adopted the policy of trying to use the best kind of labour for each task of the process,' Carter says. 'We use software to recognise faces, one set of microtaskers to identify details, another to draft parts of the description, and macrotaskers to curate parts of the process.' All of these steps are held together with a sophisticated workflow. It may sound complicated, but it works. The workflow uses the crowd to create clear descriptions of images and to create those descriptions quickly and inexpensively.

Workflow can be challenging to create. You have to design and test many different microtasks and then work out how to combine them. To help, in this chapter you find out about the basic ideas of workflow. You discover new ways of dividing complicated jobs into small tasks, and clever methods of combining the results. At the end of the chapter, I look at how you might be able to use workflow to handle real problems in crowdsourcing.

Discerning the Difference between Parallel and Serial Microtasks

To understand the nature of workflow, you first need to understand the different kinds of microtask. (If you want to know the basics of microtasking, head first to Chapter 8.) Microtasks come in two principal varieties: parallel tasks and serial tasks. (Technically, a third variety exists called a recursive task, but it's yet to find any practical application, so I won't go into that one here.) In addition to these two approaches, you can combine them in many different ways (see the section 'Combining parallel and serial tasks' later in this chapter).

Doing the job all at once: Parallel tasks

Parallel microtasks are the simplest form of microtask. You start with a large problem that you can divide into tiny tasks which you give to the crowd. For these tasks, everyone in the crowd gets the same set of instructions. Each crowd member is doing the same thing but with different data. Each member is trying to transcribe a different business card or characterise a different tweet or recognise faces in a different photograph. One set of instructions. Many people. Different data. No concern about which data is processed first and which is processed last. These things describe parallel microtasks.

In the computer world, parallel microtasks are known as single instruction multiple data tasks, or SIMD tasks.

Figure 16-1 shows how parallel microtasks work. You have a single job that you can divide into identical tasks. You give the tasks to the crowd. The crowd completes the tasks and returns them to you. You reassemble the tasks into a complete job.

For a simple example of parallel microtasks, say you receive 1,000 audio logs every day that you need to transcribe. These audio logs come from security guards who are protecting various buildings and businesses around your city. Most of your guards can't write well and some are illiterate, so you ask them to record the events that occur on their shift with a small audio recorder. You need to transcribe those 1,000 audio files into written texts, one text for each file.

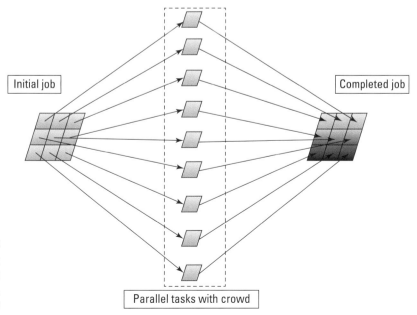

Figure 16-1:
Parallel
microtasks.

Initial job

Completed job

Parallel tasks with crowd

Each audio file contains some standard information: the date and time of the shift, the name of the guard, the location of the property, the state of the property when the guard arrived, anything unusual that happened during the hours of the shift, and the state of the property at the end of the shift. That information's followed by a list of any events and details that the guard believes to be important: a door left open, a person knocking on the door, a box of files left on the floor.

The simplest way of handling these transcription tasks is to make them into 1,000 parallel microtasks. You upload the audio files to a crowdsourcing platform and let the crowd transcribe the six elements of information from each one. You don't care which file is transcribed first and which is transcribed last. Eventually, they will all be done, and you can then use the results.

If you use this simple version of crowdsourcing, you'll discover what many crowdsourcers have found – that when you give microtasks to the crowd, you don't always get back what you hope to get back. Some members of the crowd do the work properly, but some don't. Some misinterpret the instructions. Some don't understand what they hear. Some fail to do the job properly for other reasons. When the job's finished, some of your files aren't properly transcribed, and without checking each one you can't easily tell which ones have been done correctly and which ones haven't. That's where serial microtasking comes in handy. With serial microtasking, you can get results that are often more reliable.

Putting one thing after another: Serial tasks

Serial microtasking tasks are like the stages of an assembly line. You take a complicated task and break it into little steps that you perform in order – in *series*. You begin by asking the crowd to do the first step. Next, you ask it to do the second, and then the third, and so on until the crowd finishes all the steps. Figure 16-2 shows the steps of a serial task, a task that performs six independent steps on a single object.

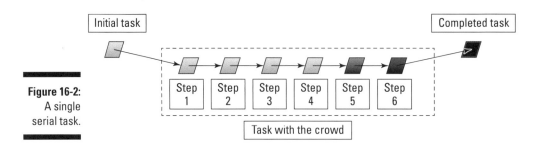

Figure 16-2:
A single
serial task.

If you take the example of the 1,000 audio logs I used in the preceding section, you could divide this transcription job into an assembly line with six steps:

1. Transcribe the date and time of the shift.

2. Transcribe the name of the guard.

3. Transcribe the location of the property.

4. Transcribe the state of the property at the start of the shift.

5. Transcribe the events that happened during the shift.

6. Transcribe the state of the property at the end of the shift.

You can create various different kinds of serial microtask to transcribe these audio files. In one way of transcribing files with serial microtasks, you first take one audio file, give it to the crowd and ask a crowdworker to transcribe the date and time of the shift. Secondly, you give that same audio file to another worker and ask that worker to transcribe the name of the guard. Next, you give the file to a third crowdworker, who you ask to transcribe the location of the property. You continue this process through the fourth, fifth and sixth steps.

Do you see what you've done there? You've divided the transcription job into six new microtasks, but you've not accrued any actual benefits from doing the work in serial. If anything, you've made your life more complicated. Whereas you once had to manage just one kind of microtask, you now have to manage six.

However, you can tweak these six microtasks just a little bit and get tasks that are crowd corrected. You get a *crowd-corrected microtask* by asking each worker to both do something new *and* to check all the work that's been done before. If the worker sees a mistake in the earlier work, she should correct it. Making this change gives you six new microtasks:

1. Transcribe the date and time of the shift.

2. Transcribe the name of the guard, check the results from step 1 and correct any mistakes.

3. Transcribe the location of the property, check the results from steps 1 and 2 and correct any mistakes.

4. Transcribe the state of the property at the start of the shift, check the results from steps 1, 2 and 3 and correct any mistakes.

5. Transcribe the events that happened during the shift, check the results from steps 1, 2, 3 and 4 and correct any mistakes.

6. Transcribe the state of the property at the end of the shift, check all the information already transcribed and correct any mistakes.

These new tasks have to be done in a fixed order. A crowdworker can't do the second task until the first task is complete, or the third task until the second is done. Furthermore, each task requires a little more work than its predecessors. The first task doesn't require any checking of previous work, whereas the second task requires a check of the work of the first task as well as doing some transcription, and the third task requires a check of the work of the first and second tasks as well as doing a little transcription. (Figure 16-3 shows how this job is divided into serial tasks for each audio file.)

When you create serial tasks, you often ask the crowd to do more work for some tasks than for others, so offering larger payments for the more complicated tasks than for the simpler tasks is a good idea. Otherwise, workers may not complete the more complicated tasks as quickly, and your tasks will stall in the crowdmarket.

The difference between serial and parallel tasks is that serial tasks need to be done in a specific order. If you divide a job into six serial tasks, you have data that moves through your crowd in six waves. On each piece of the data, a member of the crowd has to do the first step of the process before someone can do the second step. Then a crowdworker has to do the second step before someone does the third.

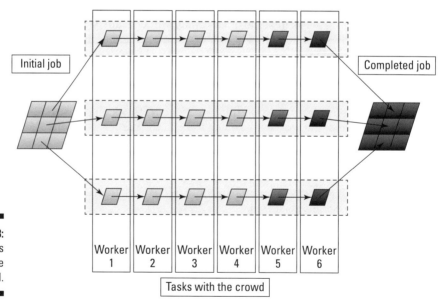

Figure 16-3:
Serial tasks with the crowd.

The crowd doesn't see serial microtasks from the same perspective as you do. In fact, the workers may not be aware that they're doing serial micro-tasks. For them, each step in the process is a microtask. Because they can see several steps, workers understand that you're offering several different kinds of microtask. However, they may not be aware that the different micro-tasks are connected.

Some members of the crowd may look at each microtask and try each one. Others may look at only one and concentrate on it. Each member of the crowd chooses which of the steps she'd like to do, but the crowdsourcing platform ensures that the different steps are done in the proper order. No one attempts to do step 2 before step 1's been completed.

In the computer world, serial tasks may be known as *pipeline tasks*.

Minimising Error

Workflow is a powerful tool where you take the results from one micro-task and combine them with the output of a second, third or even a fourth microtask to produce a complicated result. You can use workflow for many different reasons, but it's an especially useful way of minimising the effects of errors, mistakes, goofs, typos, misunderstandings and even sabotage in microtasks.

Appreciating the value of serial tasks

At first, serial tasks may not look too appealing. They tend to be more expen-sive than parallel tasks, take more time and be more trouble.

Take the example of transcribing audio files that I cover in the preceding sec-tion. If your 1,000 audio files are small, you can create 1,000 parallel micro-tasks by asking a member of the crowd to transcribe each one. However, if you create six serial tasks for each audio file, you suddenly have 6,000 tasks on your hands. And while you may not pay the same amount for each of these serial tasks as you would for one of the parallel tasks, you'll still probably pay more than one-sixth of the price of each parallel task. Suppose that you pay $1 (£0.63) for each transcription done by a single parallel task and you pay $0.25 (£0.16) for each serial task. To complete all the transcriptions, you'll pay $1,000 (£630) if you do it with the parallel tasks or $1,500 (£945) if you do it with the serial tasks. So not only do you pay more money, but you have to do more work, too. You have to follow each audio file as it goes from crowd-worker to crowdworker.

So, you may ask why do serial tasks at all. The answer is that you choose serial tasks because they offer a better way than parallel tasks of finding errors in the work. Sure, they take more time, more money and more effort, but they product more reliable results.

Among the six workers processing each audio file, for example, each worker both adds a little bit of information and checks previous workers' results. If one worker spots an error, she can correct the mistake before she sends it forward to the next step. When the job reaches the last step, it's been checked by each of the workers along the way.

Duplicating parallel tasks

Despite the benefits they bring, serial tasks can still seem like a lot of work. Because of this, many people instead try to weed out errors in microtasks by using another technique – duplicating parallel tasks and checking the results.

Duplicating parallel tasks works like this: suppose you have 1,000 audio files that you want to transcribe. You create a microtask for each audio file and send the tasks to the crowd. When the crowd has transcribed the files, you duplicate the process; you have the crowd transcribe the files a second time. You then compare the results of the two stages. If the results agree, the files are properly transcribed. If they disagree, someone in the crowd has made a mistake, so you then send the audio file to the crowd again and ask for a third transcription. If that third transcription agrees with one of the other two, you decide that majority rules. Two transcriptions that agree beats one that doesn't agree, so you accept as correct the two transcriptions that agree.

Duplicating parallel tasks does have the benefit of being a simpler alternative to doing serial tasks, but it does have drawbacks of its own. It doesn't guarantee perfect results, for one. Two crowdworkers can agree and still be wrong. Think about it for a moment. The audio file might have a voice that speaks with an unfamiliar accent or uses a word in an unusual way. When they listen to the file, both workers may misunderstand the words in the same way. They agree, but both are wrong. (For more on this blunder, see Chapter 23.)

Duplication also involves more work than you may at first think. If you transcribe 1,000 audio files with parallel workflow and duplicate all the microtasks, you expect to do at least 2,000 individual microtasks. The exact number you do depends on the percentage of mistakes you see in the work. If 10 per cent of the transcriptions contain errors, you expect to do roughly 2,222 microtasks. (Of the original 2,000 transcriptions, 200 have an error and don't match. Of those 200, you find 20 with an error when they're re-transcribed. Of those 20, you find a final 2 with errors in the transcription.)

When you duplicate work in order to detect errors, you achieve the best results if each crowd worker does the task in a different way. If the workers use different instructions, they're less likely to make the same errors. If the crowd is transcribing audio files, for example, you may have one group complete the transcriptions with parallel tasks and another group do it as serial tasks. If the results of the two kinds of tasks agree, you can be more confident that you have the right transcriptions.

Working through an Example: Devising Workflow and Making Decisions in Mechanical Turk

When you use workflow in microtasking, you take a large job and break it into a combination of parallel tasks, serial tasks and computer programs. You use workflow in order to bring the power of human intelligence to large, complex jobs.

Workflow is most important for large microtasking jobs – for the jobs you can't check yourself or assemble a trusted team to check. If you're doing microtasking jobs that are small and can be checked relatively easily, you may not need to worry much about workflow.

No matter whether you use parallel or serial microtasks – or a combination of both – an important component of workflow is decision making. When you make a decision in a workflow, you review the results of one microtask with a computer program and automatically decide which microtask should be done next.

In the preceding section on duplicating parallel tasks, my example uses workflow to compare the results of two duplicate tasks. If the two tasks produce identical results, the workflow notifies the crowdsourcer that the tasks have been done properly. If the two tasks produce different results, the workflow creates a new task and sends it to the crowd. When the crowd finishes this task, the workflow checks the result with the results of the two tasks completed earlier. If the results from two of the tasks agree, the workflow notifies the crowdsourcer that the work has been done properly.

Of course, this process may continue for a long time. If no two of the three results agree, the workflow creates a fourth task and again sends it to the crowd. The workflow continues this process until it finds that the results of two tasks agree.

Figure 16-4 gives you a diagram that illustrates this workflow. It shows how the workflow sends the tasks to the crowd, makes a decision and sends the final result to you.

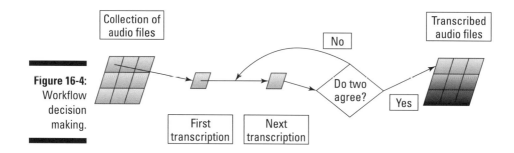

Figure 16-4:
Workflow
decision
making.

When you create workflow, you're actually creating a form of program – a program that controls your microtasks. (If you need to know more about programming, you might look at *Beginning Programming with Java For Dummies* by Barry Burd (Wiley).) This workflow sends the microtasks to the crowd and retrieves the results. Like a program, it can examine the results of microtasks in order to determine how those results should be processed. The workflow can create new tasks from those results and send those tasks to the crowd, or it can feed those results into a real computer program. In my example, such a program might put the transcribed sentences into a certain order or it might count the number of times that certain words appear in the transcripts.

See Chapter 8 for an introduction to Amazon's Mechanical Turk. *Mechanical Turk* is a general-purpose microtasking crowdsourcing platform that enables you to create your own workflow and to create rules to govern your decision-making process. You do this by writing a program to run on your own computer. That program sends commands to Mechanical Turk to create microtasks, send those microtasks to the market and recover the results of the microtasks after the crowd has done its work.

Fortunately, Mechanical Turk and most other microtasking crowdmarkets let you develop your workflow in a test environment, which it calls a sandbox. The *sandbox* looks like a standard crowdsourcing platform but is a private one that only you can see. In the sandbox, you can test your workflow. The crowd won't see your tasks, but you can look at the tasks as they would appear on the real platform.

To create a workflow in Mechanical Turk, your first step is to go to the Mechanical Turk website (www.mturk.com) to create a requestor account. This enables you to post microtasks and to deposit funds that cover the costs of your tasks and the Mechanical Turk fees. When you've done that, you can return to your own computer and create your workflow.

Here, I give you just an overview of how to create workflow in Mechanical Turk. To get the finer details of how to create and manage workflow in Mechanical Turk, read the *Amazon Mechanical Turk Developer Guide* and the *Amazon Mechanical Turk API Reference*. (An API is an application programming interface.) You can find both documents at http://aws.amazon.com/documentation/mturk. These documents describe in detail the *commands* – the operations you can send to Mechanical Turk from your workflow – and the information that you have to give them in order to create the workflow you want. The documents also point to where you can learn to use these commands with specific programming languages.

When you create workflow for Mechanical Turk or any microtask platform, you regularly use five commands. Those five commands create microtasks, send the tasks to the microtask market (in this example, Mechanical Turk), review the results of those tasks, and accept or reject them. In Mechanical Turk, those five commands are:

- ✔ CreateHIT: creates a single microtask
- ✔ GetReviewableHITs: retrieves the microtasks that have been done by the crowd
- ✔ ApproveAssignment: approves a microtask and pays the worker
- ✔ RejectAssignment: rejects the microtask and doesn't pay the worker
- ✔ GetAssignmentforHIT: gets the results for a microtask

In Mechanical Turk, microtasks are called *Human Intelligence Tasks* or HITs.

Starting with parallel tasks

To create a single microtask, parallel or serial, you use the command CreateHIT when writing your program. To create 1,000 parallel microtasks for the audio transcription job example (see the earlier section 'Doing the job all at once: Parallel tasks'), you invoke the CreateHIT command 1,000 times and give it a different audio file each time.

With the CreateHIT command, you can easily duplicate your microtasks and have multiple crowdworkers transcribe your file. When you invoke the command, you simply tell it that you want to duplicate the work, and specify the number of times you want it duplicated. Again, following the audio file example, you tell Mechanical Turk that you want each of the 1,000 microtasks to be done twice.

The programming commands GetReviewableHITs and GetAssignment forHIT give you a way to compare the results of duplicate microtasks. The first command gives you a list of microtasks that are completed. The second command gives you the results for each microtask. You can then compare the results of the two duplicate tasks. If the results are the same, you can decide that the tasks have been done well. If they differ, you can create a new microtask, again using CreateHIT, to resolve the difference.

Mechanical Turk enables you to both automatically duplicate microtasks and compare the results. You automatically compare results by telling CreateHIT that you want to duplicate those tasks three times, and you review the results with a Simple Majority HIT Review Policy. Mechanical Turk will then carry out all your microtasks three times and give you the results whenever at least two of the three duplicate results agree.

Advancing to serial tasks

You can perform serial tasks in Mechanical Turk, although you need to do a little extra work. The audio file transcription example consists of six different tasks in its serial form. Each task transcribes a new part of the file. After the first task, each subsequent task asks the crowdworker to review and correct the work that's been done already. (You can see the list of tasks in the section 'Putting one thing after another: Serial tasks'.)

Using CreateHIT, you can create 1,000 microtasks that do the first step of the serial process, and then give these tasks a name such as Step 1. When the Step 1 tasks are done, you can recover the results using GetReviewableHITs and GetAssignmentforHIT. With those results, you create the next step of the process. Using CreateHIT, you create 1,000 new tasks called Step 2. When those tasks are done you proceed to create micro-tasks for the next steps of the process until you've completed all six steps.

Combining parallel and serial tasks

When you've got to grips with handling both serial and parallel microtasks with workflow, you can combine them to create a highly reliable way of doing work. For example, you can take each audio file in the transcription job example, transcribe it with both a parallel microtask and six serial microtasks, and compare the results of the two approaches. If the results from the two differ-ent approaches agree, you can be certain that the results of the microtasking are reliable. Figure 16-5 shows the workflow for this process.

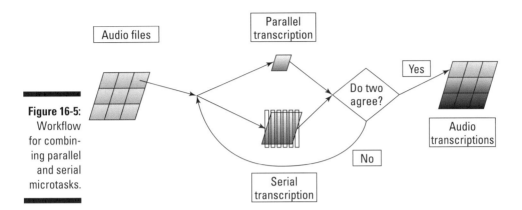

Figure 16-5: Workflow for combining parallel and serial microtasks.

This form of microtasking is more reliable than the simple approach that I describe in Chapter 8, simply because the different crowdworkers are unlikely to make the same mistakes.

Going for Gold: The Many Benefits of Workflow

Microtasking with workflow is a difficult and complex form of crowdsourcing. It's not for first-time crowdsourcers or individuals who know little about programming.

Still, workflow turns microtasking into a very powerful form of crowd-sourcing. It enables you to combine different kinds of skills and different approaches to work on a single job, to improve the ability of the crowd to tag images or transcribe text, to improve the quality of data searches, and even to edit articles and reports. It also enables you to improve the reliability of work through a process known as the Gold Standard.

The *Gold Standard* evaluates the quality of work being done as the crowd handles your microtasks. When you adopt the Gold Standard, you create special microtasks that have known answers and give them to the workers in the middle of your existing job. The workers don't know that these micro-tasks are any different from the others or in any way special. They just take on these tasks like any other task and are paid for the work just the same. Therefore, by using these tasks you should be able to capture the reliability of each worker.

If the members of the crowd do the Gold Standard tasks correctly, you can be confident that they are doing all of your work well.

If the crowd isn't doing the Gold Standard tasks properly, you should feel concerned that the results of the work being produced aren't reliable. From looking at the results of these specific tasks, you may be able to identify some workers who aren't producing good results and exclude them from your job.

Mechanical Turk makes it easy for you to implement Gold Standard questions. When you use the `CreateHIT` command, you can specify that you're creating Gold Standard questions by using what Mechanical Turk calls an Assignment Review Policy. When it uses this policy, Mechanical Turk compares the correct answers to the question with those given by the crowd and marks those that are wrong. Using workflow, you can then exclude unreliable workers form your jobs.

Many of the other companies that offer crowdsourcing services also use Gold Standard questions to improve the reliability of the results.

Chapter 17

Crowd Reporting: Using the Crowd to Gather Information and News

. . . .

In This Chapter
- Using the crowd to get a picture of events and feelings
- Editing material to piece together the story
- Using the Ushahidi crowd reporting software
- Skirting around the pitfalls of crowd reporting

. . . .

*T*he crowd isn't only a source of labour. It can also be a means of gathering news. It has eyes and ears and minds that can gather and process information. It can be deployed across a large geography and be organised at short notice. When you listen to the information that the crowd has gathered, you're engaging in *crowd reporting*. This activity is essentially a form of microtasking, although it can include macrotasking as well.

The crowd may not be a perfect means of gathering information. To see its weaknesses, all you need to do is watch a Twitter feed for ten minutes and try to follow the rumours, repetitions and odd ideas that sprint across the screen. But even with its weaknesses, the crowd is often the best means for learning about the impact of natural disasters, for monitoring large social rallies and events, or for keeping track of any detailed activity.

To get good information from the crowd, you need to be a good manager and a good listener. You need to help the crowd find the right information, you need to help it organise it, and you have to find the patterns of truth within the stories that the crowd sends you. This chapter helps you expertly handle each aspect of crowd reporting management, so you can be aware of the kinds of stories that the crowd can cover and the topics that it finds difficult.

Using the crowd to report news isn't the same thing as using the crowd to gather uniform bits of information for a business process. You may want to use the crowd to collect product prices for a market report, or find contacts for a sales campaign. In such cases, you're really doing traditional microtasking (see Chapter 8).

Understanding Why People Use Crowd Reporting

Crowdsourced news reporting brings breadth and depth to the process of gathering information. It brings breadth because it can deploy reporters around the globe in a way that no conventional news organisation can match. It can find reporters in the most distant communities and get them to the scene of a natural disaster. It can gather details from any place at any time. If you want broad coverage, you turn to the crowd.

Crowd reporting has an equal ability to find a depth of detail that's hidden to most reporting organisations. When a member of the crowd lives in a neighbourhood, he knows the residents of the area, the personalities of the leaders, the issues that touch everyone that lives there, and even the impact of the cracks in the road. If you need to know every little detail, turn to the crowd.

Sorting Eight Billion Stories

If you're going to use the crowd to report news, you need to sort the information that you receive. The world is filled with far more information than any of us can manage. Some of this information is captured by social media, where it's directed into concentrated streams. These streams give insights into the vast experience that the eight billion inhabitants of this world have every day. However, few of these streams are truly useful. To get good streams of information, you need to be a good editor. You need to choose which ideas are important and which are not.

Two crowd-based websites, Wikipedia (www.wikipedia.org) and The Huffington Post (www.huffingtonpost.com), illustrate the importance of good editors. Both solicit information from the crowd and both have a strong editorial staff. At Wikipedia, the editors are part of a volunteer community. They're writers who have earned special privileges on the Wikipedia site. They can remove contributions and suggest information that may be needed for specific entries. The Huffington Post has a paid editorial staff, a group that resembles the editors of a traditional newspaper. The editors solicit material from the crowd and choose the stories to publish.

The following sections outline key considerations for crowd reporting that help you be an expert editor.

Helping the crowd focus

When you use the crowd to report the news, you need to provide the members with help and structure, even if you're asking them to find information that you can't describe in advance. If you tell them to go and find something interesting, they may find things of interest to *them* but not necessarily to you. Therefore, you get the best results if you give the crowd fixed boundaries for its work.

In general, you find that the crowd works best if you restrict the assignment by time or space or to a specific object. So, you can ask the crowd to report on:

- ✔ An emergency that was caused by an obvious issue such as an earthquake or blizzard.

- ✔ An event that has a clear timeline, such as an election.

- ✔ Simple events that need to be observed regularly, such as common city services, For example, cities or utility companies should provide water to every neighbourhood, every day of the week. If you need to verify these services, you can deploy a crowd to check every single residence.

In each of these situations, you give the crowd a story that has missing pieces that the members can find. If you ask the crowd members to report on an earthquake, they'll look for the effects of that quake on people and infrastructure. If they're following an election, they know how the story should progress and look for deviations from that story. If they're monitoring a city service, they look for evidence that the service isn't being performed as it should be.

The crowd can't always combine news easily. Each member of the crowd has a point of view and can easily convince himself that he's at the centre of the action. With crowd reporting, you need ways of combining and weighing information to get a full and balanced picture.

Combining amateurs and experts

When journalists create reports, they try to get gather information from multiple sources and different viewpoints. They do this, in part, to be fair and open minded. However, they also do it to avoid being embarrassed. If they listen to only one side of the story, they can easily be misled.

The crowd can naturally give you many points of view if the members work independently and see the same things. However, you often deploy the crowd over a large geographic area. In such a case, one crowd member may be the only person covering a particular part of the land. To get a different point of view, you can try deploying a few experts or professionals to see whether their experience supports the reports coming from the crowd.

When you send experts to an area, you don't need to send highly trained journalists. You only need to send people you trust, people who know the information you want and can report it to you. If you want information on a tsunami, they can recognise a damaged building. If you're monitoring an election, they know how to recognise voter intimidation. If you're checking snow removal, you send people who know which streets should be cleared first and how they should be cleared.

If your experts and crowd agree, you've reason to believe that you're getting good information from the group, but it's no guarantee. Both the experts and the crowd can be wrong. Also, if the crowd and experts disagree, you shouldn't assume that the crowd is wrong and the experts are right. It may be the other way around.

When you're trying to draw conclusions from the crowd, you receive more benefit from being disciplined than from being an expert. You're an *expert* when you know a lot of facts and theories. You're *disciplined* when you approach a story in a systematic way to avoid convincing yourself that something is true when it's not.

You carry opinions and prejudices. Everyone does. But when you're disciplined, you try to keep those opinions and prejudices from letting you accept a conclusion as true when it's not. A disciplined reporter is always asking questions such as 'Is this fact true?', 'How is this fact pushing me towards a certain conclusion?' and 'Would I accept that conclusion even if I did have that fact?'

When you work with crowds, being disciplined is easier when the members gather facts than when they reason their way to conclusions. When the crowd is gathering facts, you can ask the members to double-check their sources, and you can ask multiple members of the crowd to find the same information. Getting the crowd members to check and verify the reasoning that led them towards a conclusion is more difficult. When you reason, you make jumps in logic that are difficult to explain. You might see a cloud no bigger than a man's hand and conclude that a tornado is on the way. You may reach that conclusion through years of observation, by careful reading of books about meteorology, because your neighbour has told you that tornados always follow small clouds, or you may be inventing a theory that has no basis all. When you try to get a reasoned conclusion, you tend to get better results if you can test each step of the reasoning process.

Gathering Information Geographically with Ushahidi

Ushahidi means testimony in Swahili, and is the name of a commonly used piece of crowdsourcing software. It was developed by a Kenyan, David Kobia, to monitor the 2008 elections in his country. It still retains strong ties to Kenya, even though the software is maintained by a team spread around the world and supported by a foundation based in Florida, USA.

As a type of software, Ushahidi is a kind of geographical information system. It enables the crowd to identify news and items of interest with specific locations on a map. The crowd members use the system to say that a fire has occurred at this house or a protest is happening in that square, or that food can be found at a distant office building. They can use email, text message, or a smartphone app or laptop computer to record the information. The crowd members identify an event, mark the spot on the map and then type in a description. As the crowdsourcer, you can review these reports, look at the patterns and download the information for further analysis.

Ushahidi has been used for many different kinds of crowd reporting, although the software is most commonly associated with monitoring elections and natural disasters: elections in Kenya, Namibia, India, Ethiopia, Brazil and Burundi; after the 2010 Haitian and Chilean earthquakes and the 2011 Louisiana oil spill; and to monitor other issues, such as crime in Atlanta and Washington, DC, USA.

In the summer of 2012, the London Olympic committee deployed the Ushahidi software to monitor events that affected public life and public safety during the games. The committee used the software to combine news from official press releases, official notices, reports from police and security officials, as well as incidents identified by the general crowd. Figure 17-1 depicts the summary map of Ushahidi for the Games.

The dots on the map represent reports of different incidents for one day at the Olympics. Clicking on a dot gives you a summary of the incident. (The one identified in Figure 17-1 is a road closure.) A further click on the report gives more detail about the incident, including links to further information. The record also allows further input from the crowd. The crowd members can confirm the report or indicate that they can find no evidence of the incident it describes. Figure 17-2 shows an incident report.

CrisisMappersUK
London Olympics Deployment
Road networks around the Royal Artillery Barracks - update 01.08
More information
Zoom In | Zoom Out
ALL CATEGORIES
TRUSTED REPORTS
ROAD CLOSURES
SECURITY ISSUES
FIRE
SHELTER
STOLEN PROPERTY
HELP REQUESTED
HOSPITALS
MEDICAL
OFFERS OF ASSISTANCE
OLYMPIC VENUES
PUBLIC TRANSPORT ISSUES
RENDEZVOUS POINTS
RESOLVED ISSUES

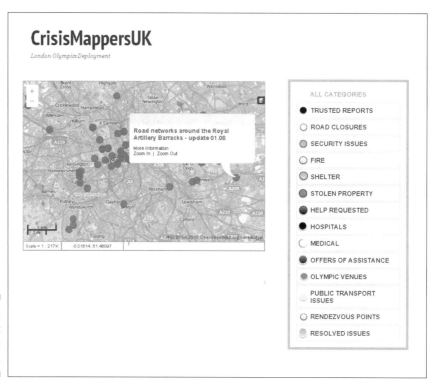

Figure 17-1: Ushahidi at the London Olympics.

Reproduced with permission from Juscomms (www.juscomms.com).

CrisisMappersUK
London Olympics Deployment
Road networks around the Royal Artillery Barracks - update 01.08
VERIFIED
22:22 Jul 31
Royal Artillery Barracks, Royal Borough of Greenwich, London SE18 UK
Road Closures
Description
As well as serving central London venues, the ORN will be serving venues in the Royal Artillery Barracks.
News Source Link
http://www.getaheadofthegames.com/bulletins/1-august.html
Credibility: 0

Figure 17-2: Ushahidi incident report.

Reproduced with permission from Juscomms (www.juscomms.com).

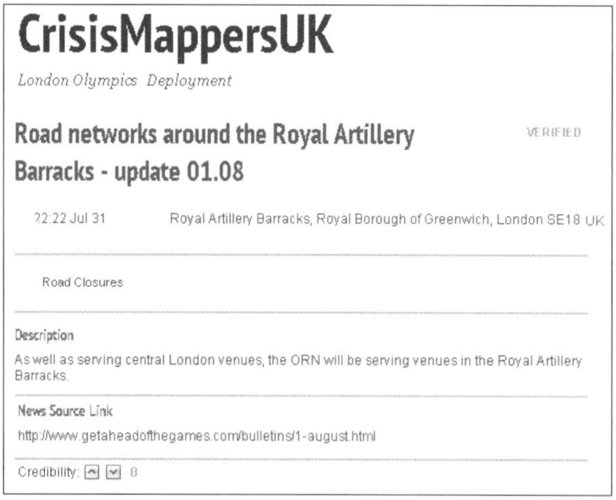

The following sections show how you can harness the power of Ushahidi for your own crowd-reporting project.

Rallying the crowd to Ushahidi

Like crowdfunding (see Chapter 6), crowd reporting requires you to recruit a crowd to your project. You can start with your social circle and then begin to search beyond it. You want the usual tools to promote your work: a web page describing the project, videos that show the issues you're trying to monitor, and tweets and emails that ask the recipient to help with the recruiting.

Because you may often organise a crowd to support civic good, you can find organisations that will assist you. You can turn to business clubs, churches, volunteer organisations, and even to companies that may be of help.

Use the recruiting process as an opportunity to train your crowd. Show the members a video of the kinds of things you're trying to monitor and ask them to take part in the project.

Deploying Ushahidi

Individuals, small non-profit organisations, large organisations and everything in between can use Ushahidi. Whichever type of organisation you come under, you can either find a site that hosts the software and allows you to use it on its servers, such as Crowdmap (`https://crowdmap.com`), or you can obtain a copy of the software and install it on your own server. Many people like the simplicity of Crowdmap, but if you have a large project you may need a server of your own.

If you need a server, you can either have a machine of your own or use a commercial web server such as one at network solutions (`http://network solutions.com`) or DreamHost (`http://dreamhost.com`). You also need a person who's familiar with the basic issues of web hosting and who can help you set up a website for your version of Ushahidi.

Ushahidi is a fairly simple package to deploy. You need to:

1. **Find space on your host.**
2. **Set up the appropriate URL.**
3. **Create a database.**
4. **Install the software.**

5. **Upload a map for your project.**

6. **Connect the appropriate email and text message accounts to the system.**

7. **Write the instructions for your project.**

Then you're ready to organise your crowd.

Ushahidi has a detailed manual that helps a technically trained individual deploy the software.

At least one organisation, Crowdmap, provides the Ushahidi software as a hosted service. Instead of installing the software on your site, you simply open an account on Crowdmap and use Ushahidi on the organisation's servers. As may be expected, the Crowdmap version of Ushahidi isn't quite as flexible as the version you can install on your site. However, many smaller organisations find the Crowdmap version perfectly adequate for their needs.

Summarising the results

After you've created an Ushahidi website and have started collecting information from the crowd, you have to summarise that information. For many applications, the basic Ushahidi map, the kind you see in Figure 17-2, is sufficient. It shows all the incidents and pins the incidents to a map.

For some applications, however, you want to create a summary of the information across geography. For the 2012 London Olympics, for example, the organisers wanted to summarise for the public the kinds of issues they faced each day. To do this, they used a word cloud to display the types of incidents. In a *word cloud*, the size of a word indicates how often that word appears in the data set.

Figure 17-3 shows a word cloud for a single day during the London Olympics. In this cloud, four words are prominent: Underground, Traffic, Emergency and Medical. These four words were the most common words that appeared in the Ushahidi postings on that day. The cloud tells you nothing about where the messages originated and nothing about how the words were used. The words might have appeared individually or together. London might have had a series of medical issues, some problems with the underground, a number of emergency calls, and roads that were relatively free of traffic. Or the city might have had a lot of medical emergencies in the underground that snarled traffic. The word cloud gives you a summary and suggests how the Olympics staff spent their day.

Figure 17-3:
Sample
analysis of
a report in a
word cloud.

Getting the Benefits while Avoiding the Perils of Crowd Reporting

Crowd reporting is one of the more challenging forms of crowdsourcing. The challenges are not found in the software or in the work of recruiting the crowd. You can install Ushahidi (see the preceding section) if you have the skills to install any modest network software, such as a blogging system.

What makes crowd reporting challenging is that it's vulnerable to errors and mistakes in a way that macrotasking or even microtasking is not. If you ask the crowd for judgements, you can easily receive inaccurate information. In the earlier section 'Combining amateurs and experts', I recommend having experts check some of the reports, but even then potential for misinformation exists. For this reason, many commentators, and even a few experts on crowdsourcing, think that crowd reporting is fundamentally flawed and can never be trusted.

Crowd reporting's unreliability comes from four different sources:

✔ Uncooperative workers who don't want to provide good information

✔ Crowds that don't represent an area or region in the way you believe they should

✔ Members of the crowd following the lead of one or more individuals rather than thinking for themselves (this problem is usually called the *crowd effect*)

✔ Bad information driving out good information (this problem is called *Gresham's Law*)

You can limit the influence of uncooperative workers with the same kind of methods that you use to screen and train workers in microtasking (see Chapter 8). You can give them a test to determine their interest and skills, and then carefully train the workers who pass the test to make sure that they know what you want.

As the following sections outline, the other problems have to be handled by careful management and by the use of trusted individuals to review the work of the crowd.

Understanding the nature of the crowd

When you gather information from a crowd, you need to know the nature of the crowd. In the simplest example, when you use Ushahidi to collect data about the damage caused by a natural disaster, you need to know where the crowd members are located. If you think the members are in one area but in fact they're in a different place, you'll get bad information through no fault of the crowd.

In many situations, you need to go beyond the location of the crowd and know something about the demographics of its members. If you believe that you have a liberal crowd, you may interpret their reports in a certain way. If the group is actually conservative, your interpretations are going to be wrong. If you believe that you're getting a picture that's balanced by equal numbers of men and women in the crowd, but in fact the crowd is entirely male, you may again make bad judgements from the information provided by them.

When you listen to the crowd, always ask, 'What can go wrong if I make a false assumption about the crowd?' In some cases, the answer is 'nothing' and you don't need to worry about the nature of the crowd. However, if you're running a project over a long period, you may assume that the nature of the crowd doesn't change. Some individuals may leave the group, but they're replaced by people who are similar. If you're dealing with a natural disaster, such an assumption may not be correct. The people who rush to a disaster are often people who get great satisfaction from working in emergency settings, and they may leave as soon as the immediate danger has passed. Those who come later are often individuals who want to see the situation return to normal.

Understanding the nature of the crowd is similar to understanding the nature of a mass market. You can do expensive and detailed market surveys, but if those surveys don't tell you about the individuals who are part of the market, they really tell you nothing at all.

Every marketing professional has a story about a survey that failed to describe individual consumers properly. It usually involved consumer products such as clothing or household furnishings. These stories usually start with a sudden rise in the demand for a product. Excited by the rise, the product manufacturer does a quick survey of the market and decides to invest in new plants to create more of the product. But just as the plants are starting to operate, the manufacturer discovers that the survey failed to capture the true nature of the market. The manufacturer had assumed that its product was being used by a stable cohort of customers: middle-aged men, perhaps, or women with two or more children. To its horror, the company discovers that its product is being purchased by the most fickle of market segments, young teenagers. In just a few weeks, the teenagers abandon their product. The manufacturer is left with excess factory capacity and low sales. In the most dramatic version of these stories, the manufacturer is deeply in debt and never recovers from the mistake.

When you gather information from the crowd, you should know something about the individuals who are responding, why they're joining the crowd, and how committed they are to your work. You can find this information during the recruiting process and in the activities you use to train the crowd.

If you're using Ushahidi to monitor an election, you probably want to know something about the politics of the people who are reporting on the political activities and the polling stations. If a group of people are reporting that one party is stuffing the ballot boxes, knowing something about the people who are reporting the abuse would be useful. Are the reporters members of the party that's accused of voter fraud? Are they from the opposition party? Do they claim to be neutral observers? If the reporters are in the opposition, you may respond to the story of fraud by sending neutral observers to confirm the stories. If the stories came from neutral reporters, you may move more quickly to file a complaint of fraud.

In this example, to give you time identify and learn about the party of crowd members, you might enable people to register early. In this early registration, you ask reporters to identify their party affiliations. You can then verify these affiliations with the voter registrar. If a reporter doesn't register or registers late, you might assume that he's reporting an event that was instigated by the opposing party. You can then try to send a neutral observer to confirm the report.

Knowing who's talking: The crowd effect

Follow the leader. That's the *crowd effect*. You get it when individual members of the crowd surrender their judgement to a few individuals. Rather than processing information independently, individuals often look to a leader and accept the judgement of that person.

Some of the recent research on the crowd effect suggests that this effect commonly occurs when each member of the crowd can see only part of the information that may be useful to him. When the crowd members find out about decisions from other members of the crowd, they conclude that those members must know something that they don't. Rather than make an independent judgement, they repeat what they hear.

The crowd effect can be so powerful that some members of the crowd ignore or discount concrete information that they possess. For example, they may be looking at a polling station that's run well and has no evidence of problems, yet because they've heard so many stories that they believe of voter fraud, they decide to report that something's going wrong, even though they see no evidence.

Limiting the crowd effect is hard. The following two sections look at your options for doing it.

Isolating the members of the crowd

The first strategy is often difficult. In some cases, you can easily isolate individual members of crowd. In certain cases, the members work by themselves and have contact with only one or two others. They don't see all the information until it's been given to you. However, in situations such as natural disasters, you have a crowd of people who want to work together and have contacts that you can't control. If you can't control the interaction of the crowd, you want to deploy experts who can guarantee to give you independent information.

To isolate members of the crowd, you often have to physically separate the individuals and prevent them from communicating with each other through text messages, emails or tweets – something you can rarely do in the real world. Most members of the crowd want to communicate with other people and resist giving up their communication tools.

Of course, the crowd effect can be influenced by many other factors: laziness, strong leaders, weak followers, contradictory information and many other things. You can't always limit the impact of these factors by isolating the members of the crowd. To reduce the impact of these factors, try to identify problematic individuals when you recruit them, just as you give a test to workers who want to do microtasks (see Chapter 8). Create a questionnaire that may test the character of a potential reporter. Ask ten questions, for example, about difficult situations. You might ask how the reporter would respond if he saw a house burning and heard people calling for help. Would he try to put out the fire, call for help or take a picture and post it for his friends? Determine the answers that you'd expect from a good reporter and select for your crowd the people who answer seven of the ten questions as you want.

Instructing crowd members to focus on the information that they can see and ignore others' opinions

You can more easily instruct the crowd to ignore other peoples' opinions. For example, you might say 'Suppose you see an event that's very different from what others see. Considering only what is before you, what do you conclude?' The problem is that the crowd doesn't always follow those instructions.

Instructing the crowd to ignore the ideas of other people is not a perfect way to avoid the crowd effect. People will still ignore your advice and listen to other members of the crowd. Instructions, however, usually have some effect, and instructing the crowd is much easier than isolating each member.

Knowing what the crowd believes: Gresham's Law

'Bad money drives out good.' Gresham's Law is an observation on economics that's named after 16th-century English financier Thomas Gresham. Applied to crowdsourcing, Gresham's Law means that the crowd sometimes loves a good story more than it loves the truth. It circulates rumours that sound interesting rather than stories that it knows to be true. If you check with the crowd, you may easily find that the Great Wall is the only manmade structure that can be viewed from space, that Elvis Presley is alive and living in Kalamazoo, and that the United Nations has appointed an ambassador for UFOs. These are interesting stories and fun to tell. However, they aren't true.

Some people confuse the crowd effect with Gresham's Law. They're not the same thing, although they are related. When you see the crowd effect without the effects of Gresham's Law, you receive the judgements of only a few people, but the information may be valid. When you get the effects of Gresham's Law without the crowd effect, you hear an odd rumour from certain members of the crowd, but most of your information is good.

In crowdsourcing, you most commonly find the impact of Gresham's Law in emergency situations. At these times, the crowd is often filled with emotion and willing to accept dramatic stories. The crowd members may report that buildings have been destroyed by earthquakes when, in fact, the structures are sound. They may report rioting in the streets when the city is calm. They may think the worst of their neighbour when they've no evidence to support their opinions. They may claim that their opinions are typical when they're not.

In some ways, crowdsourcing encourages rumours, because the transmission of rumours is a form of divided labour. Few people repeat a rumour without modifying it. They add details that make the rumour seem real, and drop information that isn't consistent with the rumour. Such things are readily done by the crowd.

You find Gresham's Law harder to address than the crowd effect. You can't simply isolate the members of the crowd from each other and expect to get better results. While communications experts know how to counteract a rumour when they know the truth, they don't have a good approach for identifying rumours without outside information.

Rumour detection is the work of professional journalists. They detect rumours by listening to different sources, comparing information and balancing different points of view. However, even the most experienced journalist can make mistakes or be misled. Sometimes, you can be fooled by false information from the crowd.

If you're using the crowd to gather information, you may find the best protection from Gresham's Law to be a small group of experts who you trust to give an accurate result.

Chapter 18

Initiating Innovation

*I*nnovation is an important part of any organisation. If an organisation doesn't renew itself with fresh ideas and new perspectives, it stagnates and dies. Innovation gives an organisation the ability to deal with the problems of a changing world.

Many individuals confuse innovation with invention. However, innovation isn't the same thing as invention. *Invention* is the process of creating a new idea, a new product or a new activity. *Innovation* is the process of getting a new view of your circumstances. Invention is one form of innovation, but it's not the only form. You're innovative whenever you:

✔ Realise that something's more important than you used to believe

✔ Discover that you can fix a problem in an office simply by rearranging the way that the workers interact with each other

✔ Appreciate that your market's been telling you what it wants

✔ Identify a new use for an existing product

✔ Uncover a way of avoiding certain mistakes

✔ Find a way of being more efficient

You can innovate all by yourself, but you often find it easiest to innovate when you work with others who have skills, experience and points of view that are different from your own. Many organisations create diverse innovation teams to develop new ideas. So to develop ways of improving its services, a company may assemble a team that consists of a manager, an engineer, a marketing director, a member of the financial office, a sales person and perhaps someone from the human resources staff. The company anticipates that the combined abilities of these individuals can better understand the problem than any one individual can, and the team is better able to identify an innovative solution. And if innovation looks to gather ideas from a diverse collection of people and identify new and practical ideas, then it's an ideal activity to crowdsource.

In this chapter, I look at how to get new ideas from the crowd, how crowd innovation is something more than holding a popularity contest on the web, and how you can build a market for your ideas by having the crowd help with your innovation.

Understanding the Forms of Innovation Crowdsourcing

The crowd can be far more diverse than any committee that you may assemble within your organisation, and it often has expertise that you can get in no other way. Your customers often understand your products better than the engineers who designed them do. Your employees often understand the operations of your organisation better than any managers do. Complete strangers can give you expertise that you'll never find within your organisation.

Innovation crowdsourcing attempts to answer questions by engaging the collective intelligence of the crowd. Except in the most extreme circumstances, a crowd of people, collectively, has a broader intelligence than any one person. The crowd has greater experience and contains more diverse points of view than a single individual. Therefore, if you put a question to a crowd, you may receive an answer that's far more useful than one you'd get from a single expert.

People who help organisations innovate usually identify two kinds of processes to develop innovative ideas:

- ✔ **Closed innovation** looks to a group of known experts to generate and evaluate ideas.

- ✔ **Open innovation** looks to a much larger class of people to be involved in the work. These people may not have been involved with the organisation before or even know of its activities.

EXAMPLE

Finding better ways of storing energy

The Office of Naval Research (ONR) in the USA worked with Innocentive (www.innocentive.com) to run an innovation process to find a new way of storing and transporting energy for the Navy. The ONR was interested in creating a new system that would be less environmentally damaging than the existing oil-based system but would be as simple and flexible as the oil drum or other ways of storing and transporting petroleum products.

The ONR offered a $250,000 (£157,500) prize for the innovation and developed detailed technical specifications. Innocentive received over 120 proposals and helped the ONR select seven finalists from the group.

The seven finalists presented their ideas in a public forum. The judges finally gave the award to Celle Energy, a British company that proposed a hydrogen storage system. Celle Energy proposed that hydrogen could be used as a fuel additive to increase the energy in petroleum products. In this mode, the US Navy would not have to modify its existing engines but could replace them with hydrogen engines as the old ones wore out and were retired.

In general, crowdsourced innovation is considered to be a form of open innovation, although in some cases it can be a form of closed innovation as well. As with all forms of crowdsourcing, innovation crowdsourcing utilises markets to combine the ideas of the crowd. The crowdmarket will help you understand how the crowd values different ideas.

You can use two types of crowdsourcing to drive innovation:

✔ **Crowdcontest:** In the simplest form of crowdcontest, you put a question to the crowd and offer a prize for the best answer. That prize can be a monetary reward, publicity for a good idea, a stake in your corporation or even the opportunity to turn the winner's idea into a real product or service. After you've announced the contest, you wait for submissions, evaluate the ideas, and reward the one that seems to be the best answer to your question. (For more on crowdcontests, head over to Chapter 5.)

The crowdcontest form of innovation crowdsourcing can also be seen as a form of market research. Through a crowdcontest, you try to understand how a group of people understand your question and, from that understanding, extract a good answer. Like market research, an innovation crowdcontest can involve much more than a simple contest. You can engage the crowd members in a discussion to help them refine their ideas. You can encourage the crowd to talk to itself in order to generate as many ideas as possible. You can utilise the crowd to evaluate ideas and tell you how they can best answer your question. You can get information that you can't out of a survey or questionnaire, because you can uncover ideas that you didn't expect.

✔ **Macrotasking:** You can also consider innovation crowdsourcing to be a form of macrotasking, of engaging outside expertise. In this form of crowdsourcing, you recognise that you need a solution to a specific problem, and you identify the kind of expertise that you may need to address that problem. You then ask the appropriate experts to propose answers to those questions. Using this form of innovation crowdsourcing, organisations have developed new algorithms, created new chemical compounds, and discovered ways of removing environmental threats. (For more on macrotasking, see Chapter 7 and the nearby sidebar, 'Finding better ways of storing energy'.)

Asking for a Little Insight: Classes of Innovation

Innovation can be something much more than invention. Invention creates a new product, service or idea, but innovation creates a new way of looking at your organisation, your activities, your ideas. Inventions can create new ways of looking at the world, but many are simple improvements that do little to change your point of view. Often, real innovation comes from finding out that a certain idea is more important than you previously thought, or that a particular concept is really worth all the attention you've been giving it.

Innovation divides into three different classes of idea. You can find innovations that:

✔ Discover new ideas

✔ Suggest substantial improvements over old ideas

✔ Create a true advantage or altered world view

Before you start innovation crowdsourcing, you need to determine the kind of idea you want to find. Each class of innovation requires its own approach to crowdsourcing.

Crowdsourcing for novelty

When you crowdsource for novelty, you look for something that's truly new. The new idea may offer no real advantage other than a changed package or a slight alteration that breaks people out of their old habits. However, you look for something that's not been seen before. You rely on the crowd to tell you that the innovative idea hasn't been seen before in this setting.

Although novel ideas may not change the fundamental way in which you think, they still have value. Many a company's been able to reposition a product and gain market share by redesigning the box and then advertising its 'new, improved packaging'.

Even some of the simplest novel ideas can spark innovation that proves to be important. Organisations have often discovered that big changes came to the way they operated when they adopted small changes merely for the sake of novelty. They processed applications in reverse alphabetical order, for example, or reorganised the columns of a spreadsheet that was important to their operations.

In crowdsourcing for novelty, you seek something that may have no obvious value beyond its newness. Crowds can react in inconsistent ways to novel ideas. If the members of your crowd are talking among themselves, they can easily start following the opinions of a few vocal people who believe that one of the ideas is truly new. This is an example of the *crowd effect* – the crowdsourcing version of mob rule, in which the crowd starts following the ideas of one or two people without thinking. (You can learn more about the crowd effect in Chapter 17.)

Crowdsourcing for improvement

Crowdsourcing for improvement is a common form of crowd innovation. You consider an idea and try to fix it, improve it with established criteria, or utilise it in a new way. Often, you look for only minor modifications, although you have to be prepared for suggestions that can produce radical changes. The crowd may see an entirely new market for a product or suggest how to completely restructure some activity.

By looking for improvement, you generally have clear, concrete goals for your innovation. You can provide concrete measures that you can use to judge the improvement of the evolving ideas.

Concrete measures were a key part of a crowdsourced innovation run by Netflix. The movie website Netflix improved the process that it used to recommend movies to its subscribers by running a crowdcontest. In that contest, Netflix posted a set of data and showed that its current method produced recommendations that customers liked a certain percentage of the time. Netflix offered a prize for the first method that offered a 10 per cent improvement over that figure. (For more about Netflix, see Chapter 22.)

Because crowdsourcing for improvement relies on concrete measures, it's less prone to the crowd effect (see the preceding 'Crowdsourcing for novelty' section). Hence, you often get better results when you encourage your crowd to discuss the problem and collaborate.

Crowdsourcing for advantage

In looking for an innovative advantage, you seek to improve or restructure a product or service substantially. You want that new idea to be a thorough improvement over its predecessor, but you place few or no restrictions on the changes you're seeking. You ask primarily that the new ideas create an advantage by being cheaper, generating more revenue, being easier to operate, or opening an entirely new market.

Often, crowdsourcing for advantage looks to engage untapped expertise. Usually, you're not trying to create a new product or make radical changes to a service. You're trying to find a more advantageous position for your goods or services in the market.

Kimberly-Clark, a manufacture of disposable nappies for babies, has used innovation crowdsourcing to build an advantage in the market for general baby products. It attempts to engage the expertise of mothers, who generally understand the needs of their peers far better than any product designer does.

In crowdsourcing for advantage, Kimberly-Clark puts out a request to the crowd, which consists of mothers or others who have experience with young children. The company asks the crowd to submit ideas for products and 'businesses that nurture the relationship between mother and child'. Each member of the crowd has to submit a simplified business plan for the product or business. Kimberly-Clark then employs a panel of experts to judge each application according to four criteria:

- ✔ Originality and creativity
- ✔ Ability to solve a problem important to parents
- ✔ Commercial viability
- ✔ Stage of business development

Typically, the company gives the mothers with the best ideas a grant to help start or develop a business. Some of the top ideas are brought into the Kimberly-Clark company and used to expand the company's line of baby products.

Planning for Innovation

Planning to innovate is almost a self-contradictory idea. You tell yourself that you'll have a new idea at a certain time, in a certain place and under certain circumstances. Innovation, though, is closer to inspiration, which comes in its own time and on its own terms. Innovation is not like being able to think of an impossible thing each morning before breakfast, as the Red Queen in

Alice's Adventures in Wonderland claimed she could do. Indeed, you can't force inspiration and you can't dictate innovation to arrive on schedule, as a large literature on the subject suggests. Still, you need innovative ideas in order to progress and, if you're offering goods or services in a market, you need to make plans for yourself and your organisation. In such a world, unplanned innovation is too haphazard to trust.

Planned innovation is further complicated by the fact that you're usually constrained by your own actions, your history, your community, your market or your customers. You can't simply put out a call and ask, 'Teach us to think in new ways or do new things.' You have to fit your new ideas into your existing world.

The following sections help you pin down which aspects of crowdsourcing innovation you can plan, and how.

Planning for new ideas

All innovation needs new ideas, so when you start to plan for innovation, you need to start by determining how you'll get new ideas.

In planned innovation, with or without crowds, you generally move through a series of steps that seem far more orderly on paper than they are in practice. In these steps, you generate ideas, refine ideas, test the ideas and finally deploy the ideas. You rarely follow these steps in a linear order. Instead, you move in circles, cycling among them as you see that a particular combination of skill, experience, insight and occasional serendipity produces a valid, usable new idea. The basic process is shown in the diagram in Figure 18-1. These four steps are sometimes called the *process of ideation*.

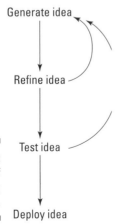

Figure 18-1:
The steps of
generating
new ideas.

Generate idea

Refine idea

Test idea

Deploy idea

To use crowdsourcing to create and gather new ideas, you put the first three steps of the idea-generating process into a crowdcontest. You use that contest to generate, develop and test new ideas. Figure 18-2 shows the role of the crowdcontest (for more on crowdcontests, take a look at Chapter 5).

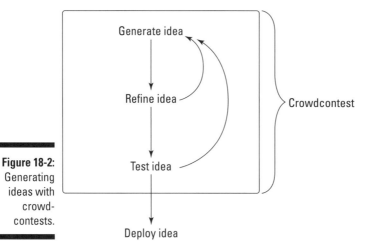

Figure 18-2:
Generating ideas with crowd-contests.

Bringing the unexpected into your plan with a crowdcontest

If you need to create new ideas that satisfy the deadline of your plan, you can always try a crowdcontest. Crowdcontests don't really create new ideas according to plan, but they do pull new ideas out of the crowd to a deadline. If you think that the crowd has a new idea, you can easily use a simple crowd-contest to innovate:

1. **Describe the kind of innovation you're seeking.**

2. **Offer a reward for the best idea.**

3. **Establish a deadline for the contest.**

4. **Promote the contest to the crowd.**

5. **Collect the results.**

6. **Select the best idea.**

7. **Implement the result.**

Rather than look for a specialised crowdmarket that handles innovation, you can run this contest on your organisation's web page. You create the page, notify the crowd and get the process started.

However, when you hold a crowdcontest for innovation, you may discover that you need to create a more complicated process. Innovation crowdsourcing involves a sophisticated process of communication between you and the crowd. You may need to spend extra time explaining the kind of idea that you're seeking. The crowd may require extra time to develop and refine its ideas. You may also need a little more time to understand what the crowd's telling you and to test its ideas.

Defining the problem

When you begin to plan for innovation crowdsourcing, you need to describe the idea that you're seeking: the novelty you hope to create, the improvement you need, the advantage you hope to establish. This step is similar to drafting a statement of work in macrotasking or microtasking (see Chapter 11). However, unlike the problem of defining a job for those forms of crowdsourcing or describing a product in an ordinary crowdcontest, this task can be daunting. Your goal isn't always obvious. You may understand the need for innovation, but you may not see all the possible solutions.

You can have a simple crowdcontest if you can clearly describe your problem at the start. Remember that you've been involved in this innovation process longer than any of the crowd have, and hence you may have ideas and you may have made assumptions that aren't obvious to the crowd. Start by describing the problem as best you can. Be as concrete as you can but leave enough freedom for the crowd to be creative. You want to let the crowd members' intelligence, experience and expertise lead you to a useful set of ideas.

As in other forms of crowdsourcing, you want to test your problem statement on others. Let some of your colleagues read your text and comment on it. Ask them what ideas they may want to submit to such a contest. Listen to their feedback. If they give responses that appeal to you, you probably have a good description.

If your problem is complex or if you can't clearly anticipate the kinds of ideas you need, allow yourself the option of revising the statement of the problem. You have a choice of two easy ways of doing this:

> ✔ **Update your problem description during the course of the contest.**
> You follow the cycle back to the start of the innovation process illustrated in Figure 18-1. Updating the problem description has some obvious drawbacks. In some cases, members of the crowd may take offence and object to your changes. However, if you tell the crowd that you'll be engaged in a dialogue with them and will help them refine their ideas, you're more likely to get a positive response.

> You can establish the contest so that you update the project description on a regular basis, whether you make any real changes or not. If you have no real updates, you can report on the state of the contest. You can tell the crowd about the number of submissions or general nature

of the submissions and the ideas that may work. By making these statements, you emphasise that innovation crowdsourcing is indeed a dialogue with the crowd.

✔ **Run your innovation crowdsourcing as a two-stage contest.** As with an ordinary crowdcontest, you identify the most promising ideas in the first stage, give the creators of those ideas a modest award, and then allow those creators to participate in a second stage to refine their ideas.

When you start the second stage, you can give feedback to the participants, refine your problem description or even encourage the participants to collaborate. The Netflix contest (see the earlier section 'Crowdsourcing for improvement') is a good example of a two-stage contest. In the second stage, Netflix not only refined its instructions and gave feedback to the crowd, but it encouraged certain teams to collaborate and submit a single entry.

Refining the ideas

In planned innovation, you often want to encourage the crowd to refine its ideas. This refining is part of the dialogue with the crowd. The crowd members read your description and offer responses. When you see the responses, you better understand how the crowd members perceive your problem. In the process, you may realise that they didn't fully understand your description of the problem, or that they saw aspects of your problem that you hadn't anticipated. Therefore, the process of innovation works best if you communicate with the crowd and help to refine the ideas.

Much of the communication with the crowd is like the feedback in ordinary crowdcontests (see Chapter 5). You correspond with individual members. You tell them that you like a certain aspect of their work but not another, or suggest that they may not understand the problem, or that their work is promising and should be extended in a certain way. You usually conduct such correspondence in a private manner so that each of your suggestions is seen only by specific members of the crowd.

However, you can use the crowd itself to refine ideas. In this model, you post all the submissions on public pages and let the crowd comment on them. The owners of those ideas can read the comments and make new submissions that incorporate the feedback from the crowd.

You can incorporate your feedback with the feedback from the crowd. One way to do so is to have the contest organiser rank each submission on a scale from 1 to 10. You rank as 1 an idea that's ill formed and not particularly useful, and rank a complete, useful and highly valuable idea as a 10. The crowd can see all the submissions and their ranking scores. The crowd members can then suggest ways of modifying their submissions to improve their scores. If a member of the crowd submits a revised idea, you review it and offer a new score.

As with all forms of crowdsourcing, you need to define intellectual property rights carefully and clearly. Commonly, you say that all submissions become the property of the contest organiser. You also say that you'll disqualify any submission that's improperly borrowed from another source or uses the intellectual property of others. If you let the crowd comment on submissions, you may find that many members of the crowd can claim that they've contributed to a winning submission. Therefore, you need a way of resolving such claims.

If you create your innovation crowdsourcing contest properly, you have a record of all comments on the submissions and a record of the dates of all revisions. With that information, you have a record of all the public contributions to an idea. (You don't have a record of any private communications among the crowd, but the exchange of information in this manner isn't your responsibility.) With the public record, you can establish a simple way of rewarding people who contributed to winning ideas. You may, for example, announce that any suggestion that improves a submission will be rewarded with 5 per cent of the prize for each point of improvement.

Testing the concept

In innovation crowdsourcing, you have to test the best ideas to see whether they actually work. To do this, you may choose to divide the evaluation process into two parts:

1. **A panel of judges reviews each entry and selects the idea (or ideas) that seems the most promising.**

   The people who generated these ideas then receive part of the payment that you're offering for the crowdcontest.

2. **You try to use the chosen ideas.**

   If you're trying to create a novel marketing plan, you use the idea to create such a plan and then try to follow it. If you're trying to fix a process, you try to apply the idea and observe the result. If you're trying to create a new product with the idea, you manufacture the product and try to market it. You give a full payment to the winning idea only if it works.

Integrating the idea into the organisation

After you select an innovative idea, you have to integrate it into your organisation. As with any organisational change, you'll find this step easiest if you've prepared your organisation and given it a stake in the process. If the organisation isn't ready to accept a new idea, it can easily thwart any innovation.

The best way to prepare is to create an organisation that views itself as an innovative group and judges its own success on the quality of innovation. You can create such an organisation by engaging members of the organisation in the crowd innovation process. You can engage your current organisation to help define the contest, generate new ideas, refine ideas and judge the submissions.

You can easily include your organisation in the work that defines the crowd-contest and judges the submissions. Your employees may be in the best position to understand the kind of innovation you need and judge the kind of results you want.

However, you may want to change your organisation, to develop a new product or service that's quite different from the work that the group's currently doing. In such a case, you may want to define the crowdcontest by yourself and create a panel of judges that's independent of the organisation. By excluding your organisation from this work, you can demand fresh ideas and fresh points of view.

As you prepare your crowd innovation, avoid having your organisation involved in all the steps of the innovation process. If people in your organisation are submitting ideas, they shouldn't be the ones to define and judge the contest. If people are defining and judging the contest, they shouldn't submit ideas. You don't want the same group to set goals and then be able to determine whether their own ideas meet those goals.

Innovation crowdsourcing and the suggestion box

As with other forms of crowdsourcing, innovation crowdsourcing has historical roots. The idea's connected with the suggestion box, the tool that companies once used to collect ideas for improving their operations. Although suggestion boxes are now generally mocked, at one time there was a professional organisation, The National Association of Suggestion Systems, and a body of theory about suggestion systems.

The theory of suggestion boxes has several good practices for innovation crowdsourcing. It argues that the people who define the problem and judge the ideas shouldn't be the ones who submit ideas. It also suggests that ideas should be judged by a two-stage process that utilises a panel of judges and the results of the actual implementation. The ideas receive a partial reward when they're selected by the judges and a full reward when they show that they can produce innovation in an organisation.

Suggestion boxes probably had their greatest impact during the Second World War, when organisations were under great strain and often filled with temporary workers.

Running with the Right Crowd

As with all forms of crowdsourcing, innovation crowdsourcing demands that you have a crowd that's well matched for the innovation that you're trying to develop. If someone in the crowd doesn't have the right experience, right skills or right connections to the problem, you get nothing of value from her.

You don't need to think that everyone in the crowd needs to have the right set of skills or the special kind of insight that you need. You just need one person in the crowd, just as with crowdcontests. Still, the more your crowd understands your problem and has the skills to solve it, the better you can match your crowd to the problem and the better result you're likely to get.

The problem of finding the right crowd is much like a similar problem in market research. In market research, you try to understand the preferences and inclinations of your customers by assembling a small group of people who represent your customers. You try to ensure that your small group has the same preferences and inclinations by using methods that are statistical selection techniques.

In innovation crowdsourcing, you try to get skills and ideas that come from a known body of people such as your employees or customers. Unlike market research, you rarely need to have a crowd that perfectly represents these groups of people. If anything, you want to have the best customers or most insightful employees in your crowd.

Knowing the different types of crowd

In innovation crowdsourcing, you can use two classes of crowd:

- ✔ **Public crowds** are recruited through a public invitation. They may be built out of people who come to your website.

- ✔ **Private crowds** begin with a group of people that you already know. They may be assembled from your employees, customers or members.

Both kinds of crowd can be further divided into two classes:

- ✔ In **open crowds**, you take everyone who comes as a member of your crowd.

- ✔ In **curated crowds**, you restrict membership to people who have specific experience, skills or positions.

Figure 18-3 shows the different types of crowd and gives an example for each.

	Public crowd	Private crowd
Open	Everyone who comes to an invitation. Example: People who come to your website.	Everyone in a pre-existing group. Example: Your customers.
Curated	A restricted public crowd. Example: The visitors to your site who are mothers of young children.	A restricted private club. Example: Employees who use your product.

Figure 18-3:
Different types of crowds for innovation.

Matching your plans with the best crowd

You can use the same kind of crowd to crowdsource for any kind of crowd-sourced innovation: novelty, improvement or advantage (see the earlier section 'Asking for a Little Insight: Classes of Innovation'). However, each of the three categories of innovation requires a slightly different approach, as the following sections outline.

For all crowds, you need to ensure that:

- ✔ The crowd has the ability to provide you with good ideas.
- ✔ The crowd isn't committed to your current products, services and procedures. If the crowd members think that everything you do is fine and good, they won't be able to give you a fresh vision.

Crowds for novelty

In crowdsourcing for novelty, you generally try to determine how a group of people perceive an idea and what they would need to perceive it as new. You want to find the crowd that's in a position to identify novelty and can communicate that novelty to other groups. Often, you start with a private crowd, a crowd that understands the way your organisation currently operates or the ideas it promotes. You probably restrict the crowd to a group with specific skills.

However, if you hope to change your organisation radically, perhaps move into a new area of activity, you may want a crowd that knows a little about your organisation. In this case, you probably want a curated public crowd. You invite a large group of people to join your crowd and then restrict yourself to a group who understand what you're trying to do. You restrict the group by asking each potential member a set of questions, and you take only those who answer in the way that you want.

Crowds for improvement

When you crowdsource for improvement, you generally try to find a solution to a concrete problem. Your product isn't working as planned and you need a solution. Perhaps your website seems to be functioning well but 70 per cent of the visitors spend more than five minutes on the site and don't find the information they need; or your main service seems to be working well in the English language market, but you want to expand it to the Spanish market.

In this form of crowd innovation, you look for a specific set of skills or experience. Often, you find it easy to use the open private crowd of your employees and the one of your customers. Crowdsourcing for improvement is a means of utilising expertise that's often difficult to engage. It utilises the things that your customers have discovered about your products and that your employees know about your business processes.

You can deal with specific problems or general questions that look for any kind of improvement. However, in both cases, you need to guide the crowd or you get answers that are of little use. If you merely ask 'How can we improve this process?' you're likely to get odd opinions that offer little real insight.

Ask the crowd a series of questions that cause the members to focus on the issue or aspect that needs improvement. You may find it productive to have a series of questions that moves from general issues to specific. Often, you find the best suggestions in the middle of the answers. For example, you may write:

> *We are attempting to improve our website to make it more useful to our clients. We would like your ideas that may address one or all these questions:*
>
> - *What general change would improve the website?*
> - *How would you change the opening page and the first impression of the site?*
> - *What can be done to improve the navigation between pages?*
> - *How can we best display the products on the shopping page?*

Crowds for advancement

Crowdsourcing for advancement is the most sophisticated form of innovation crowdsourcing and often demands a crowd that's been chosen with care. The crowd needs to be able to address open-ended questions and to have enough distance from your current products or approach to operations not to be trapped in old ideas.

Commonly, you crowdsource for advancement with a curated public crowd. You invite a large group of people to join the crowd and then select those who are the most prepared. However, you can successfully use private crowds, such as a crowd drawn from your employees.

In the Kimberly-Clark crowdsourcing example in the earlier section 'Crowdsourcing for advantage', the company uses a curated public crowd. It announces on its website that it's looking for new ideas. It advertises this search widely and only excludes its employees and a few others who do business with the company. Kimberly-Clark curates the crowd through the application that accompanies the idea. This application asks not only for a description of the idea but also for a description of the business that the applicant's creating to support the product. Because Kimberly-Clark reviews the applications not only on the quality of the idea but also on the development of the business, this naturally restricts the crowd.

Communicating effectively with the crowd

In innovation crowdsourcing, you need to ask your questions in a way that your crowd not only understands but can also answer.

You must also balance general approaches with specific problems. Give the crowd some guidance so that the members can think about your problem in depth, but don't constrain them by preparing an overly detailed specification. If you ask a general question like 'How can we improve our product?' you're likely to receive a range of ideas from the utterly trivial to the completely incomprehensible. You may get suggestions that tell you to paint the product blue, make it heavier or have it advertised by a famous actor. However, if you ask a *specific* question in order to get a more useful answer, you often get no responses at all. For example, if you're trying to improve the services of your organisation and ask 'What can we do to reduce by 50 per cent the time between our first contact with a potential client and our first full interview?' you may receive no answers at all. Such questions require a detailed knowledge that the crowd may not have, or they may intimidate the crowd by suggesting that the question has one specific technical answer.

Opinions and indications of popularity have a place in innovation crowdsourcing, but they're not the only input you need. It may be useful to know that someone agrees with you or that the crowd believes that it'll benefit from a certain idea. However, you're likely to want stronger evidence that an idea's good and can solve your problem. You may also want concrete reasons that show how one idea is superior to another. You may want a story that shows how a proposed idea has worked in other settings. You may want an explanation of how an idea can improve your organisation. Such reasons, stories or explanations come from opinions or popularity polls.

For example, you may start a crowd innovation process to improve the city services in your neighbourhood. If you merely ask the crowd 'What needs to be done in your neighbourhood?' you're likely to get a lot of submissions that are important only to the person who's suggesting the idea. 'Pick up the rubbish behind my house,' one may say, 'Fill the pothole in front of my driveway' or 'Put up a fence to keep kids from crossing my lawn.'

However, if you broaden the question that you put to the crowd and ask for an explanation, you're likely to get much more useful answers. The two-part question: 'What should the city do to improve the quality of life in your neighbourhood?' and 'What problem would the improvement address?' is far more likely to get responses that move beyond limited opinions and personal needs.

Building New Products and Services with Co-creation

Co-creation is a form of innovation crowdsourcing that develops new products and services. You use the crowd to identify new ideas, define a potential product, design that product, test the product, and release that product. Many commentators describe co-creation as a form of new product development that uses a market to create products for itself, but it's actually a much broader activity. Co-creation uses the skills and experience of a crowd to create fully formed products and bring them to market. Often, that crowd may be creating products for its own use; however, it can also create products for other markets.

In the artistic world, the term *co-creation* has come to mean an artistic project that involves multiple people who coordinate their activities over the Internet. In this arena, an individual conceives a project and solicits submissions. The creator then chooses the best submissions and combines them into a new artistic work.

A good example of artistic co-creation is the Johnny Cash Project. After the death of the country singer Johnny Cash, California artist Chris Milk proposed creating a new version of Cash's final music video. Individuals were invited to draw a version of any frame in that video and submit it to the project. They were also invited to vote on the different versions of each frame. One version of the project presented a new video with all the most popular frames. Another showed the frames that the directors of the project chose. A third allowed the viewer to scroll through all the different submissions.

In some areas of business, the concept of co-creation is merely another form of design contest. The European site eYeka (`http://en.eyeka.com`) portrays itself as a co-creation site. It runs crowdcontests to develop packages, adverts, videos and logos for existing products and brands.

When you use co-creation to develop a new product, you do far more work than when you merely create an advert or logo. You typically go through five different steps:

1. **Generate new ideas.**

2. **Define the product.**

3. **Design the prototype.**

4. **Test the prototype.**

5. **Release the product to the market.**

Each of these steps can be done as a crowdcontest or as a macrotask.

Generating ideas and defining products

When co-creating as a form of crowd innovation, you usually combine the first two steps into a single process. You generally identify an area or field in which you'd like to develop a product. You don't need the crowd to identify that field, although you may easily ask it to do so. Instead, you state the area that you want to develop and ask for ideas that will make good products. This activity can easily be done as a crowdcontest and is really a form of crowdsourcing innovation for advancement, similar to what Kimberly-Clark is doing to develop new products with the expertise of mothers (see the earlier section 'Crowdsourcing for advantage').

Designing with the crowd

After you have an idea for a product, you can easily create another crowd-contest to design it. If the product is simple, you can do your crowdsourcing as a simple contest in which you look for the best work of a single designer. If it's a complicated product, you'll oversee a self-organised crowd. In this kind of crowdsourcing, you place a description of the product on the crowdmarket and offer a prize for the team that produces the best versions of the product. You let the crowd develop self-organised teams to do the work.

In many circumstances, you may find it easiest to design the product with macrotasking. With this strategy, you determine the way in which the product needs to be designed and divide the work into steps. You describe each step, place the description of each step on a crowdmarket, and select individual workers to compete those steps. (See Chapter 7 for more on macro-tasking.)

Because you're crowdsourcing, you can duplicate the work. You can hire two or three individuals to work on a single step, and you can then compare the results and choose the one that best meets your needs.

Testing, testing, testing

When you have a prototype product, you need to test it. If the product's highly technical, you are likely to handle this step with macrotasking. You describe what needs to be done to test the product, post the description on a crowdmarket, and hire individuals to do the testing. Again, you can (and should) hire multiple people to do the tests and you then compare the results.

You can test some products, such as computer applications and programs, with companies that offer crowdsourcing test services. These firms have developed regimented ways of testing products and guide a crowd through the process. uTest (www.utest.com) and TopCoder (www.topcoder.com) are examples of firms that test software.

If the product's fairly simple, you can create a crowdsource test yourself. You create a crowdcontest that offers a reward for the first identification of specific problems with your product. You offer the product to a specific number of members of the crowd and wait for their results. You can even continue this process after you move beyond testing and are selling the product.

Giving the product to the world

Finally, you can move the product to market with the crowd. Crowdsourcing offers a variety of ways to do preliminary marketing:

- ✔ In a crowdcontest (see Chapter 5), you can reward people for distributing the product.

- ✔ In microtasking (see Chapter 8), you can pay the crowd to promote the product in one or two places.

- ✔ In crowdfunding (see Chapter 6), you can use the crowd to simultaneously sell an initial offering and raise funds for production.

A good example of a product that was marketed with crowdfunding is the Pebble watch from E-paper (`www.getpebble.com`). The Pebble watch uses Bluetooth technology to take information from your mobile phone and display it on your wrist. After the E-paper had designed the product, it offered an initial sale of the watch to the public in order to raise funds. It asked individuals to pledge a certain amount to the company. In return, the individuals each would receive a certain number of watches, depending on the size of their pledges. The sale brought $10 million ($6.3 million) to the company and substantial new publicity for the new product.

Considering an Example: Restructuring a Business with InnoCentive

To better understand how innovation crowdsourcing works, consider the problem of restructuring a small business.

Riordan owns a mid-size storage and transfer warehouse business. He'as reached a point where he knows that he needs to restructure the business in order to stay profitable. At the same time, he'd like to use the business to do a little social good.

Most of Riordan's employees are young men who have limited prospects because they have only limited reading and writing skills. Riordan decides to determine whether his business can be restructured to help educate these young men. He's aware of the perils of combining education and work, and has long been suspicious of companies that try to achieve social goals. He claims that such companies always fail at both efforts, are never very profitable and rarely do any good. Still, Riordan has reached a point in his life where he feels that he has to do something to improve the lot of his workers.

He decides that a combination of new technology and a management system may help him accomplish his goals.

In planning his innovation, Riordan identifies a few basic goals. He needs to ensure that the new technology and system:

- ✔ Do not interfere with the operation of the warehouse – capacity and speed of operation are unchanged
- ✔ Teach mathematics and reading skills
- ✔ Give the workers an incentive to engage with the lessons and learn

In addition to these goals, Riordan has a few financial constraints. He has outside investors and a board that keeps him to a tight budget. He has $250,000 (roughly £160,000) to invest in this innovation, and after three years, he'll need to see a regular 5 per cent return on that investment.

Before he goes any further, Riordan needs to determine whether this approach is feasible. A simple way to get feedback on the idea is to pose it as a challenge on an innovation website. Because the idea involves technology and social good, Riordan could try posting it on InnoCentive (`www.innocentive.com`), which offers a variety of crowdsourcing services.

Despite myths to the contrary, innovation doesn't occur in a flash of inspiration. Ideas need to be refined before they can solve the problem at hand. So the first step in this process is to assess Riordan's idea, to determine whether it has any merit at all or is merely the dream of an idealist who hopes that somehow capitalism may be able to accomplish a little more than merely providing a steady return on investments.

To assess the idea, Riordan utilises the InnoCentive Brainstorm Challenge. The Brainstorm Challenge is a simple product, common to many innovation sites, that enables him to post a question to the crowd and receive their proposals in return. To run one of these contests, he needs to describe his problem. In addition to the information given at the start of this section, he may need to describe the nature and size of his business, the size of his workforce, and the nature of the employees who work for him.

Before posting the challenge, Riordan also has to set a prize. The InnoCentive Brainstorm Challenges are small-prize contests, offering between $500 (£315) and $2,000 (£1,260). For a contest like this, in which he really wants an assessment of his idea, Riordan probably needs to offer something close to $2,000 (£1,260).

Riordan also needs to create a process to judge the contest. The contest runs for 30 days before the submissions are reviewed. For the simple InnoCentive contests, he needs to recruit a panel of judges. If he wants Innocentive to organise the panel, he needs to move up to the next category of crowd-sourced innovation.

Riordan needs to keep the support of his board throughout the process, so he asks a couple of board members to serve as judges. Because the board members are likely to prefer ideas that are more focused on profit than on social good, he also recruits a local social worker and a couple of professors from the local college. He's aware that he may have a panel that has too many different opinions to come to a consensus, but overall he thinks that the individuals make up a good panel and that if they can agree on any idea then Riordan should be able to make it work.

For the first weeks of the innovation contest, Riordan receives few viable ideas. Most ideas involve simply giving money to the workers rather than trying to educate them. Indeed, one of the judges complains that they should stop trying to change the company and merely give half the money to a local soup kitchen.

However, eventually a programmer suggests a new computer system to manage the warehouse that could also be used to train workers. The system he proposes uses computer simulation to find the best way of managing storage. The same program could be adapted to train workers how to manage a facility and combined with some distance-learning systems to improve the workers' reading and mathematical skills. The crowd refines the idea, and suggests how Riordan could give workers time to train themselves and how he could use badges and other incentives to motivate the workers.

The cost of the new system is slightly more than Riordan wanted to pay, but the board members accept the idea because they had a hand in creating it. Riordan then begins the process of starting the new system.

Chapter 19

Preparing Your Organisation

*I*f you plan to make crowdsourcing a permanent part of your organisation, you need to start thinking about your organisation in a new way. Most people still think of organisations, large companies, small non-profit organisations and everything in between in terms of a hierarchy. At the top of the hierarchy is the president or CEO. Below the top officer is a row of vice presidents. Below them, you find directors and project managers. Everyone has a place and all have a role to play in keeping the organisation moving.

When you start talking about crowdsourcing in a company, people think about the hierarchy and ask questions such as 'Which part of the organisation chart will be cut and replaced by the crowd? Which part of the company will be outsourced?' These questions miss the main point about crowdsourcing. Crowdsourcing isn't outsourcing. It's not the activity of taking some division of the company and moving it to some place where the cost of labour is lower. Crowdsourcing, especially crowdsourcing that takes place within an organisation, is about rethinking how the organisation operates and using market mechanisms to create the scale, scope and capacity of different activities. Crowdsourcing is a way of bringing new talent into an organisation.

This chapter helps you look at your organisation and bring crowdsourcing into it. I show how to look at processes, and I describe how to develop crowdsourcing for these processes and how you can deploy crowdsourcing as a means of expanding your company's operations.

Focusing on Crowdsourcing Elements of Processes

When crowdsourcing from within an organisation, you are the most creative and do the most good if you think about processes rather than organisational structure. Instead of looking at the organisation chart, look instead at the activities your organisation engages in and the processes it has in place in order to produce goods and services. By looking at the processes, you see points where crowdsourcing can improve your operations by increasing efficiency and adding skills that you don't currently have in your company.

If you're working with a large organisation, you'll already have process charts. If you're in a smaller organisation, think about drawing such a chart. Process charts show the steps that your organisation needs to take in order to function.

Airy owns a small business that makes leather accessories for women: purses, bags, wallets and belts. Her company has operated for about eight years and has six employees: two sales people in her store, a web master, a finance person and a worker who helps Airy make the products. The company expanded quickly, largely based on the clever and quirky nature of the Airy's leather designs. However, revenue stagnated about three years ago. She considered adding an employee to expand her business, reasoning that if she could make more products, she might be able to sell more and increase her revenue. Airy, however, felt that she couldn't take the risk, because her sales have been flat.

If you think about how Airy's organisation chart would look, you may struggle to see where she might use crowdsourcing to improve her business. As things stand, the organisation structure is simple: Airy's in charge and everyone reports to her. If, however, you look at the diagram in Figure 19-1, which illustrates the main process of her business, you can see that the process itself suggests the areas in which she can expand her business by using crowdsourcing.

Figure 19-1:
The central business process for a leather accessory company.

In Airy's case, she can employ crowdsourcing in any step of the process. She ultimately decided to focus on the design step and the sales step, because both are activities that can be improved by bringing in new talent. In the design step, she crowdsourced some of the product designs. By doing this, she expanded her product line and began to reach new customers.

After she'd crowdsourced some of the design work, Airy next brought some new talent into sales. To this end, she crowdsourced some marketing work. First, she hired some macrotask workers to test new products before she put them into full production. Next, she hired some other macrotask workers to handle customers after the sale. These workers kept the customers engaged through a blog and Twitter accounts. They circulated stories about how the products were used, offered fashion tips and handled any problems that customers found.

As the crowdsourced workers began to contribute to Airy's company, they also changed the basic process of the company. She and her sales employees spent more of their time managing the process and were able to accomplish more than when they were doing most of the work. The design step of her process became a design curation step. In it, Airy selected the designs, both those that she'd created and those she received from the crowd, to create a product line. The sales step became a real sales and marketing activity that provided useful information to Airy and which expanded her customer base. Figure 19-2 shows how crowdsourcing changed Airy's process.

Airy's company became more sophisticated after she began to use crowdsourcing, was able to reach more diverse markets and showed a steady increase in revenue as the public began to purchase the new products.

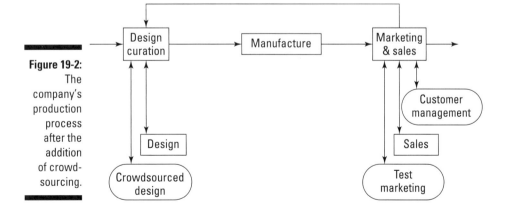

Figure 19-2: The company's production process after the addition of crowdsourcing.

Planning for the Future

Crowdsourcing isn't a guaranteed way to achieve a better company and increased revenue. Neither of those benefits automatically comes from crowdsourcing. You can just as easily see your company collapse and your revenues decline. For crowdsourcing to be an asset to your organisation, you have to prepare your organisation for crowdsourcing, test the skills of your employees and co-workers, and make sure that the organisation can gain the benefits that crowdsourcing promises.

Ultimately, crowdsourcing demands that an organisation improves its ability to manage work. It has to manage that work without some of the usual tools that conventional organisations have. The organisation won't have all the workers in one place, for example. It won't have a single schedule to structure the day. It won't have a common lunch room or water cooler where workers can learn about their colleagues and begin to appreciate the strengths and weaknesses of each other.

You start preparing your organisation by identifying places where you might employ crowdsourcing. Generally, you do this by looking at one of your business processes and asking simple questions such as 'How can I improve this process, and what kind of talent do I need to achieve that improvement?' Initially, you ask this question in an abstract way without worrying about where you might get that talent and where that talent might fit.

When you've identified the steps in your process that may benefit from crowdsourcing, you need to determine how to connect the crowdworkers to the business process. To do that, you need to recognise that crowdsourcing involves management of crowdworkers, and that you have to find suitably skilled and talented people within your organisation to manage the crowd-sourcing work.

Have a clear point of contact for your crowd. Not only does the crowd need to have a clear reporting line – a single person who gives it direction – your organisation needs to know who's communicating with the crowd. Few things confuse an organisation more than allowing it to think that anyone can communicate with the crowd and give it direction.

When you have managers in place, you need to start creating statements of work – describing the activities that the crowd will do (see Chapter 11). As you complete those statements, you can start to call for a crowd and begin a trial run.

Navigating a Trial Run

After you identify the tasks your organisation can crowdsource and prepare the statements of work, you're ready to conduct a trial run. A trial run will teach you many invaluable lessons. You may, for example, discover that you need to revise your statement of work. You may discover that your organisation can't easily manage crowdsourcing. You may find that the particular talent you need isn't easily found on the crowdmarket. You don't want to make discoveries like these after you've committed to using the crowd in your daily operations. Trial runs are important – don't ever think of leaping into production without doing one.

You can usually try three kinds of trial run. You can try crowdsourcing for:

- **A single product or order.** This type of trial run's usually the simplest. You decide that you'll create a single product. You hire the crowd, make the product and test the result. (See Chapter 15 for more on testing your results.) If things go well, you go ahead and expand your use of crowdsourcing.

- **A single customer or market.** This kind of trial run's probably most useful when your organisation's providing a service rather than a product. You choose a single customer and create a crowdsourced process to serve that customer. Again, you do the work and test the result (using the ideas in Chapter 15). If things go well, you expand your use of crowdsourcing.

- **A finite time.** Crowdsourcing work for a single product or a single customer is often not enough to show how crowdsourcing's really going to change your organisation. You obtain more information by creating a full crowdsourced operation, running it for one week, two weeks or a month, evaluating the results and then making your decision.

When conducting your trial run, monitor these three things (following the ideas of the cycle of continuous improvement in Chapter 15):

- **The crowd:** Does it have the skills your need? Is the crowd working properly? If you can't assemble the right crowd and the right work, then you need to use conventional workers.

- **The process:** Is it providing the goods or services you need? Is it working well? If not, you need to make corrections and do a second pilot run. If you can't produce the right results, you need to return to the conventional way of working.

✔ **Your organisation's response:** How are other workers engaging with the crowd? Are you seeing any resistance from members of your organisation? Is crowdsourcing causing part of your organisation to malfunction?

As you work on the pilot test, you may need to adjust other parts of your organisation. You may need to change the person who's managing the process that now includes crowdsourcing. You may need to find a way of better coordinating the work of the crowd with the work of the rest of your organisation, because the crowd may operate on a different schedule than your office does.

If you're incorporating crowdsourcing into several steps, such as in both marketing and sales, you may want to do your trial runs one step at a time. Identifying problems is easier if you change only one aspect of the process.

Building Commitment

As you start to crowdsource, you need to build commitment to crowdsourcing within your organisation. While some people immediately embrace crowdsourcing, many do not. They quickly reject the idea and conceive reason after reason why it should fail. They claim that workers can't be trusted, that crowdsourcing won't produce quality results or that it will undermine your position in the market. You can't dismiss these ideas with a wave of your hand and expect them to vanish, and you also can't expect that everyone will eventually see the value of crowdsourcing. You have to build commitment.

Start building commitment to crowdsourcing from the moment you decide to try it. Work with the rest of the organisation to explain the benefits of crowdsourcing, addressing individuals' concerns about how they'll benefit from crowdsourced workers and how they'll be able to do new things with the new process.

The time at which you hold a trial run (see 'Navigating a Trial Run' earlier in this chapter) is a good point at which to address employees' doubts and to build commitment. You can start a trial run even when some people in the organisation may not be thoroughly convinced of your ideas. You can't, however, start full production if you have a lot of doubters in the organisation.

In the trial run, make sure that you have a means of addressing concerns that members of the organisation may have. If someone's concerned about quality, have a way of comparing crowdsourced work with work produced by conventional means. If someone's concerned about timeliness, be sure to collect data on how quickly the organisation's working. Hold a group meeting after the trial run to review the results and discuss the impact of the new ways of operating.

A good way to bring crowdsourcing into your organisation is by creating a small group that does special projects. As the rest of the organisation sees value in the projects, you can move crowdsourcing into other units. Also, should the project fail, you can quickly end the special group and let the organisation return to its old ways.

At the end of the day, you may not be able to get the kind of commitment that you want. You may have someone in your organisation who just doesn't like crowdsourcing and thinks that it can't be trusted. In such a case, you need to ask two questions before you proceed with crowdsourcing. Firstly, is the crowdsourcing process working properly? If it is, then the objections of a single individual may not be that important. Secondly, are the people who are objecting to the process in positions where they might thwart or disrupt the crowdsourcing? If they are, you should consider your options.

Knowing the Limits

Not everything can be crowdsourced. Not everything is good to crowdsource. If crowdsourcing doesn't improve your business process, then you shouldn't use crowdsourcing.

As you make your plans, you may come across three different reasons to use conventional processes rather than crowdsourcing. You shouldn't crowdsource if:

- ✔ **Crowdsourcing doesn't bring in the talent you need.** You can't always find the talent that you need in the crowdmarket. Some kinds of workers simply don't go there.

- ✔ **Crowdsourcing hurts quality or quantity.** Crowdsourcing can easily lower the quality or quantity of goods that your process produces. This kind of problem often occurs when you do sophisticated things that need to be monitored constantly. If crowdsourcing isn't working well for you, it shouldn't be part of your organisation.

- ✔ **Crowdsourcing makes things too complicated.** If you need to give more to crowdsourcing than the benefits you get back from it, you shouldn't crowdsource. Effective crowdsourcing generally requires managerial skill from your organisation, and you can easily find yourself devoting more to management than you receive in return.

For some activities, you spend more time planning and managing your crowd than you get in return. In such cases, the conventional way of doing the work is better than crowdsourcing. Microtasking is the form of crowdsourcing that most commonly has this problem. You have to expend a great deal of effort to plan, deploy and test a microtask project, but in some cases you won't achieve enough benefit to justify the work.

Bracing for the Unknowns

Things don't always go the way you planned, especially when you crowd-source. Crowdsourcing expands the capacity of your organisation but it demands more managerial work from your staff, management work that's based in crowdmarkets. Since crowdmarkets can deliver unanticipated problems, you need to be braced for the unknown.

When you introduce a new crowdsourced activity to your organisation, you may see three different kinds of problems:

✔ The crowdsourcing process may not work properly.

✔ Your organisation may resist the introduction of crowdsourcing.

✔ Your organisation may resist the product of the crowdsourcing (and would have resisted that product if it had been produced conventionally).

Of course, you can't anticipate everything that might occur, but you can make yourself ready for potential problems. As you and your organisation explore crowdsourcing, you need to be prepared to have:

✔ **Plenty of trial runs.** Try as you might, you won't learn everything in a single trial run. You may find that you're going to be testing crowdsourcing for a long time.

✔ **Plans to adopt crowdsourcing step by step.** When you try to do too much at once, you may create problems that you can't easily debug. If you take as many as three new crowdworkers on initially and the process isn't working, you may not be able to find the fault quickly.

✔ **A way to easily fall back on conventional means.** If crowdsourcing isn't working, you have to be ready to go back to the old ways. Of course, if your organisation knows that it can always return to conventional methods, it may not put all its heart into crowdsourcing. Still, it's a good idea not to jump into a new process without having a safety net.

✔ **Readiness to exploit new opportunities.** Plan for unexpected success as well as unexpected trouble. You may find that crowdsourcing works well, that your organisation likes it and that you should adopt more crowdsourcing as quickly as possible. Be prepared.

Part V
The Part of Tens

To read about a selection of quirky crowdsourcing cases, head to www.dummies.com/extras/crowdsourcinguk for a bonus Part of Tens chapter.

In this part . . .

- ✔ Keep track of how the crowdsourcing industry is developing and where it's heading by checking out a select group of websites.

- ✔ Apply best practices to whichever form of crowdsourcing you employ to improve your effectiveness and get the best possible results.

- ✔ Gain inspiration and learn valuable lessons from ten varied tales of outstanding crowdsourcing success.

- ✔ Watch out for roots along the path that can trip the unsuspecting crowdsourcer and turn a potential success story into a disappointment.

Chapter 20

Following the Future of Crowdsourcing: Ten (Or So) Websites to Watch

In This Chapter

▶ Checking out the sites that crowdsourcers follow

▶ Going global

▶ Following the progress of crowdsourcing

▶ Building new platforms

*A*s soon as you become a crowdsourcer, you might start to wonder how crowdsourcing itself is developing and where it's heading. You might find yourself asking how you can keep track of trends and stay ahead of the field. Who knows – you might even decide to crowdsource your dilemma. You could go to your favourite microtasking site and post a task: 'Tell me the latest trend in crowdsourcing' and offer $1.41 (£1) for the answer. When you get the answer, though, you're likely to be disappointed. You've not created a clear statement of work with concrete instructions (see Chapter 11), so you're likely to get an arbitrary opinion from someone in the crowd. An arbitrary opinion's an arbitrary opinion, no matter who holds it. It may be right. It may be wrong. You can't tell.

Rather than you creating a well-crafted crowdsourcing job to tell you about the future (which is entirely possible), instead you'll get a better picture of the future by following the select group of crowdsourcing sites that I name-check in this chapter. Some of these sites give you information about the crowdsourcing industry; others are trying to create new crowdsourcing services that may – or may not – work. By keeping a close watch on all these sites, you can keep your finger on the pulse and discover where the industry's going and what the futures holds for it – and for you.

Discovering the State of Crowdsourcing: Crowdsourcing.org

To know where crowdsourcing's going, you need to know where it is at present. You can get a clear picture of crowdsourcing by going to the crowdsourcing.org website (www.crowdsourcing.org). This industry information website is the closest thing in the crowdsourcing field to a trade association. Crowdsourcing.org is, however, a private company that offers consulting and advice on crowdsourcing issues. Don't be fooled by the address, which suggests that it's a non-profit organisation.

Crowdsourcing.org provides some of the most complete and comprehensive information about the current state of the crowdsourcing industry. Among the information available on this site, you can find:

- **A crowdsourcing providers list:** Crowdsourcing.org provides the most complete listing of crowdsourcing platforms on the Internet. Its list includes companies that use crowdsourcing, those that offer software to help others who are crowdsourcing, and companies that offer services.

  This list is organised by topic: crowd labour (microtasking and macro-tasking), crowd creativity (crowdcontests), crowdfunding, distributed knowledge (self-organised crowds and microtasking) and tools (software platforms for industry and organisations).

- **A crowdfunding accreditation programme:** About half the website is devoted to crowdfunding. Crowdsourcing.org has created a set of standards for crowdfunding that guarantee a minimum level of transparency and accountability. The programme certifies crowdsourcing sites that follow the standards, so you have a means for checking the trustworthiness of crowdfunding sites.

- **Expert commentary on crowdsourcing media:** Crowdsourcing.org offers videos and articles about crowdsourcing, prepared by experts in the field or by leaders of the crowdsourcing industry. Many of these commentaries describe crowdsourcing problems and applications of crowdsourcing that may be difficult or unusual, and show how they can be handled on a commercial crowdsourcing platform. Some of these commentaries deal with problems in the industry and are of interest to people who work within the industry.

- **Reports and infographics on the crowdsourcing industry:** Crowdsourcing.org is one of the few organisations of any form that gathers information about the crowdsourcing industry. It offers a collection of reports that are complete and thorough. Most of these reports are of interest to people who want to work with the crowdsourcing industry. From these reports you can learn about the different companies that offer crowdsourcing, the amount of business these firms have and the amount of capital they've raised.

Reading the Morning News: Daily Crowdsource

For up-to-date information about what's happening in the world of crowd-sourcing – indeed, if you want to know what events have happened overnight – turn to Daily Crowdsource (`http://dailycrowdsource.com`). This web-site is an industry trade journal based in the USA. It publishes company press releases, stories and research reports on the industry, and provides a forum for industry leaders and observers to discuss the trends that they're observing.

On DailyCrowdsource.com you can keep abreast of the crowdsourcing indus-try and find out about new crowdsourcing sites and services, get news of upcoming crowdsourcing conferences and meetings (and read reports from those meetings), and keep up with trends in the crowdsourcing industry by following the comments of leaders and experts.

Highlights of the website include:

- A regular trade show for users, called Crowdopolis. (The audience for this trade show consists of people who are interested in using crowd-sourcing in their business or work. Crowdopolis is a good place to get an overview of the field and learn about the business aspects of crowd-sourcing.)
- An archive of useful crowdsourcing tips.
- A collection of crowdsourcing case studies.
- The daily news wall and email notifications.
- Whitepapers and statistics on the crowdsourcing industry.

The Daily Crowdsource and crowdsourcing.org (see the preceding section) offer some of the same information. However, each site has its own approach to the industry and each offers material that can't be found on the other.

Getting the European Perspective: crowdsourcingblog.de

If you're looking at the future of crowdsourcing, you can't limit yourself to just the US perspective. The news from Europe is just as interesting and sug-gests that crowdsourcing may be tightly connected to entrepreneurship and small newly formed companies (often called *start-ups*). You can get a good perspective on the European news from crowdsourcingblog.de (`www.crowd sourcingblog.de`), a site based in Germany.

Crowdsourcingblog.de presents some of the same information that you can find on crowdsourcing.org or Daily Crowdsource. Indeed, you occasionally see these three sites cross-link each other's stories. However, crowdsourcingblog.de has a directory of European crowdsourcing firms. It also divides the field in its own way, offering lists of sites that specialise in creative activities, crowdfunding, charitable organisations, innovation crowdsourcing and microtasking. Crowdsourcingblog.de is closely connected to the German business start-up community, and participates in start-up conferences in Germany and hosts information and conferences on start-ups. It also holds an annual conference for the European crowdsourcing community.

If you need to move beyond the stories from continental Europe, you can see stories from the UK at Crowdsourcing Gazette UK (`www.crowdsource-gazette.com`). As with crowdsourcingblog.de, this site publishes a lot of news that you can also get at Daily Crowdsource or crowdsourcing.org. However, it also runs stories about crowdsourcing in the UK that you can't find anywhere else.

Meeting the Leaders: CrowdConf and Crowdopolis

You can get good stories and good information about the future of an industry by meeting the industry leaders. In crowdsourcing, a good way to meet these leaders is by going to crowdsourcing conferences. Some of the best conferences are small impromptu gatherings called business mashups, or sometimes just mashups. *Mashups* are meetings where information is distributed informally, there are opportunities to meet people who are starting businesses that may be similar to yours, and there are social events where a few people give brief presentations on a subject.

You can find out about mashups by following Facebook pages that support entrepreneurship, by subscribing to business school newsletters and by being part of an active local business community. Since mashups often deal with the problems of starting new innovative businesses, speakers often talk about how to use technology and people to do work more efficiently – subjects that are part of crowdsourcing.

Mashups are often associated with business schools or cities that have a strong tradition of entrepreneurship, so you can find mashups on the subject of crowdsourcing in places such as Silicon Valley or New York or Berlin. If you can't go to one of these mashups, an alternative is to visit CrowdConf or Crowdopolis – two of the big industry meetings.

CrowdConf (www.crowdconf.com) is currently the big crowdsourcing industry gathering. It meets every autumn in San Francisco and is the one place where all parts of the crowdsourcing industry meet to share their insight and lessons. The conference is affiliated with the microtasking company CrowdFlower (www.crowdflower.com) and tends to draw a lot of companies that are interested in microtasking.

Crowdopolis is targeted more at companies that may want to use crowdsourcing. It's associated with Daily Crowdsource and is held in difference cities around the globe. You can find out more about Crowdopolis meetings at the Daily Crowdsource website (http://dailycrowdsource.com).

Both of these conferences maintain significant websites and post videos of the presentations. If you can't go the meetings, you can at least go to the websites and learn a little bit about what's happening to crowdsourcing and how you can use it.

Tracking Equity Crowdfunding: Crowdcube and Indiegogo

One of the big questions about the future of crowdsourcing concerns the future of equity crowdfunding – when will it be made legal in the USA and how will it work around the world? (Chapter 6 tells you more about equity crowdfunding.) You can get some great information from websites such as crowdsourcing.org, but you can also learn a great deal by looking at crowdsourcing platforms such as Crowdcube and Indiegogo that are doing or preparing for equity crowdfunding.

Crowdcube (www.crowdcube.com) is a British site that's already engaged in equity crowdfunding. It's associated with the Innovation Centre at the University of Exeter. The university has used the site to raise funds for the new companies formed by its students and faculty, but other firms that are incorporated in the UK can also use Crowdcube for small-scale equity crowdfunding.

Indiegogo (www.indiegogo.com) is one of the groups in the USA that's been pushing for equity crowdfunding. It supported the change in US law that'll make equity crowdfunding legal, and is preparing to be among the first platforms to offer equity crowdfunding. Indiegogo.com will probably reflect the strategies of the US crowdfunding industry as that industry adopts the equity funding model.

By looking at these two sites, you get a first impression of how equity crowd-funding works. These platforms are likely to provide some of the first ideas about how equity crowdfunding will work and how successful it may be.

Monitoring the Growth of the Global Crowd: Clickworker and Trabajo

Slowly but steadily, crowdsourcing is growing beyond its base in the English-speaking world. Europe is starting to create a crowdsourcing industry, and Latin America has created its first crowdsourcing companies. You can monitor the growth of crowdsourcing in these two regions by monitoring the fortunes of two crowdsourcing platforms: Clickworker and TrabajoFreelance.

Clickworker (www.clickworker.com) is a German microtasking platform that's trying to build a presence in the European market by offering crowd-sourcing services in multiple languages. It draws a crowd from 70 countries and offers four standardised services in all the major European languages:

✔ Search-engine-optimised content

✔ Tagging and metadata

✔ Translation

✔ Web research

The fortunes of Clickworker will be a measure of how well the industry can grow beyond its English-language base.

In Latin America, crowdsourcing has a very small presence. At the time of writing, only a few companies offer crowdsourcing services in the region. Brazil has an annual crowdsourcing conference (http://conferencia crowdsourcing.com.br) but it's dominated by organisations that are interested in collaboration and co-creation, which isn't quite the same thing as crowdsourcing.

Latin America does, however, have at least one macrotasking website – TrabajoFreelance (www.trabajofreelance.com), based in Argentina. You can follow the prospects of crowdsourcing in Latin America by following Trabajo.

Trabajo is really a cross between a traditional macrotasking firm – a company such as Elance or oDesk – and a traditional freelance agency. The company not only offers macrotasking services such as web creation, graphic design and financial services, but also light construction and repair. At the moment, Trabajo is able to do both crowdsourcing and contracting because it primarily serves Buenos Aires, which contains half of Argentina's whole population.

Some crowdsourcing platforms have already started to build a strong presence in multiple countries. Amazon's microtasking platform, Mechanical Turk (www.mturk.com), has a crowd in the English-speaking world, and Clickworker is building a strong position in Europe. If Trabajo expands as a crowdsourcing firm and starts offering crowdsourcing services to other countries, it will be a sign that crowdsourcing's arrived in Latin America.

Expanding the Scope of Crowdcontests: Kaggle

Crowdcontests are a successful form of crowdsourcing, but they tend to be applied only to creative problems: designing business cards, designing posters and designing T-shirts, for example. Several industry leaders believe that the potential applications of crowdcontests could be wider in scope, that crowdcontests can be used to provide other services as well. As yet, however, they haven't provided much evidence to sustain their point.

One crowdcontest platform that doesn't provide design services is Kaggle (www.kaggle.com). Kaggle uses crowdcontests to carry out statistical analyses and predictions. The success of the platform may mean that the world can learn from it about potential uses of crowdcontests for new applications.

Kaggle follows a process that's remarkably similar to the design contests run by the crowdsourcing platform 99designs (http://99Designs.com) and to the video production of Genius Rocket (http://geniusrocket.com). Kaggle's process allows you to post data and a description of the kind of analysis or projection that you want. Members of the crowd then submit their solutions to the problem and you choose the one that best meets your need.

Kaggle does seem to be successful and is marking out a path that others may follow. It's certainly shown that crowdcontests tend to be successful when contestants feel that they learn something from the process even when they don't win. At Kaggle, each contest gives the crowd the chance to test its skills on a new data set.

Promoting Innovation: AHHHA and Innovation Exchange

Many companies, especially those that sell consumer products to the mass market, were quick to embrace innovation crowdsourcing (see Chapter 18). Other companies, however, were cautious. They weren't sure that innovation crowdsourcing was any better than conventional methods for developing new products, and were concerned that innovation crowdsourcing exposed the inner workings of any company to the public. The fortunes of AHHHA and Information Exchange may give clues as to the future of this application of crowdsourcing.

AHHHA (www.ahhha.com) is a small-scale innovation firm and works with entrepreneurs and inventors. It not only provides a crowdmarket to develop products, it also provides other services for bringing products to market. AHHHA has had a few early successes but is still working to bring innovation crowdsourcing to a large market. If it succeeds, AHHHA will have demonstrated that innovation crowdsourcing can move beyond large companies.

Innovation Exchange (www.innovationexchange.com) works at the other extreme of innovation crowdsourcing. It deals with large, grand challenges. It advertises that it works with the largest companies in the world (companies that are often called the Global 5000) and with the top 100 global non-profit organisations. It wants to present problems that are on the scale of the Netflix challenge (see Chapters 18 and 22) or the Darpa Red Balloon Challenge (see Chapter 9). While Innovation Exchange has also had some success, it's still working to be identified as a major innovation platform. Should it get the success it desires, the company will establish innovation crowdsourcing as a good way to deal with big, difficult problems.

By keeping an eye on these two platforms, you'll be able to track the future of innovation crowdsourcing.

Building New Microtasking Platforms: MobileWorks and Tagasauris

Microtasking, although already a firmly established form of crowdsourcing, may need a new generation of crowdsourcing platforms to appear before it can advance much further. At the moment, microtasking is limited to a certain number of fields: handwriting recognition, sentiment analysis, data cleaning and search optimisation. You can apply microtasking to other problems, but better ways of controlling and combining the results of these tasks may be needed for the application to be effective. The progress of two platforms,

MobileWorks and Tagasauris, may suggest the future direction of this form of crowdsourcing.

MobileWorks (www.mobileworks.com) is a general-purpose microtasking platform, like Amazon's Mechanical Turk. However, MobileWorks is trying to expand the microtask market so that it can engage the members of the crowd no matter where they are and what kind of computing device they have. The crowd members can be sitting at their desks, looking at their phones or reading from a tablet computer. Because MobileWorks can be easily used from any kind of device, it may prove to be a simple way of creating self-organised crowds for gathering data and pictures.

Tagasauris (www.tagasauris.com) is a platform that's been very active in developing the concepts of workflow. As a business, it offers the services of photographic tagging. You can give the platform a set of images and it asks the crowd to create descriptions of these images. Originally, Tagasauris used microtasking to do the work, but as it developed its tagging services, it developed a sophisticated method of handling workflow and began incorporating some macrotasking as well. As a result, Tagasauris now uses multiple crowd-markets and has many ways of combining the work from the crowd.

Both MobileWorks and Tagasauris are working to have a larger presence in the marketplace and to support more and more applications. The success of these companies, or at least the success of the technology they support, should suggest the future of microtasking.

Macrotasking in the Boardroom: 10EQS

Traditionally, crowdsourcing has been a form of labour and not of management. It certainly can tag and translate and transcribe and design, but can it also guide a company? Can it be a presence in the corporate boardroom? Can it create a strategic plan or produce tactical memos? The Swiss firm 10EQS (www.10eqs.com) is working to develop crowdsourcing as a business strategy service.

10EQS provides companies with short-term access to business or subject experts, and has access to a crowd with substantial training and business expertise. These experts can help with a variety of business needs:

- Data collection and benchmarking
- Economic and business projections
- Market and competitive analysis
- Strategic planning and forecasting

10EQS faces a tough task. Crowdsourcing usually doesn't do a good job of dealing with company history, conflicting views or investors' long-term goals. If, however, 10EQS proves to be a success as a business strategy firm, it will show that crowdsourcing can indeed work at all levels of a corporation.

Chapter 21

Ten Best Practices to Adopt

In This Chapter

▶ Keeping channels of communication open at all times

▶ Shouting about the good stuff

▶ Rewarding the crowd

Generally, the best practices for one form of crowdsourcing aren't always the same as the best practices for another. The five forms of crowdsourcing are united by only one common feature: they utilise a crowd-market to control and coordinate activity. Nonetheless, that one common feature allows me to identify best practices that you can apply to all types of crowdsourcing.

Doing Things Step by Step

You can crowdsource a lot of things. When you understand the fundamentals of crowdsourcing, you can look at a business process, a not-for-profit activity or even the things that you do in your own life and see two or three or four things to crowdsource. As much as you may want to run away and do everything with crowdsourcing, though, build your expertise first and learn the right ways to do things.

Do things in small steps and you'll quickly see that the difference between microtasks and macrotasks is smaller than you may have believed. For example, you might see that your activity, which you thought looked like a macrotask (a task that requires a single worker to handle every step of the process), can be done instead as a series of microtasks. You may choose to do it as a macrotask, because that may be the easiest way to approach it, or you may see some benefit by doing it as a series of microtasks.

Amazon's Mechanical Turk platform urges crowdsourcers to break jobs into small tasks before doing them. This advice is good for microtasking, especially for series of microtasks that have to be handled by workflow (see Chapter 16), but is also good advice for all forms of crowdsourcing.

Copying What Others Have Done

Anything that you want to do has been done before, somewhere, by someone. Or at least something close to it. Look at what other people have done and learn from them. Go to the blogs associated with the different crowdmarkets, find out how other people have organised their crowdsourcing, and structure your plan along the lines of one that's worked successfully.

Most crowdsourcing platforms (or websites) have sections displaying jobs that people have successfully done on those sites:

- ✔ **Crowdcontests:** For crowdcontests, you can find some guidance in the 99designs customer blog (`http://99designs.com/customer-blog`). These blog entries contain descriptions of projects that have been highly successful. They also offer advice from customers who had to learn how crowdcontests work the hard way.

- ✔ **Crowdfunding:** If you want to find successful crowdfunding projects, go to the Kickstarter Most Funded page (`www.kickstarter.com/discover/most-funded?ref=sidebar`). All the projects there have been highly successful, and some can serve as good models for your projects.

- ✔ **Macrotasking:** You can find good examples and advice for macrotasking at the Elance Water Cooler page (`www.elance.com`).

- ✔ **Microtasking:** For microtasks, Amazon's Mechanical Turk offers a set of case studies (`https://requester.mturk.com/case_studies`). While many of these studies lack sufficient detail to enable you to duplicate their approach, they do contain links to typical Amazon jobs. You can start with these jobs and modify them to fit your needs.

- ✔ **Self-organised crowds:** If you're looking for examples of self-organised crowds as they are used for innovation, you can find a good collection of stories on the Innocentive website (at `www.innocentive.com/open-innovation-crowdsourcing-research-resources`). Like many company websites, this page offers plenty of success stories and few examples of hard lessons. Still, many of these studies provide useful models for innovation crowdsourcing.

Borrow whenever you can. Doing so fits with the spirit of the crowd.

If you're looking for inspiration, check out the examples in Part II and the success stories in Chapter 22.

Paying Attention to the Price

Crowdsourcing involves markets, and markets involve prices, so being able to choose a good price to suit the market and adjust prices so that you get the best work is a valuable skill. Doing this is somewhat similar to learning to bargain. Some people can bargain easily. They identify the price they want to pay for an object and quickly get it at that price. Other people have to start with an initial bid that's far below their target price and then slowly bargain until they get a deal with the seller. In crowdsourcing, you usually put yourself in the best position if you can name a price that's close to the price that the workers will accept and then get to a final deal as quickly as possible.

Most crowdsourcing websites offer advice about paying workers and setting the prices for tasks. This advice is a good starting point. However, you really don't get a feel for setting prices until you've worked in the market and begun to understand how the market works.

Macrotasking provides the best example of a dynamic market that can be tricky to use. Most markets allow you to set a range for the amount that you're willing to pay. You may be inclined to set the range low in order to keep your costs down. However, setting the range of pay to a high value may not actually increase your costs and is quite likely to draw a larger number of workers to your job, who will then compete for your job. With the extra competition, the workers may bid the price down to a value that's close to the amount you originally wanted to pay.

Of course, different crowdsource markets have different dynamics. You only understand a market after you've spent some time working in it. That's the way you learn to set your price.

Talking with Your Crowd

If you're managing the crowdsourcing, you need to talk with your crowd. Blog. Tweet. Post progress reports. Let them know how the job's progressing. Encourage the crowd. Crowdworkers work best when they feel engaged in the work and feel they have a stake in the outcome. If you don't talk with them, the workers can easily believe they're anonymous people who are labouring away by themselves. Keep in touch with the crowdworkers so they know what you're doing and how the work they're doing fits in with your goals.

You absolutely must talk with the crowd if you're doing a crowdcontest or a similar activity that has a clear goal. By talking with the crowdworkers, you guide them towards that goal and help produce a good result.

Macrotaskers can easily feel disconnected from you and from your work. If you're not talking with them, they can wander. After all, they have plenty of incentives to look beyond their current job and to worry about the source of their next task. Some macrotaskers juggle tasks. They contract for too many jobs and try to divide their time among them. They do two hours for you one morning and do nothing more for you for several more days. By talking with your workers, you keep your work in front of them. You're also more likely to find out when workers are doing multiple jobs for many people.

For more on communicating with the crowd, visit Chapters 10 and 15.

Listening to the Crowd

Don't just talk at the crowd, listen as well. Crowdworkers have something to tell you. Sometimes the things they want to tell you aren't interesting, but some can be vitally important. They may show you an easier way to organise the work; a task that can better meet your needs; an approach that's simpler than the one you developed. An important part of crowdsourcing is drawing out the good idea from the crowd, separating the wheat from the chaff.

Sometimes, you listen to the crowd by reading the crowd members' words. Sometimes, you listen by observing their actions. They bid for your job quickly but return it undone. They submit material that looks suspiciously familiar. They don't respond to your call to raise funds. When you see patterns of behaviour, investigate them. You can start by talking to the crowd.

For more on listening, see Chapter 14.

Using Social Media

The web allows you to post messages in many ways. You can write blogs, post videos, record audio, tweet, assemble groups and do other things to engage the crowd. Try as many methods as possible to connect with the crowd.

Of course, you should use social media in a way that makes sense. Do only the work that you need to do. If you're hiring a single macrotasker for a month, you may not need to send a daily tweet reporting on the progress of the job. Likewise, if you're doing a large collection of microtasks, you may find that you need to post a short video about the work, but that you don't need to repeat your explanations while the job is running.

When you use social medial in crowdsourcing, set a goal. Use only as much social media as you need to meet that goal. Choose the platform and the message that make sense for your work (and take a look at Chapter 10, on engaging the crowd, too).

You're trying to get the job done well, and sometimes you train people best by doing or demonstrating. A short YouTube video that shows how to do a microtask may be worth far more than a carefully written description of the same task. A weekly Skype call may help your macrotask workers to better understand your goals. A regular Google discussion group may fire the enthusiasm of the core contributors to your crowdfunding campaign.

Publicising Accomplishments

When something good's happened, tell the crowd about it. Doing so is good for the crowd, for other crowdsourcers and, ultimately, for you.

Publicise the winners of crowdcontests. You make the winner feel good and you tell other crowdsourcers about a high-quality worker. Announce when you've reached major goals in your crowdfunding campaign. More often than not, you can encourage people to give more to your efforts. Generally, people like to give to a winning activity. Use badges and leaderboards to identify top contributors to a microtasking effort. You encourage the best and show the others what they may accomplish.

Chapter 15 gives you more information about promoting your work.

Bringing the Crowd into the Decisions

Involve the crowd and bring members into decisions you need to make. The crowd has a broader viewpoint and may see things that you don't. And by asking their opinion, you get them more firmly connected to your work.

In macrotasking, you can require the crowdworkers to be part of your decision meetings, and you can ask the crowd to vote on different ways of proceeding. Just make sure that the crowd understands how the decision is being made. You don't want the crowd members to believe that they're able to make decisions when they're only one part in a complex organisation.

Crowd decision making is vulnerable to the crowd effect, to a group of people following the opinions of a select few. In general, you get the best result if you solicit the crowd's opinions in a way that encourages all individuals to reach their own conclusions. Don't put them in a position where they can be unduly influenced by a single person or a small number of people.

Doing the Same Job Two Ways

When appropriate, consider using different methods or approaches for tasks done multiple times to minimise errors. (You know this method intuitively. If you're summing a column of numbers, you may double-check your work by summing the numbers from top to bottom and then reversing the process and summing from the bottom to top.) This best practice is a way of avoiding the consequences of Babbage's Law. Charles Babbage argued that two people doing the same task with the same methods tend to make the same mistakes.

If you're duplicating tasks in microtasking to avoid errors, try to have at least two methods of doing the same work. You can sum numbers in different ways. You can identify elements in a different order. (Chapter 16 explains how to approach microtasking jobs in different ways.)

This practice also applies to macrotasking. If you're doing a complicated job, break it into tasks to give to multiple crowdworkers. If you're designing a website, for example, you may let two workers design the basic architecture of the site independently. You can then compare their results and ask one of the workers to incorporate the best elements of both designs into a final plan.

Giving a Gift to the Crowd

Have a gift for people who pledge money to your campaign. The gift can be a small token that identifies workers with your project. You may offer gifts of increasing value: a basic gift for small contributors, a more expensive gift for mid-level contributors, and an expensive gift for high-end contributors.

You can also apply this practice to microtasking, macrotasking or crowdcontests. You can offer workers a gift to thank them for good work, to recognise accomplishments or just to help them identify with your activity.

Most crowdsourcing websites allow you to tip workers. Even Amazon's Mechanical Turk, one of the busiest crowdsourcing sites, has a mechanism for giving a tip to the crowd so that, in the midst of a complex workflow, you can stop and tell a worker that he's done well, that his efforts are appreciated and that you're able to offer him a little something extra in return.

Chapter 22

Ten Success Stories

*W*hen you start crowdsourcing, make a start by looking around at other people's successes – projects that worked well, by one measure or another. Every success story can teach you a little lesson about crowdsourcing that you may not be able to learn any other way.

In this chapter, I serve up ten varied stories of crowdsourcing projects. Some of these projects started a new business; many of them helped individuals do something that they couldn't have done by themselves. All are examples of how crowdsourcing has worked successfully.

Creating the SXSW Festival T-shirt

More than any other form of crowdsourcing, crowdcontests show you what the crowd's thinking. You discover ideas that the crowd thinks are cool, interesting and intriguing. Because of this, many art festivals use crowdcontests to design their advertisements.

The SXSW festival, a major arts fair in Austin, Texas, USA, has long been promoting audience participation. The organisers were crowdsourcing before they entirely knew what crowdsourcing was. They asked for help from the crowd to prepare programmes, design posters and create T-shirts. When they started, such things were identified as audience outreach or market engagement. Now they're known as crowdsourcing and they reach a much, much larger audience.

In 2010, SXSW organisers (the initials stand for South by Southwest) used the crowdsourcing platform 99designs to crowdsource its T-shirt. They followed the standard process, paid less than $1,000 ($630) for a contest, received back about 500 designs, reviewed the submissions and selected a winner. The designs they received from the crowd suggested that SXSW is seen as a global phenomenon, one which presents ideas that engage people in their early 20s. As a result of this, the T-shirt designs repeated images of music, technology and games. Few made any reference to the Texan culture that had once been a hallmark of the festival. (You can check out the designs the organisers received at `http://99designs.com/t-shirt-design/contests/design-official-t-shirt-sxsw-30498`.)

The success in this story is found both at the festival and in crowdsourcing itself. In using 99designs, SXSW organisers acknowledged that they were ready to reach a larger audience and get a more professional group of designers working on their festival. SXSW was once just a small regional festival, whose organisers chose designers from the music fans who attended the concerts. Designing for the festival has now become a much bigger activity that covers more topics and deserves a more professional approach.

The SXSW contest demonstrated not only that event organisers can obtain good and inexpensive designs through crowdsourcing, but also that they were able to understand their audience better by reviewing the submissions to the contest. They saw a tool that can give them a lot of useful information.

Developing Smith & Kraus's Mobile App

Smith & Kraus is a publisher of plays (about as far from high technology as you can get!). The company's experience of crowdsourcing showed that not only can a first-time crowdsourcer get a good result from a macrotasking website, she can also get a good technical product.

The managing partner wanted a mobile phone app to sell the publisher's material to actors and directors. She decided that the company couldn't afford a full-time developer and concluded that the best way to get an app would be to advertise for a student. However, she didn't know any students, didn't know how to find students, and really didn't know how to tell a student what she wanted or how she'd know when the app was doing what she wanted it to do. She really wanted a professional app developer, but didn't think she could afford one.

After looking at different alternatives, she was directed to the macrotasking sites oDesk and Elance. She gave these sites a try even though she wasn't sure she could make them work properly or could even communicate with a professional software developer. She was a professional publisher who'd spent her career in theatre. She knew how to talk with artists, but had no idea how to talk with engineers.

The macrotasking sites proved to be easier to use than she anticipated. She got some help writing a description of her app and found a macrotasker who both understood what she needed and had the experience to fill in the gaps in her description. The app worked when it was delivered and was deployed on schedule. The project was all done, much to the publishing manager's surprise, under her own control.

Spending Time with Mr Bentham

The philosopher Jeremy Bentham (1748–1832) would probably have been sympathetic to crowdsourcing. He was, after all, an eminently practical man who promoted a philosophy called utilitarianism. 'It is the greatest good to the greatest number of people,' he said, 'which is the measure of right and wrong.'

Mr Bentham also had an innovative side that would have enjoyed working with the crowd. He stated that he wanted his embalmed body, dressed and upright, displayed in University College London (UCL). It remains on display there and apparently even attends faculty meetings.

Only Bentham's published works and a few documents are currently in print, so UCL's library is running a crowdsourced project to transcribe his manuscript papers (see http://blogs.ucl.ac.uk/transcribe-bentham). The project follows the usual kind of process. The library is posting Bentham's 8,178 manuscripts and calling in the crowd to transcribe and check them. At the time of writing, about 60 per cent of the manuscripts have been transcribed. Scholarly transcription is an expensive and time-consuming job. Crowdsourcing lowers the cost of this work and speeds up the process.

The impact of this project will be measured over decades, not days. Jeremy Bentham helped lay the foundation for the Victorian period and for the modern age. His writings encouraged the political leadership of the UK to measure social progress in concrete ways. An yet, without the transcriptions, we really don't know the nature of his influence. We don't know with whom he corresponded, how he combined ideas or how he worked with others. The transcripts will provide that information and help everyone to spend a little more time in the company of Jeremy Bentham.

Generating a New Movie Recommendation Method for Netflix

Often, self-organised crowds can tell you the most about crowd behaviour because they're finding out about themselves as they're doing their work. The Netflix prize remains one of the great successes of self-organised crowds, because it produced a new way of understanding how people make purchasing decisions. To achieve that understanding, members of the crowd had to cooperate and compete. The contest staff closely monitored the progress of the crowd and encouraged the participants to work together.

Netflix, a company that distributes movies over the Internet, created the contest to generate a new method of recommending movies to customers. The company posted a set of data on the web that showed what customers had rented and offered $1 million (£630,000) to devise a method that could predict the movies that customers would like.

The company ran the contest in two stages. It used the first stage not only to identify good ideas but also to push the best contestants into teams. The final team, BellKor's Pragmatic Chaos, combined researchers from two groups that had done well in the preliminary round. The goal of the contest was to create a program that could predict which movies customers would rent based on the movies they'd already watched. Netflix already had a program that made such predictions, but it sometimes made errors and predicted the wrong movie. The combined group ultimately created a new program that reduced the error rate by 10.6 per cent.

Building a National Treasure Trove

The Australia National Library Trove Project (check it out at `http://trove.nla.gov.au`) is more than just a crowdsourcing project. It's a collection of material about Australia that combines the resources of a thousand libraries, offers issues of newspapers and other publications, presents manuscripts and even offers archives for old websites. Several aspects of Trove involve crowdsourcing. The project offers a *wiki* – a reference website that's built and edited by the crowd – to enable members of the public to accumulate their knowledge, and gives the crowd the ability to tag and describe elements of the collection.

Trove also maintains a large collection of modern photographs of Australia that it's collected with the help of the photo-sharing site Flickr (`www.flickr.com`). With Flickr, Trove has been able to request photographs from the crowd and allow anyone to view and use them. Over 3,000 people have contributed over 100,000 images.

The Trove archive enables Australians to document the present without going through the traditional process of curation. It allows the crowd to identify the images that are important to them and to create a portrait of modern life. According to the project managers, Trove is already one of the most used collections of images that depict current life. (You can see the images at `www.flickr.com/groups/pictureaustralia_ppe`.)

Running a Video Campaign for Audio-Technica

Audio-Technica used a crowdcontest to help it get a stronger position in the US headphone market. The company hadn't done well in the USA in spite of producing critically acclaimed products. To overcome this problem, the company decided to start a new video advertising campaign. Instead of going to a conventional ad agency, it went to GeniusRocket, a crowdsourced video production firm.

GeniusRocket held a curated crowdcontest for Audio-Technica, a type of contest in which the judges review the submissions and offer suggestions before making the final decision. The winner captured the desire of the crowd in a way that few could explain in words. The video says that music gives life and the headphones bring music. Called 'Audio 911', it shows an emergency – a young man trembling on the brink of death. A pair of headphones pulsing with the beats of the day are placed over his ears and restore his life. The video has had over a million views on YouTube and gave a market share to Audio-Technica. (Check out the video at `www.youtube.com/watch?v=R-Kz12Ijanw`.)

Getting USA Today on Mobile Phones

USA Today is skilled at dealing with technical services. For 30 years, the company has published a global newspaper, a task that's required it to coordinate the efforts of writers, printers, delivery drivers and others employers around the globe. In 2011, the company decided to deliver the news to a mobile app. Despite the experience of those at *USA Today*, they knew that this task wouldn't be easy. As they prepared it, they quickly realised that their app would have to operate in hundreds of different environments, even though it was perceived as a single app.

To test the new app, *USA Today* turned to uTest, which crowdsources software testing. The result was highly successful. The company realised the app on time and was able to show that it had few bugs. 'There is no way to hide poor quality in the world of mobile,' explained the app designer.

The *USA Today* mobile app has quickly become a major distribution channel for the newspaper. Recent statistics suggest that it accounts for roughly 25 per cent of the network views of the paper. The paper wants to be connected to its readers, and the mobile app is the quickest link for the crowd. A spokesman for the paper said that the mobile app makes *USA Today* 'only an arm's length away'.

Analysing Viruses with Foldit

Foldit is a form of self-organised crowd, although it can be viewed as a form of microtasking or even as a game. It was created by researchers at the University of Washington, USA, as a means of analysing the structure of natural proteins – but that isn't why the crowd uses it. To the crowd, Foldit's a game, a game in which the players try to fold a complex three-dimensional shape into a compact structure. The fact that these three-dimensional shapes represent proteins isn't important to many of the players. It's just part of the game.

The researchers created Foldit because they were trying to understand how proteins behave in the human system. If they could understand how proteins changed from long strings of molecules to compact structures, they reasoned, they'd better understand how the immune system works. In particular, the researchers would gain insight into the structure of one particular protein – the AIDS virus.

The researchers had written computer programs as a way of trying to fold the proteins. The programs weren't that difficult but they demanded substantial computer time, because they blindly tested every possible combination of every possible way of folding the molecules. Humans are able to do these folds much faster. By looking at the molecule, they can judge where the molecule might fold and how it might be manipulated into a small shape.

Using Foldit, the crowd was able to analyse the structure of a virus that causes AIDS in monkeys. They analysed this structure by playing a game that encouraged them to manipulate these three-dimensional forms that happened to behave like the AIDS virus. The computer program would have taken thousands of hours to find a way of folding that virus. The crowd found one in just ten days.

Writing Descriptions for Magnum Photos

Magnum Photos is a collective founded by Henry Cartier-Bresson, Robert Capa and other well-known photographers. It possesses some of the most famous images from the 20th century, but most of its photographs have no description. They often have nothing more than the name of the photographer and a number.

Magnum wanted to organise, identify and describe its collection of some 600,000 images. To prepare descriptions, it had two choices. It could either hire experts to study each photo and write a summary, or it could put the photos to the crowd and let the crowd members prepare the descriptions. Magnum knew that if it hired experts, the process would cost at least $12 (£8.50) per photo, possibly more. The people at Magnum thought that the crowd would be able to do the work faster and more cheaply than experts could. However, they weren't certain that the crowd could do the work well.

Magnum ultimately decided to employ the crowd to write the photo descriptions. The collective organised a serial crowdsourcing process that passed each photo through the hands of several members of the crowd and allowed each one to add some new information and check the work of other members. (See Chapter 16 for more on serial crowdsourcing.)

Magnum's project isn't yet over, but the signs of success came early on. In the course of processing some of the first pictures, the crowd discovered a file of photos taken on the set of the 1973 movie *American Graffiti*. They not only identified the movie stars, who didn't always look like the characters they played in the film, they were also able to identify where the pictures were taken and what the people were doing. It was a quick demonstration of how well crowdsourcing can work.

Setting Up Coffee Joulie with the Crowd's Backing

A modest success story suggests that coffee is almost as important to the crowd as is technology.

The company Dave & Dave came up with a new product called the Coffee Joulie, a large metal bean that you place at the bottom of your coffee mug. It absorbs heat from freshly brewed coffee and as the coffee cools, the Coffee Joulie slowly releases heat and keeps your drink warm.

Dave & Dave put a request on Kickstarter. They wanted $9,500 (£5,974) to finance the production of the first Coffee Joulies. Anyone who pledged $100 (£63) or more would receive a free set of Coffee Joulies. 'This took off really fast, way faster than we thought it was going to,' explained one of the Daves. 'We just completed leapfrogged that goal in a month.' On Kickstarter, the donors offered nearly $307,000 (£196,000).

Chapter 23

Ten Crowdsourcing Blunders to Avoid

. . . .

In This Chapter

▶ Preparing for the crowd's mistakes

▶ Protecting yourself from failure with a trial run

▶ Guarding your reputation

. . . .

*T*he basic idea behind crowdsourcing is simple. You have a problem that you can't solve by yourself or work that's too much for you to do. You turn to the crowd and ask the crowd for assistance. If you ask in the right way, the crowd comes to your aid and all's as right as can be.

However, obvious crowdsourcing blunders exist, roots along the path that can trip the unsuspecting crowdsourcer. But forewarned is forearmed, so steer well clear of the following mistakes as you prepare for your first attempt at crowdsourcing.

Thinking Crowdsourcing Is Easy

Hubris brought down the Greeks and it can also bring down the crowdsourcer. If you think that crowdsourcing is so easy that you don't have to pay attention to details, then you are overconfident and heading for a fall.

Liang, a graduate student in psychology, learned about crowdsourcing as he was doing his doctoral study. Assured by other students that crowdsourcing platforms are easy to use, he decided to use the crowd at Amazon's Mechanical Turk to proofread his thesis. He created a collection of microtasks by dividing the paper by paragraphs. He posted the paragraphs on Mechanical Turk with the request to rewrite the paper into standard English and offered

$0.25 ($0.15) per paragraph. When the tasks were complete, Liang assembled the work into a complete paper and submitted it. Judgement came quickly. His professor said the paper was terrible. Some of the paragraphs had been written properly but most had not. For some, the crowdworker had changed only one word (and not always for the best). For other paragraphs, the worker had copied text from Wikipedia or just typed nonsense. Liang's blunder was to crowdsource without first thinking about the right way to do it.

You make the mistake of thinking that crowdsourcing is too easy when you forget about the details of the process or believe that those details will magically take care of themselves. If you don't think about the details of how to divide your job, how to engage the crowd and how to check the results, you're likely to get work that's done badly, delivered late and filled with errors.

When you do it, you need to remember that crowdsourcing is a powerful technique that requires attention to detail. You need to think about your job and the kind of approach that you need. Choose an appropriate platform and have a means of checking the quality of the work you receive. Above all, think about what you're doing.

Failing to Review the Work of the Crowd

Some people believe that you can always trust the work of the crowd. After all, trusting souls are out there who believe in the fundamental virtue of the common man, and who transfer that trust to crowdsourcing. The truth, though, is that you can't trust the work of the crowd any more than you can trust the work of any other group of human beings. You always need a mechanism to check the work that the crowd does.

If you want an example of why you should check the work of the crowd, talk with any experienced crowdsourcer. You'll hear stories of tasks undone, work copied from websites and arbitrary answers given to clearly written questions. To try to understand the quality of crowdsourced work, Michael, a crowdsourcing researcher in California, did an experiment. He put a job on Amazon's Mechanical Turk that asked the crowdworker to flip a coin and report whether the coin landed heads up or tails up. He did 100 replications of the experiment and found that 70 of the crowdworkers responded that the coin landed heads up. Standard statistical theory states that only 50 of the crowdworkers should have reported that the coin landed heads up, with a margin of error of 15. It would be extremely unusual for as many as 70 workers' coins to land heads up. From this, Michael concluded that some of the crowdworkers never bothered to flip a coin and were lying.

If you commence any form of crowdsourcing without planning to check the results of the workers, you're committing a blunder. This problem's most common in microtasking. In macrotasking, self-organised crowds and crowd-contests, you can usually check the work of the crowd fairly easily, and in crowdfunding, the money is as good as the bank says it is. In microtasking, however, you need a process for checking each result.

You may be tempted to believe that you can check the results of microtasks by duplicating or triplicating the work and then comparing the results. Duplicate tasks are definitely better than single tasks, but they still aren't perfect. First, you can't duplicate every task. You can't double-check Michael's experiment by duplicating the coin flips, for example. Second, sometimes duplicate tasks merely duplicate errors. Two people can do the same task and both do it wrongly.

When you put a job to the crowd, have a way of checking the quality of the work you receive back. If you're doing macrotasking or crowdcontests, or even working with self-organised crowds, you can probably review all the submissions yourself. When you're microtasking, though, you may need a more sophisticated process that allows the crowd to check the work or that duplicates the work.

Not Knowing Who's in the Crowd

Believing that the crowd is a great teeming mass of people who possess any skill you may need and who can do any job you may put to it is an easy trap to fall into. The crowd members are, indeed, a diverse group, but you usually can't see all of the crowd at one time. From your perspective, or from the perspective of the crowdsourcing platform you use, you may not see the skills that you need or get the help that you want.

Two years ago, my neighbourhood was struck by an earthquake, the Great Millennial Hoover Park Earthquake, as the residents have come to call it. It was as bad as anything I've ever seen, but it was nothing compared with the kinds of quakes that have hit Japan, Haiti and Iran. It cracked some plaster, knocked some books off the shelves, broke a favourite bowl and tipped over recycling bins up and down the street.

Within a few minutes, someone organised a crowd reconnaissance of the neighbourhood. The organiser told us to tweet news reports of what we saw and use the tag #hooverquake. The first reports were of broken windows and cracked walls, but the stories quickly escalated. Collapsed buildings; fires in the street; children trapped in schools calling for their parents. None of these latter events were true. The local primary school had actually hurried the children onto the playground, where they stood screaming because they thought the earthquake was the most exciting thing that had ever happened to them.

These stories came from people with great imaginations who lived nowhere near Hoover Park. Some of them even had Twitter IDs that suggested they were from Florida or Ohio or North London. Still, readers were inclined to believe the stories. Some of the commercial media outlets picked up the stories and repeated them. None of them bothered to check whether the tweets came from part of the crowd that was actually in Hoover Park.

You don't need an earthquake in your neighbourhood to appreciate the diversity of the crowd. If you scan Wikipedia, for example, you'll see that it's the work of quite a diverse crowd and that it hasn't yet found a crowd that can give it a complete, balanced reference work. Some of the articles – those that teach with technology, for example – contain mathematical descriptions and almost require a Masters degree to understand them. Articles about science fiction may contain incredible details that can't possibly be of interest to most readers. But other articles – articles on social or historical topics that may have some general interest – may still be incomplete, and may contain vague generalities and statements that really don't describe the subject. The Wikipedia crowd, at least the part of the crowd that contributes to the work, doesn't yet have all the skills and knowledge it needs to complete the encyclopaedia.

Don't assume that you always have the crowd that you need. Be sure that the crowd members have the experience or skills that they need to do data work or gather your data. You do this by qualifying your crowd.

The quality of the work that you can get from the crowd depends on the kind of crowd that comes to your project. You can't great expect technical work from a crowd of teenagers on Facebook, nor can you always get good marketing advice from a team of Java coders. Know your crowd, and be sure that you have a crowd with the right skills and the right experience. You can get a sense of your crowd in macrotasking, because you get to see information that gives the background of the workers. However, if you're doing microtasking, crowdcontests or self-organised crowdsourcing, you may have to do something extra when you qualify your workers, in order to ensure that you have the right crowd. You can find out more about how to qualify the crowd for microtasking in Chapter 8.

Failing to Do a Trial Run

The trial run is so important, especially in microtasking, that it almost doesn't deserve comment. In crowdsourcing, you learn by doing, by creating a crowdsourcing job, writing a statement of work and instructions, posting the job, observing how it works and assessing the results. A trial run's a great way to do all this. (You can find out more about learning from your results in Chapter 14.)

Brigid attempted to do a crowdfunding project on Facebook for a charity. She faced a tight deadline and decided that she didn't have time to do a trial run. Rather than prepare her materials and test them with a small group, she posted them and started urging everyone she knew to contribute to the cause. Little happened. A few people pledged to the cause, but not enough. Eventually, a friend contacted her and said that she didn't understand the purpose of the campaign. A review of the campaign showed that several problems existed. The description was not as clear as it could have been, some links pointed to the wrong web pages and a video which had been lovingly prepared didn't display properly. The deadline came, and Brigid had nothing to show for it.

If you don't do a trial run, you take the risk that your job will fail. By doing a trial run, you learn by doing and give yourself an opportunity to learn without paying for a full, complete and expensive job.

In crowdsourcing, doing trial runs is easy. For microtasking, you just send a small number of tasks to the crowdsourcing platform. In macrotasking you ask your worker to do a small job before you try the big job. In crowdcontests or self-organised crowds, you do a small contest first so you can see if you have the talent for your project. In crowdfunding, you try to raise a small amount of money first.

Putting the Crowdsourcing Ahead of the Job

Getting excited about crowdsourcing is easily done. Crowdsourcing is a novel and powerful way of doing work. It can achieve things that other forms of work cannot. However, crowdsourcing isn't the only way to work, and it may not be the best way to do a job. When you're preparing a project, ask yourself 'Is this the best way to do the job?' and 'Am I attempting to crowdsource an activity that would be done better another way?'

Min and Sasha were preparing a business plan for a start-up company that they wanted to create. Both of them had seen their friends use crowdsourcing in their companies and decided that they wanted to use it to create a business plan. They wrote a job description, posted it on a macrotasking site, selected a worker and started the process. Thirty days later, the crowdworker delivered the business plan. It was an impressive document, but it had little value as a business plan. The descriptions were general and could have been applied to any business. The financial projections were based on assumptions that weren't explained, and the marketing section didn't seem to say anything specific about the service that Min and Sasha wanted to produce. The investors in the company read the document and announced they were withholding funds until Min and Sasha created a better plan.

Complete business plans are probably not good things to crowdsource, although perhaps some parts of them can be addressed by macrotasking. Good business plans require a variety of skills, much knowledge, an understanding of the founders' skills and a vision for the organisation. Much of this can't be gained from the crowd. In general, don't ask the crowd to do things that you don't know how to do, and don't ask it to do things that require a detailed knowledge of you and what you're doing.

Don't crowdsource just because it's new, because it seems special or because it'll impress your market, your boss, your neighbour, your girlfriend or you. Crowdsource because it's the right way to do your particular job. Keep your attention focused on your goal and avoid becoming fascinated with crowdsourcing. Crowdsourcing is indeed fascinating and it has the ability to transform many kinds of activities and do things that can't be done in other ways. However, it can't transform anything if it's unsuccessful, and it can't be successful if you spend more time thinking about crowdsourcing than you spend thinking about your goal.

Losing Your Reputation

Not only do the members of the crowd have a reputation; you do too. Furthermore, the crowd talks. Sometimes you like what crowd members say and sometimes you don't.

You're going to find it hard to crowdsource if the crowd views you as incompetent, hostile or unorganised. There are many ways to lose your reputation on a crowdmarket. You can give bad descriptions, offer difficult jobs or set arbitrary deadlines. However, you usually get in trouble with issues that involve money and payments.

Purna manages the crowd for Tinitasks, a microtasking firm that offers two kinds of microtasking service: microtasking jobs that are prepared by Tinitasks' staff and microtasking jobs that are prepared by its customers. Purna knows which jobs are which, but the crowd doesn't. The crowd members think all jobs come from Tinitasks.

In the middle of the spring, Purna noted that fewer and fewer workers were accepting work from Tinitasks. Soon, Tinitasks was running at only 70 per cent capacity. It was able to attract only 70 per cent of the workers it needed to do its work. In reviewing the blogs and forums for the Tinitasks crowdmarkets, Purna concluded that the company was in danger of losing its reputation. The workers were saying that instructions issued by Tinitasks were difficult to understand and that the company was slow to pay workers. So, Purna quickly reviewed the customer jobs and found many with poorly written instructions. She also found one customer who had been placing large jobs with Tinitasks without ever reviewing the work or paying workers.

Purna needed three or four months to rebuild Tinitasks' reputation in the market. She created a process that edited the text for all jobs, and got the vice president of marketing to bring the non-paying firm into line. She also started a small publicity campaign among the workers. 'We've heard you and we've changed' was the message. Still, Purna knows that Tinitasks still carries a little stain from the incident. Every now and then, someone will post on the worker blog 'You know Tinitasks, they don't pay.' Mud sticks.

The easiest way to ruin your reputation is to change the rules of your project with no warning or explanation. For example, if you suddenly change the price that you offer for your tasks, you may get the reputation of being stingy. If you raise your prices too many times, the crowd resists taking your tasks. They assume that you will raise your prices again and that they may as well wait until you do. And if you change the rules in the middle of a job, even if you do so in an effort to improve the quality of work, you get the reputation of being arbitrary or not knowing what you want.

Two rules will generally secure your reputation. Firstly, treat the crowd as you would like to be treated. Secondly, be as consistent and transparent as you can be in all your decisions. (Should you find yourself under attack from a disgruntled member of the crowd, take a look at Chapter 14.)

Hiding from the Crowd

You can't do crowdsourcing without a crowd, and you can't get a crowd unless you make the effort to call the crowd together. In some forms of crowdsourcing, finding a crowd isn't difficult. For example, if you're macro-tasking on an established crowdsourcing platform, you should have little trouble finding a crowd. However, if you're running a crowdcontest from your own website or doing crowdfunding in any form, even from one of the major crowdfunding sites, you can't just assume that the crowd will come or that pledges will flow to you; you need to make an effort to attract a crowd. If the crowd can't find you, you can't do crowdsourcing.

Hamish, a marketer with Benedict Foods, organised several crowdcontests to promote the Benedict brand. He wanted to produce a Benedict Foods cookbook and organised contests for recipes, for designing the site and for writing the text. The prizes for the contest were generous, and the contest description was enticing. However, few people submitted entries. After he concluded that the contest was unsuccessful and closed it, Hamish investigated the process. In publicising the event, the company had largely reached older customers who didn't regularly use the Internet. It had failed to reach a crowd.

When you crowdsource, be sure that you can draw a crowd. Just because your website is connected to billions of people on the web, don't assume that enough of them will visit that site and be ready for work. Use a commercial crowdsourcing platform unless you have solid evidence that you can draw an adequate crowd at your site. And when you use a crowdsourcing platform, be sure that the platform has the kind of crowd you need.

Crowdsourcing works best when you have a natural crowd on the web, a group of people who use all aspects of the Internet and are interested in your work. But even when you're using an established crowdmarket for macrotasking or microtasking, you need to be prepared to take steps to draw the crowd to your work. Describe your work in words that are clear and attractive. Give the crowd a reason to rally around you. Make sure that your project is visible on the web. Have a place where the crowd can offer feedback. Publicise the results.

Assuming That All Crowdworkers Understand

You can make bigger blunders when you're getting good results from the crowd than when you're getting bad results. When you get bad results, you know that something's wrong. You know that the instructions aren't clear and that the crowd is misunderstanding you.

When you get good results, you're tempted to believe that all's well. Usually, everything is well, but occasionally it's not. Sometimes the crowd is doing the right things by luck. In other words, the crowd is doing the right thing but not for the right reason. Something changes and the crowd no longer does what you want.

This kind of problem isn't common but it can occur when you try to reuse a crowdsourcing job. It worked the first time, and it may have worked a second time. You try it a third time, however, and you watch things go wrong. The crowd does the wrong things and get you the wrong results.

Elmira used crowdsourcing to help translate small texts into different languages. She had access to a translation program that did a fairly good job. However, she wanted simple, colloquial translations that read as if they were written by a native speaker. To do this, she put each text through the translation program and then gave both the original text and the translated text on a crowdsourcing market. She asked the crowd to put the text in 'common speech' without exactly saying what common speech might be. The process worked well on a couple of occasions. Then people started editing the English text rather than the translated text. They'd rewrite the English text as a very informal document filled with slang. In reviewing her instructions, Elmira recognised how the crowd could misinterpret them. She pulled the job, rewrote the instructions and then reposted the tasks. In the end, she was only a little surprised that she'd not seen a problem earlier.

Just because you understand what you want, don't assume that the crowd knows what you want. Make sure that your instructions are clear. Ask the crowd to test them. If you don't, you'll find that at least some of the crowd, or maybe all of the crowd, will interpret the instructions in their own way and give you information that you can't use.

Always assume that you'll have trouble communicating with at least certain parts of the crowd. They are many. You are one. Some members of the crowd may have backgrounds that are quite different from yours. They may tend to interpret your instructions in ways that you didn't intend. No matter how many times you've used a job description or set of instructions, you may want to give it one more review before you use it again. (You can look at Chapter 11 for more information about writing instructions for the crowd and how to test those instructions.)

Having Too Much Faith in the Market

Having faith in the crowdmarket isn't a blunder, but thinking that markets are the only way to manage people definitely is a blunder. Sometimes, you can be better off using a more conventional technique to get your job done.

Fred, who runs a small technology firm, fell in love with crowdsourcing. To him, crowdsourcing represents a return to the fundamental truths of economics, to the ideas of Adam Smith and the invisible hand that guided the actions of business people. He vowed that he'll use crowdsourcing for every aspect of his business.

Fred began using macrotasking throughout his business: financial planning, bookkeeping, marketing and even sales. Eventually, he realised that some crowdsourcing jobs were wasting his time. In these jobs, he had to teach the crowdworker the history of his company, explain the context of the market and revisit decisions he'd made three or six or nine months before. Eventually, he concluded that some of his jobs were better done by long-term contractors or permanent employees than by crowdworkers.

Fred didn't completely revert to his old way of doing business. He still does a lot of work through crowdsourcing, but he resists the idea of hiring long-term contractors. The idea doesn't seem right to him. He's so in love with the idea of a free market that he can't accept that crowdmarkets may involve too much extra work to make them the best way to manage some workers or do some tasks.

Don't crowdsource because you love the idea. Crowdsource because it's the best way to do your job. If you crowdsource just because you love the idea of markets, or because you're in love with technology or you think it's the wave of the future, you're likely to give a badly designed task to the wrong workers and get an unusable result.

You may sometimes meet business people, like Fred, who are so in love with the idea of free markets that they don't see the shortcomings of crowdsourcing. Markets are indeed lovely things and they make crowdsourcing possible. You can love them all you like, but they sometimes involve costs that you'd rather not pay again and again. You have to train your new crowdworkers. You have to integrate them into an existing organisation. You have to tell them the history of your activities. Never assume that crowdsourcing is the best way to manage an activity just because it involves a market.

Index

About the Author

David Alan Grier is a writer and consultant on issues regarding computing and labour. He claims to be one of the original second-generation computer brats, as his father, Thomas Grier, was an early employee of Univac Computer Corporation and then became Director of Customer Relations for Burroughs Computer Corporation. David learned his first lessons of programming in his father's office. You can learn something of his father's career from the book *Too Soon To Tell* (Wiley, 2009).

David did not set out to become an expert in crowdsourcing. If anything, crowdsourcing chose him. In 2005, he published a book on how we did computing before we had machines to do it for us. This book, *When Computers Were Human* (Princeton University Press, 2005), was well received and earned the 2006 Independent Press Award for the best book on computing technology. At the time, no one recognised that this book contained the basic ideas of crowdsourcing, as the term *crowdsourcing* wasn't invented until 2007. However, someone was paying attention. Eventually, the organiser of a crowdsourcing conference asked him to address their meeting. At that conference, he realised that he'd been studying crowdsourcing for decades – he just never knew it.

David has worked as a writer, as the editor-in-chief of the *Annals of the History of Computing,* and as the lead columnist for *Computer* magazine. His writing has appeared in publications as diverse as the *American Mathematics Monthly* and the *Washington Post*. He has been the publisher of the Computer Society of the Institute of Electrical and Electronics Engineers (IEEE) and has served as the president of the Computer Society of the IEEE. His video podcasts are available at the Daily Crowdsource (`www.dailycrowdsource.com`) and at other places around the web.

To be clear, the author is not David Alan Grier, the talented actor and star of stage and screen. However, both this David Alan Grier and that David Alan Grier were raised in Detroit, Michigan. Detroit is a good place to call your home, especially if you are named David Alan.

David now makes his home in Washington, DC, where is a professor at the George Washington University. He has a PhD in Mathematical Statistics from the University of Washington in Seattle. He also teaches courses in technology policy, technology and labour and crowdsourcing, as well as teaching a great ideas course entitled *Difficult and Obscure Texts*. David regularly works with companies large and small, old and new. You can reach him at `dagrier@djaghe.com` or on LinkedIn (`www.linkedin.com`).

Dedication

To Gertrude Blanch, who knew more about crowdsourcing at the Works Progress Administration than we will ever understand. To all the friends who taught me that I knew something about crowdsourcing. And to Jean, who taught me everything else.

Publisher's Acknowledgements

We're proud of this book; please send us your comments at http://dummies.custhelp.com. For other comments, please contact our Customer Care Department within the U.S. at 877-762-2974, outside the U.S. at (001) 317-572-3993, or fax 317-572-4002.

Some of the people who helped bring this book to market include the following:

Acquisitions, Editorial, and Vertical Websites

Project Editor: Steve Edwards

Commissioning Editor: Claire Ruston

Assistant Editor: Ben Kemble

Development Editor: Charlie Wilson

Copy Editor: Kim Vernon

Technical Reviewer: Candice Novak

Proofreader: Mary White

Production Manager: Daniel Mersey

Publisher: Miles Kendall

Cover Photos: © chuwy/iStockphoto

Composition Services

Project Coordinator: Kristie Rees

Layout and Graphics: Joyce Haughey

Indexer: Sharon Shock

Brand Reviewers: Jennifer Bingham, Zoë Wykes

FOR DUMMIES®

Making Everything Easier!™

UK editions

BUSINESS

978-1-118-34689-1

978-1-118-44349-1

978-1-119-97527-4

MUSIC

978-1-119-94276-4

978-0-470-97799-6

978-0-470-66372-1

HOBBIES

978-1-118-41156-8

978-1-119-99417-6

978-1-119-97250-1

Asperger's Syndrome For Dummies
978-0-470-66087-4

Basic Maths For Dummies
978-1-119-97452-9

Body Language For Dummies,
2nd Edition
978-1-119-95351-7

Boosting Self-Esteem For Dummies
978-0-470-74193-1

Business Continuity For Dummies
978-1-118-32683-1

Cricket For Dummies
978-0-470-03454-5

Diabetes For Dummies, 3rd Edition
978-0-470-97711-8

eBay For Dummies, 3rd Edition
978-1-119-94122-4

English Grammar For Dummies
978-0-470-05752-0

Flirting For Dummies
978-0-470-74259-4

IBS For Dummies
978-0-470-51737-6

ITIL For Dummies
978-1-119-95013-4

Management For Dummies,
2nd Edition
978-0-470-97769-9

Managing Anxiety with CBT
For Dummies
978-1-118-36606-6

Neuro-linguistic Programming
For Dummies, 2nd Edition
978-0-470-66543-5

Nutrition For Dummies, 2nd Edition
978-0-470-97276-2

Organic Gardening For Dummies
978-1-119-97706-3

FOR DUMMIES®

Making Everything Easier! ™

UK editions

SELF-HELP

978-0-470-66541-1

978-1-119-99264-6

978-0-470-66086-7

LANGUAGES

978-0-470-68815-1

978-1-119-97959-3

978-0-470-69477-0

HISTORY

978-0-470-68792-5

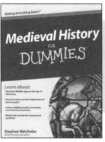

978-0-470-74783-4

978-0-470-97819-1

Origami Kit For Dummies
978-0-470-75857-1

Overcoming Depression For Dummies
978-0-470-69430-5

Positive Psychology For Dummies
978-0-470-72136-0

PRINCE2 For Dummies, 2009 Edition
978-0-470-71025-8

Project Management For Dummies
978-0-470-71119-4

Psychology Statistics For Dummies
978-1-119-95287-9

Psychometric Tests For Dummies
978-0-470-75366-8

Renting Out Your Property For Dummies, 3rd Edition
978-1-119-97640-0

Rugby Union For Dummies, 3rd Edition
978-1-119-99092-5

Sage One For Dummies
978-1-119-95236-7

Self-Hypnosis For Dummies
978-0-470-66073-7

Storing and Preserving Garden Produce For Dummies
978-1-119-95156-8

Teaching English as a Foreign Language For Dummies
978-0-470-74576-2

Time Management For Dummies
978-0-470-77765-7

Training Your Brain For Dummies
978-0-470-97449-0

Voice and Speaking Skills For Dummies
978-1-119-94512-3

Work-Life Balance For Dummies
978-0-470-71380-8

Making Everything Easier! ™

COMPUTER BASICS

978-1-118-11533-6

978-0-470-61454-9

978-0-470-49743-2

DIGITAL PHOTOGRAPHY

978-1-118-09203-3

978-0-470-76878-5

978-1-118-00472-2

SCIENCE AND MATHS

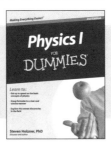

978-0-470-92326-9

978-0-470-55964-2

978-0-470-90324-7

Art For Dummies
978-0-7645-5104-8

Computers For Seniors For Dummies, 3rd Edition
978-1-118-11553-4

Criminology For Dummies
978-0-470-39696-4

Currency Trading For Dummies, 2nd Edition
978-0-470-01851-4

Drawing For Dummies, 2nd Edition
978-0-470-61842-4

Forensics For Dummies
978-0-7645-5580-0

French For Dummies, 2nd Edition
978-1-118-00464-7

Guitar For Dummies, 2nd Edition
978-0-7645-9904-0

Hinduism For Dummies
978-0-470-87858-3

Index Investing For Dummies
978-0-470-29406-2

Islamic Finance For Dummies
978-0-470-43069-9

Knitting For Dummies, 2nd Edition
978-0-470-28747-7

Music Theory For Dummies, 2nd Edition
978-1-118-09550-8

Office 2010 For Dummies
978-0-470-48998-7

Piano For Dummies, 2nd Edition
978-0-470-49644-2

Photoshop CS6 For Dummies
978-1-118-17457-9

Schizophrenia For Dummies
978-0-470-25927-6

WordPress For Dummies, 5th Edition
978-1-118-38318-6

Think you can't learn it in a day? Think again!

The *In a Day* e-book series from *For Dummies* gives you quick and eas[y] access to learn a new skill, brush up on a hobby, or enhance your personal or professional life — all in a day. Easy!

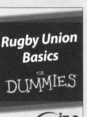

Available as PDF, eMobi and Kindle